CATHAL BRUGHA

Cathal Brugha

'An Indomitable Spirit'

DAITHÍ Ó CORRÁIN & GERARD HANLEY

FOUR COURTS PRESS

Typeset in 10.5 pt on 13.5 pt CaslonPro by
Carrigboy Typesetting Services for
FOUR COURTS PRESS LTD
7 Malpas Street, Dublin 8, Ireland
www.fourcourtspress.ie
and in North America for
FOUR COURTS PRESS
c/o IPG, 814 N. Franklin St, Chicago, IL 60610.

A catalogue record for this title is available
from the British Library.

ISBN 978-1-80151-017-2

Printed in England
by CPI Antony Rowe, Chippenham, Wilts.

DÓC
For Bernadette Fagan

GH
In memory of my parents Eddie (1914–86) and Kathleen (1917–2020),
and my brother Éamonn Hanley (1946–2018)

Contents

Abbreviations

BMH	Bureau of Military History
CAB	Cabinet Office, TNA
Cd.	Command paper
CSORP	Chief Secretary's Office Registered Papers
DIB	*Dictionary of Irish biography*
DJ	Department of Justice
DMP	Dublin Metropolitan Police
FJ	*Freeman's Journal*
GHQ	General Headquarters
II	*Irish Independent*
IMA	Irish Military Archives
IP	*Irish Press*
IPP	Irish Parliamentary Party
IRA	Irish Republican Army
IRB	Irish Republican Brotherhood
IT	*Irish Times*
ITGWU	Irish Transport and General Workers' Union
MP	Member of Parliament
MS	Manuscript
MSPC	Military Service Pensions Collection
NAI	National Archives of Ireland
NLI	National Library of Ireland
RIC	Royal Irish Constabulary
TD	Teachta Dála
TNA	National Archives, London
UCDA	University College Dublin Archives
UVF	Ulster Volunteer Force
WS	Witness Statement to the Bureau of Military History

Illustrations

CREDITS

Illustrations 1, 19, 20: Cashman Collection, RTÉ Photographic Archives; 2: courtesy of Andrea O'Reilly; 3, 8: Keogh Photographic Collection, National

Library of Ireland; 4, 7: from J.J. O'Kelly, *Cathal Brugha* (1942); 5, 9: National Library of Ireland; 6: Irish Political Figures Photographic Collection, National Library of Ireland; 10, 14, 15, 17: Hogan-Wilson Collection, National Library of Ireland; 11: Political Personalities Photographic Collection, National Library of Ireland; 12: Éamon de Valera papers, UCD Archives; 13: British Pathé; 16, 21: Poole Collection, National Library of Ireland; 18: The Independent Newspapers (Ireland) Collection, National Library of Ireland; 22 Civil War Figures Photographic Collection, National Library of Ireland; 23: Dublin Corporation Photographic Collection, National Library of Ireland.

Acknowledgments

THAT WE WERE ABLE TO PRODUCE this detailed study over the past four years, despite multiple Covid lockdowns, is due to the extraordinary commitment and professionalism of a host of librarians and archivists. We owe a particular debt of gratitude to the staff of the Cregan and the O'Reilly Libraries in Dublin City University, Dublin City Libraries and Archive, the National Library of Ireland, the National Archives of Ireland, Military Archives, University College Dublin Archives; and, in the UK, the National Archives, London and the Bodleian Library, Oxford. We are especially grateful to Cathal and Catherine MacSwiney Brugha for their generous help and encouragement. We have accrued significant debts to many people who have helped in ways large and small, and often at heroically short notice: Frank Boucher-Hayes, Noel Carolan, Seamus Cullen, Mel Farrell, Belinda Griffin, Fr Tom Looney, Mary MacDiarmada, Pat McCarthy, Andrea O'Reilly, Joe Rodgers and Deirdre Stuart. The support and encouragement of our colleagues in the School of History and Geography at Dublin City University, especially James Kelly and Susan Hegarty as successive heads of school, is greatly appreciated. The acquisition of photographs for this book was assisted by financial support from the Faculty of Humanities and Social Sciences Book Publication Scheme at Dublin City University. As ever, it has been a pleasure to work with the team at Four Courts Press. Particular thanks are due to Martin Fanning for his patience, encouragement and understanding. Our greatest debt is to our respective families for their unwavering support as they too 'lived with Cathal' for several years. DÓC thanks his parents Esther and Teddy; his siblings Aoife, Éanna and Tadhg-Iarla; Bernadette Fagan; Ailís, without whom he would be lost; and the treasured Brían and Íde, whose arrival since this book project first started has been a daily source of joy, happiness and great fun. GH thanks his siblings Marian, Carmel, Declan and Paul. *Buíochas ó chroí libh.*

Daithí Ó Corráin & Gerard Hanley
Dublin City University
March 2022

Prologue

WITHIN SEVEN WEEKS in July and August 1922, Cathal Brugha was joined in death by Harry Boland, Arthur Griffith and Michael Collins. All were significant figures in the Irish Revolution. Brugha and Boland opposed the Anglo-Irish treaty of 1921 and took the republican side in the Irish civil war. Griffith and Collins were the most prominent members of the Irish delegation that negotiated the terms of settlement with Britain and vigorously defended it. Of the four figures, Collins has attracted the most interest from writers, historians, film-makers and commentators of all kinds.[1] Boland and Griffith have also been the subject of several studies.[2] By some distance, Brugha has been the most neglected of the quartet, a sort of leading personality also-ran, despite being a member of the Gaelic League, Irish Republican Brotherhood (IRB) and Irish Volunteers; a celebrated survivor of the 1916 Rising; a crucial figure in the post-Rising reorganization of the Volunteers and Sinn Féin; speaker at the first sitting of Dáil Éireann and president *pro tempore* until Éamon de Valera's return in April 1919; minister for defence in the underground Dáil government during the War of Independence; passionate and acerbic opponent of the Anglo-Irish treaty; a reluctant participant in the civil war, having tried to prevent it, and that conflict's first high profile fatality. Austin Stack's contention in 1929 that Brugha 'is not sufficiently known to the Irish people' has largely remained intact.[3]

Three reasons may be advanced for Brugha's relative neglect by historians. The first was that he left little by way of personal or ministerial papers. There are no diaries or runs of correspondence on which prospective biographers could construct a detailed and textured life story. One consequence of this has been a stilted view of Brugha the soldier, remembered for his heroic defiance in 1916 and again in 1922 rather than for his other involvements in the Irish Revolution with one notable exception. Brugha's fractious relationship with Collins between 1920 and 1922 has attracted considerable commentary but largely from the perspective of Collins rather than of both men.[4] In this regard, Brugha's furious contribution to cabinet meetings in December 1921 and the subsequent treaty debates damaged his reputation at the time and shaped subsequent perceptions of him. A second reason lies in Brugha's personality. A reticent and reserved man, he was not a flamboyant or charismatic figure like Boland or Collins. J.J. O'Kelly recalled how Brugha 'loathed limelight' and 'was so retiring except when there was fighting'.[5] As a worker in Brugha's firm reflected, 'very few people really knew Cathal'.[6] Likewise, Robert Barton, later wondered if, apart from de Valera, any of Brugha's political colleagues had close relations with him.[7] Among his contemporaries, Brugha was a figure more respected than loved. Third and relatedly, that sense of regard was due to Brugha's extraordinary physical courage and his resolute and lifelong pursuit of an Irish republic. James Quinn commented in his *Dictionary of Irish biography* entry on Brugha that 'even in a movement of zealous men and women, Brugha's zeal was exceptional'.[8] In 1919, for instance, Brugha remarked, prophetically, that 'the death he would like to die would be fighting for the Republic'.[9] When that wish transpired on 7 July 1922, the *Irish Times* produced a biting obituary comment of 'Ireland's stormy petrel':

> Of all Ireland's many extremists he was the most extreme. The manner of his death was typical of his life. Cathal Brugha died, as he lived, in the last ditch … All his life he hated England with an intensity of feeling which is rarely found even in this country of painful memories. Whenever there was talk of a rebellion he was at the head of the insurgent movement. Whenever there was talk of a surrender he was found fighting to the last.[10]

While this captured Brugha's noted tenacity, it ascribed to him a simplistic extremism. Ever since, this view has dominated how he has been portrayed and remembered.

Brugha did, however, have his ardent defenders, none more so than the Valentia Island-born J.J. O'Kelly, also known by his *nom de plume* Sceilg. He was a journalist, an Irish language activist, a founder of the Keating branch of the Gaelic League, a member of the first and second Dáil, and a prolific writer.[11] O'Kelly had closely identified with Brugha since their days in the Keating branch. As editor of the *Catholic Bulletin*, a monthly magazine, he played a pivotal role in proclaiming the reputations of those who took part in the 1916 Rising. O'Kelly shared Brugha's opposition to the treaty but did not take up arms. He wrote a great deal about Brugha; the first piece appeared in the *Catholic Bulletin* in August 1922. Twenty years later, this was developed into a 348-page biography called *Cathal Brugha*.[12] Its immediate impact was limited because it was published during the restrictions and tightly regulated censorship of the Second World War and because it was written in Irish in

Gaelic script (cló Gaelach). Overdrawn in style, it offers several defences of Brugha which, beneath thickets of hyperbole, provide valuable life details as well as useful insights on his character and concerns. In 1948 O'Kelly produced a précis of his biography in an anniversary lecture on Brugha, Austin Stack and Terence MacSwiney delivered at Sinn Féin headquarters. This was subsequently published as a pamphlet.[13] O'Kelly's work was infused with his own particular political stance. He had been engaged in a contest for 'republican primacy and purity' fought between Fianna Fáil and Sinn Féin in the 1920s and 1930s.[14] In 1969 Tomás Ó Dochartaigh, general manager of Comhar Linn and the son of Brugha's sister Eveleen, published a complimentary portrayal under the title *Cathal Brugha: a shaol is a thréithe* that drew substantially on O'Kelly's 1942 work.[15] Partly because the biographies by O'Kelly and Ó Dochartaigh were written in Irish and partly because of their hagiographical style, they did little to shake the enduring popular image of Brugha the militant extolled by republican propagandists during and after the Irish civil war. Brugha's only son Ruairí claimed never to have been 'satisfied with the Sceilg book from an objective point of view'.[16]

Predictably, the story of Brugha's courage, defiance and sacrifice in 1916 and 1922 was frequently rehearsed in republican periodicals such as the *Wolfe Tone Annual* published between 1932 and 1962 by Brian O'Higgins, a veteran of the 1916 Rising, anti-treatyite and republican campaigner.[17] Each issue proclaimed a hero or epic episode of Irish history in narrative articles and also occasionally in ballad or verse. Between September 1937 and September 1939, O'Higgins also produced the short-lived *Wolfe Tone Weekly* with the assistance of fellow republican and 1916 veteran, Joseph Clarke. It was supressed by the Irish government on the outbreak of the Second World War but not before aspects of Brugha's career were aired in several issues.[18] Brugha's valour was also instanced in *Guerrilla days in Ireland*, Tom Barry's bestselling memoir of his role as commandant of the West Cork Brigade IRA, first published in 1949: 'Brugha's place in Irish history, high amongst our great patriots, will of a certainty be determined, not by those virtues [of integrity and unselfishness], but because of his incredible courage'.[19]

The approach of the fiftieth anniversary of the 1916 Rising prompted Ruairí Brugha to gather information from his father's contemporaries. These included Richard Mulcahy, who was IRA chief of staff and succeeded Brugha as minister for defence after the treaty split, and Robert Barton, minister for economic affairs in the second Dáil and treaty signatory. Mulcahy compiled valuable 'notes' on Brugha that are among his papers in the University College Dublin Archives. In early 1966 Ruairí corresponded with Florence O'Donoghue, who was Cork No. 1 Brigade intelligence officer during the War of Independence but remained neutral during the civil war and later resurrected his military career in the 1940s, rising to the rank of major. Having served on the advisory committee of the Bureau of Military History (BMH), which collected over 1,700 witness statements from participants in the Irish Revolution in the 1940s and 1950s, O'Donoghue turned his attention to writing about the Irish Revolution in the 1950s and 1960s.[20] On 25 April 1966 he delivered a lecture on Brugha before a meeting of the Fianna Fáil Cumann Tír Chonaill in the Royal Hibernian Hotel in Dublin. Attended by President Éamon de Valera, members of the Fianna Fáil front bench and the Brugha family, it received extensive coverage in the press.[21] The hope expressed by Ruairí Brugha that O'Donoghue's paper would be published was not realized as O'Donoghue died in 1967.[22] Members of Cumann na mBan, who served with Brugha before his death, criticized O'Donoghue for not eliciting their recollections during his research.[23]

The fiftieth anniversary of Brugha's death was marked on 9 July 1972 by a commemorative pageant in Dublin's Olympia Theatre. Produced and scripted by Noel Mannix, the lead role was played by Brugha's grandson and namesake in a performance that ran to over two hours. One theatre critic described it as a folk hero story and 'just as expected in its fervid patriotic aura and in its utter devotion to its subject'.[24] The most arresting performance came from the audience when 91-year-old Joseph Clarke interrupted the show to draw the attention of Taoiseach Jack Lynch and President de Valera to republican prisoners on hunger strike in the Curragh.[25]

Writings about Brugha remained remarkably few in the decades that followed. In 1985 Micheál Ó Cillín contributed a useful article, particularly on Brugha's early life, to the *Dublin Historical Record* and there was a piece about Brugha in his daughter-in-law's memoir published in 2006.[26] More recently in 2015, Fergus O'Farrell completed a MA thesis in UCD under the title 'Cathal Brugha: Peter the painter, candlestick maker, 1916–1921'. This was subsequently published in the new Life & Times series of short biographies by UCD press.[27] Drawing on the BMH, O'Farrell's brief but highly informative account sheds new light on aspects of Brugha's revolutionary career, particularly his involvement in a plot to assassinate the British cabinet during the conscription crisis in 1918.

Cathal Brugha: 'an indomitable spirit' is *not* a biography in the conventional sense of that term. The frustrating paucity of personal papers left by Brugha ensures that he remains an elusive figure; a minute account of his life, thoughts, impulses, concerns, what he read and who he met cannot be constructed. That, however, is not to suggest that a detailed reassessment of his various involvements in the Irish Revolution cannot or should not be attempted. Far from it. The abundance of source material on the Irish Revolution – the 'best documented revolution in modern history', according to one prominent historian – reveals an array of perspectives on Brugha as others (friends, political allies and opponents) saw him during the complexities and strains of an extraordinary period.[28] This wealth of surviving evidence allows the simplistic and reductionist depiction of Brugha to be replaced by a nuanced and multilayered reappraisal of him. That in essence is the goal of this study. What follows is not a defence or rehabilitation of Brugha but rather an attempt to chronicle his public and private life and the influences that shaped him, to examine his uncompromising commitment to an Irish republic that dominated his life, to appraise his complex involvement in the Irish Revolution, to contextualize his relationships with contemporaries such as Collins, de Valera and Mulcahy, to explore how his premature death at the age of forty-seven affected his young family and how his wife, Caitlín, upheld his political principles by standing as a Sinn Féin TD, and to comment on how Brugha's indomitable patriotism was propagandized after his death. Based on exhaustive research of the personal papers of Brugha's numerous contemporaries in the National Library of Ireland and UCD Archives, state papers in Britain and Ireland, press and parliamentary material, the records of the BMH and Military Service Pensions Collection (MSPC), among other sources, we present a broad and multifacted portrait of a complex, tenacious, and often maligned figure.

CHAPTER 1

Beginnings: early life, career and the Gaelic League

Iᴺ 1909 CATHAL BRUGHA WROTE an article on the significance of the Irish language and the importance of the work of the Gaelic League in consolidating it.[1] Like many cultural revivalists in the early twentieth century, his reference point was Thomas Davis, the profoundly influential Young Irelander, whose writings had highlighted the vital connection between language and nationality. Fr Michael Hickey, a Gaelic League stalwart, expounded on this link in a well-known pamphlet: 'the Irish language is the mind, the soul, the great bulwark, the most manifest expression of Irish nationality'.[2] Brugha was inspired by this credo and his deep commitment to the Irish language remained a constant throughout his foreshortened life. When Brugha was born in 1874, the United Kingdom of Great Britain and Ireland had existed for almost three-quarters of a century but in many ways the union was only partial. Although Ireland was relatively tranquil, demands for change in the domains of political status, land ownership and cultural identity intensified in the late nineteenth and early twentieth centuries. Five months before Brugha's birth, sixty Home Rulers were returned at the February 1874 general election with the political goal of restoring an autonomous Irish parliament. Subsequently, the demand for home rule dominated the Irish political landscape until a small band of revolutionaries, Brugha among them, sought a republic by force of arms in 1916. It was a hinge moment for the future of Ireland. As will be shown in this and the next chapter, Brugha's embrace of the zeitgeist of projecting a distinctive cultural identity was the foundation on which his later republicanism was developed.

Brugha's ancestors are believed to have originated in Picardy in northern France and may have been Huguenots (French Protestants of the Calvinist tradition). They moved to Cornwall around 1600. Their original name was probably de Burgo which was anglicized to Burgess. In the mid-seventeenth century, the family settled in the Borris area of County Carlow where they purchased land and became fully absorbed in the Irish way of life. The Burgesses were not landlords but craftsmen who retained their Protestantism.[3] Three Burgess brothers – Edward, Richard and William – moved to Dublin in the early nineteenth century. Edward and Richard became tobacconists with premises at 19 St Mary's Abbey off Capel Street. William (Brugha's grandfather) lived at 1 Salisbury Place off Richmond Road in Drumcondra and in 1846 was listed as a furniture broker on Liffey Street.[4] He and his wife Roseanne had five children and their eldest son, Thomas, born in 1827, was Brugha's father. Some accounts have erroneously suggested that Brugha was the son of a Yorkshireman, which he patently was not.[5] On 17 May 1860 Thomas married Marianne[6] Flynn from 31 Boot Lane.[7] A Roman Catholic, she was the eldest child of Edward Flynn, a partner in an auctioneering firm in Dublin's fish market. Their fourteen children – ten girls and four boys – were all raised as Roman Catholic (and are named in the accompanying note).[8] Charles William St John Burgess, their tenth child and our protagonist, was born on 18 July 1874 at 13 Richmond Avenue, Dublin. According to Ó Dochartaigh, after the birth of six girls in a row Thomas Burgess celebrated the boy's arrival with champagne for himself and the attending doctor.[9] Charlie Burgess, as he was known in his youth, did not become Cathal Brugha until the early years of the twentieth century.

Following somewhat in his father's footsteps, in 1861 Thomas Burgess began to buy and sell furniture at 6 St Mary's Abbey in Dublin before announcing in the press in August of that year that he was moving his business to Great Strand Street.[10] By September 1862 he was trading at 6 Lower Ormond Quay, advertising the sale of household furniture at competitive prices, and also his desire to purchase similar stock from the public.[11] Burgess sourced goods from auctions around Ireland and expanded his repertoire to include fine art, bronzes, statuary, carved oak, rosewood and mahogany furniture, and rugs.[12] A press advertisement in October 1864 announced that the pictures offered for sale by Burgess included works from the collections of the late Arthur Guinness (the brewer), Christopher Coppinger (a distinguished Dublin lawyer) and Arthur Cane (a prominent civil servant).[13] In addition to a substantial showroom on Ormond Quay, from where he also operated as an upholsterer and undertaker, Burgess had a shop at 23 Nassau Street. Until 1867, he regularly placed classified advertisements in the press. Some were addressed to the 'Nobility, Gentry and Parties requiring superior fashionable and antique furniture' and promised the 'most select and grandest collection on sale in the city'.[14] They were indicative of a thriving business.

In November 1867 John Littledale & Co. auctioneers were instructed to dispose of Burgess's stock and his interest in the lease at Ormond Quay on which he had spent £1,100 'in substantial and ornamental improvements and rendering it most suitable for carrying on any first class business'.[15] This was in preparation for relocating his family to London where he had taken a stake in a large furniture wholesale business. In 1870 Burgess was listed in *Kelly's London Directory* as 'an antique furniture dealer' at 72 Newman Street, off Oxford Street, where several antique and curiosity businesses were located.[16] A London press advertisement in September 1870 indicated his willingness to buy furniture stock for ready money.[17] The 1871 census of England, Wales and Scotland recorded Burgess, his wife and six children living at 72 Newman Street; they subsequently moved to No. 78.[18] On Marianne's insistence, all their children were born in Ireland. By 1874 the Burgess family had returned to Dublin and lived at 13 Richmond Avenue until they moved to a more substantial house at 29 North Frederick Street three years later. Burgess maintained both his London business and his premises on Nassau Street and was listed in *Thom's Directory* as an importer and valuer of works of art and decorative furniture.[19] During the 1880s, however, he appears to have concentrated his business efforts in Britain. Burgess may have experienced financial difficulties in 1881 when there was a hurried disposal of his Dublin premises on Nassau Street, although stores at 4 Great Strand Street were retained until the end of his life.[20] The English census in 1881 listed him as a cabinetmaker living in Cheltenham along with his older sons, Edward and Thomas.[21]

In the late 1880s Burgess experienced financial ruin. In August 1887 he sent a shipment of pictures, furniture and statuary worth £6,100 (some accounts suggest £10,000) to Sydney for auction.[22] The consignment was accompanied aboard the SS *Austral* by Edward and Thomas junior. In February 1889 Burgess senior told a bankruptcy court in Sydney that Edward, who was given £80 in cash for expenses, was in sole charge and had instructions to sell the goods and to account for the money realized to him. Nothing more was heard from Edward, who, on arrival in Sydney, placed the goods in the hands of James R. Lawson, an auctioneer. Apparently unknown to Burgess senior, a sale took place on 5 December 1887 that realized £2,900; there were two further sales in August and September 1888 that yielded £2,153. None of the proceeds were remitted to Burgess senior. Instead, they were placed in a trust account in Lawson's name on which Edward drew freely for various expenses.[23] Thomas junior took no active part in the business, but while Edward was in Melbourne for a few months he sold a number of articles and spent the money. In consequence, Thomas junior was sent back to England by Edward. Only then did Burgess senior learn of what had transpired. As one Australian headline put it, he had been 'ruined by his sons in Australia'.[24] On 16 April 1888 he sequestered his estate in Ireland for the benefit of his creditors and was adjudged bankrupt.[25] Burgess told the bankruptcy hearing in Sydney that the shock was so great that his wife became seriously ill.[26] It also made a searing impression on 14-year-old Brugha, who as an adult developed an abhorrence, as we will see in chapters 2 and 5, of financial impropriety and was sometimes accused of parsimony in both his business and political life. The cost of the trip to Australia and legal representation there further increased Burgess's debts.[27] The blow of having to sell the family home at 29 North Frederick Street and their furniture was softened somewhat by Marianne possessing her own property. She had been bequeathed 12, 13 & 14 Great Charles Street by her father. She had gifted No. 14 to her eldest daughter Elizabeth as a wedding present two years earlier. Marianne moved the family into No. 13.[28] Brugha's older brothers never returned to Ireland. Thomas went back to Australia from England and worked variously as a miner, labourer, and station hand. From 1899 until 1940, he lived a pauperized and eccentric existence in a rock shelter on Balmoral Beach in Sydney. Known as 'Dublin Tom', he died in 1943 at the age of seventy-nine.[29] Edward (by now known as Éamonn) moved to South Africa and died in Johannesburg in 1952.

The deterioration in the family's financial situation had significant implications for the younger children's education. Brugha first attended the Colmcille Schools on Dominick Street near his North Frederick Street home. In 1888 he and Alfred, his younger brother by four years, were pupils in Belvedere College. Their enrolment lasted only two years due no doubt to the bankruptcy that also ended the boarding school education of Brugha's sisters. Brugha was regarded as a good all-round pupil with a particular interest in Irish history. He provided some home-schooling for his sisters but according to Eveleen taught them nothing but Irish history.[30]

Although short in stature, Brugha, who was strong and wiry, excelled in a wide variety of sports. An expert swimmer by a young age, he won several prizes as a member of the Pembroke Swimming Club and the Half Moon Club on Dublin's South Wall (which sponsored a trophy in his honour after his death).[31] As a 17-year-old, Brugha swam from Howth pier to Ireland's Eye.[32] He played rugby at half back for Belvedere, Clontarf and Santry. While at Belvedere he took up cricket and eventually became a bowler for Pembroke Cricket Club, earning the accolade of 'the best fast bowler in Leinster'.[33] Brugha had a particular talent for gymnastics and was a member of the National Club. In the mid-1890s he transferred to Dublin Gymnasium (also known as City of Dublin) and enjoyed considerable success. He was a member of the team that defeated Dawson Street at the Earlsfort Terrace skating rink in April 1897 to win the Irish Shield. The *Freeman's Journal* reported how Brugha's side prevailed by thirteen points in 'a great contest' before a large

crowd with Charles Burgess earning the second-highest number of points for
his team.[34] Two years later and again at Earlsfort Terrace, Brugha was one of
an eight-member Gymnasium team that triumphed over a highly rated team
from Dundee. He was the second-highest points scorer for his team in the
rings event and third in the rope competition.[35] In April 1899 an inaugural
international gymnastics competition was held in Dublin with an
amalgamated England and Wales team competing against teams from
Scotland and Ireland. Brugha was on the Irish team that gave 'an indifferent
display' to come third on 496 points; the victorious Scots scored 655.[36] He
was back to winning ways with Dublin Gymnasium who defeated the
Birmingham Athletic Institute, one of the foremost clubs in England, in the
first round of the Adams Shield in March 1901.[37] J.J. O'Kelly described
Brugha in gushing terms as 'amongst the best all round athletes and gymnasts
of his weight in Ireland at the close of the last [nineteenth] century'.[38] He was
also a fine boxer, a keen cyclist, and played Gaelic football and hurling.

After his stint in Belvedere College, Brugha studied medicine for two
years.[39] However, family circumstances militated against a medical career. His
father's health declined following his bankruptcy and efforts to revive his
business failed. Aged seventy-two, Thomas Burgess died of heart failure on 6
April 1899 at 12 Glenarm Avenue, Drumcondra; he was buried in Glasnevin
cemetery.[40] As Alfred Burgess noted, his father was by then a comparatively
poor man and his estate, which was left to Marianne, was valued at just £20.[41]
Brugha became the family's chief breadwinner. He initially secured
employment in London, but his stay there was short as he disliked his
voluntary exile.[42] On returning to Dublin he secured a position in 1891 as a
clerk with Hayes & Finch, a Liverpool company founded in 1882 that
manufactured and supplied church candles and other ecclesiastical goods. Its
Dublin office was at 3 Eustace Street. Brugha's abilities were soon recognized
and he was promoted to travelling salesman, a position that required travel
throughout Ireland.[43] His occupation was given as commercial traveller on the
1901 census. At that time, he lived at 1 Ardilaun Terrace, beside Croke Park,
with his mother, his aunt Lucy Flynn, his mother's nephew, a boarder,
his brother Alfred, who was a clerk in Dublin Corporation, and four
unmarried sisters: Mary, a governess; Pauline and Adelaide, described as
having no occupation; and Eveleen, a shop assistant.[44] Sometime after
this, Brugha took up residence at 36 Cabra Road and his mother is recorded
as dying there after 'a lingering illness' on 7 March 1907.[45] Adelaide and
Alfred also lived there as lodgers.[46] Tomás Ó Dochartaigh, who was Brugha's
nephew, draws attention to the familial support that Brugha provided. At one
point when Ó Dochartaigh's parents and three siblings could find no suitable

1 Cathal Brugha in the 1910s. Regarded as a natty dresser, this was
appropriate for his work as a commercial traveller.

accommodation, Brugha took them all to live with him. Before Brugha got married he bought a small shop and a house for his sisters, Madeline and Adelaide.[47]

Brugha's pursuits were not confined to the sporting realm. He had a keen interest in literature, was a good linguist and 'a pleasing singer' who was fond of music, particularly classical.[48] Known for his dapper and well-groomed appearance (see plate 1), russet hair, sallow skin, a broad forehead, penetrating blue eyes and tight lips dominated his features. Brugha's reticent and generally aloof disposition often obscured a more genial inclination. At times characterized as intense and austere, some of his closer acquaintances noted a charm of manner. He did not smoke, drink or swear. He was devout and attended Mass and prayed the rosary daily.[49] A revealing portrait was sketched by Robert Barton who suggested that Brugha's taut mouth and long upper lip created the impression of 'a hard and stubborn character, unyielding to persuasion or force. His smile however revealed an inner self that made an instant appeal'.[50] Brugha developed a reputation as a pugnacious opponent when opinions were divided. For Barton, he 'made up in willpower … for what he lacked in argumentative acumen'.[51]

A pivotal moment of awakening in Brugha's life occurred in 1899 when he was introduced to the Gaelic League by John Carrig, a friend of his brother Alfred.[52] Founded in July 1893 by Eoin MacNeill and Douglas Hyde 'for the sole purpose of keeping the Irish language spoken in Ireland', the League was the most influential of the various organizations devoted to the preservation or revival of the Irish language in the late nineteenth and early twentieth centuries. Through the language it was hoped to appeal to people of all political and religious persuasions. The League sought to revive Irish as a spoken and literary language by organizing language classes, publishing existing Irish literature and promoting new literary output. Hyde, the organization's most important public figure, was the first president and retained that position until 1915. He was the Sligo-born son of a Church of Ireland rector who grew up in Roscommon and was educated in Trinity College. MacNeill was born in County Antrim and served as first vice-president of the League. He was also the inaugural editor of *An Claidheamh Soluis*, the League's newspaper, which provided an outlet for new verse and prose.

The Gaelic League sought mass membership and was enthusiastically received. By 1908, according to the League's own figures, there were an estimated 671 branches in Ireland.[53] They were affiliated to the governing council or central executive of the League known as the coiste gnótha. The League was involved in a number of high-profile campaigns. It lobbied for the rights of Irish speakers to give testimony in court in 1897; the Dublin branches secured Irish as a requirement for employment in Dublin Corporation; in 1899 the League opposed attempts to have Irish removed from the school syllabus for the intermediate examination; and in 1908–9, following the establishment of the National University of Ireland (NUI), it campaigned to have Irish made a compulsory matriculation subject. Fittingly, Hyde became the first professor of Modern Irish at University College Dublin from 1908 until 1932, and MacNeill became the first professor of Early and Medieval Irish History there. In addition to cultural revival, the league served social needs for the urban lower middle classes of English-speaking Ireland. Dunleavy and Dunleavy argue that it had 'a faddish attraction for hundreds of young men and women drawn to it more for its collateral social activities than for its language classes'.[54]

Brugha's interest in the Irish language and in Gaelic culture generally became intense. He increased his fluency by regularly attending classes in Parnell Square, where he also participated in céilí-dancing, singing, lectures and debate. Brugha took part in the Fleming Companionship, inaugurated in 1901 in Cork to continue the work of John Fleming (Seán Pléimeann) to systematize the study of the language. He passed examinations in 1902 with honours and won second prize in the 'Hall of Readers' category, a feat repeated in 1903.[55] Brugha was one of several Irish-speakers and people interested in Irish-Ireland ideas who met informally in An Stad on North Frederick Street, a shop and guesthouse owned by Charles McGarvey. Patrons included Arthur Griffith, The O'Rahilly, John MacBride, Oliver St John Gogarty and James Joyce.[56] In 1906 Brugha entered six competitions in Oireachtas na Gaeilge, winning five first places in the language competition.[57] When his work as a salesman brought him to various parts of the country, he sought out and attended local Gaelic League classes and functions. In this way, Brugha became well known in League circles across Ireland. Peadar Ó hAnnracháin, a Gaelic League organizer in Munster, recalled meeting Brugha one day in his hometown of Skibbereen when Brugha emerged from the local post office indignant that the Irish form of his name was not accepted on a postal order.[58] Brugha developed a preference for Munster Irish, especially the dialect of Gaeltacht na nDéise in west Waterford, a place with which he developed a personal and enduring bond. When on business in Waterford city, he regularly stayed at the Metropole Hotel on Bridge Street. He used these occasions to visit Martin Coleman, a native of Kill parish then in his eighties who was regarded as 'the finest Irish speaker and the greatest repository of Gaelic lore in prose, verse, proverb, prayer and every class of folklore' in the area.[59] Brugha often stayed with him until late into the night conversing in Irish and taking

notes on Irish sayings and local history. When business took him to
Dungarvan, he cycled to Ring and immersed himself in the company of local
Irish-speakers of all ages. Brugha quickly acquired both fluency and a perfect
blas (accent) such that he could pass as a native speaker.[60] By 1910, Brugha,
along with Piaras Béaslaí, the journalist, member of the Gaelic League and
later revolutionary, regularly attended the League's summer college, Coláiste
na Mumhan at Ballingeary in the Muskerry Gaeltacht of west Cork, as both
a student and a teacher of Irish.[61]

Alfred Burgess located the origins of Brugha's republican or separatist
outlook as springing from the family's nationalist political background, which
was further developed through his involvement in the Gaelic League.[62]
Politically, Thomas Burgess senior was an ardent supporter of Charles Parnell,
the Irish Party leader. There are some suggestions that he may have been a
Fenian.[63] In 1873 the *Irishman* recorded that he contributed £1 to a national
testimonial for John Mitchel, the militant journalist, Irish nationalist and
defender of slavery in the US, who had fallen into poverty and poor health.[64]
Through his association with the Gaelic League, Charlie Burgess gaelicized
his name to Cathal Brugha. Reports in *An Claidheamh Soluis* and elsewhere
indicate that this was a gradual process. The English version of Brugha's name
appeared in the early years of the twentieth century, then for a time he was
Cathal Burgess, then variously Cathal Mac Burgéasaigh, Buirghéis and
Buirréas before settling on Brugha. Whereas he recorded his name in English
in the 1901 census, he was the only male 'Brugha' in Ireland in the 1911 census
and for good measure he entered the surnames of his sisters Ada (Adelaide)
and Madeline as Brugha also.[65] In addition, he concentrated more intently on
native games such as handball, hurling and Gaelic football rather than 'Saxon'
sports.[66] Piaras Béaslaí suggested that the League exerted a 'considerable
influence' on the outlook of Brugha and others.[67] This was also the subject of
reflection by fellow revolutionary and future president of Ireland Seán T.
O'Kelly:

> When he knew Cathal Brugha first, almost a quarter of a century ago,
> he was just a typical Dublin youth, a little more serious minded than
> the average, full of the joys of living … Suddenly he, like Padraic Pearse,
> Eamon Ceannt, Joseph Plunkett, Tom MacDonagh, and thousands of
> others were touched by the fire of Gaelic enthusiasm enkindled
> through the foundation of the Gaelic League.[68]

Roy Foster points out that radical nationalism seemed to thrive among
medical students. As well as Brugha, other advanced nationalist medical
students included Ernie O'Malley, James Ryan, Patrick McCartan, Daniel T.

Sheehan, Eimar O'Duffy, Kathleen Lynn, Dorothy Stopford and Brigid Lyons Thornton.[69]

Brugha was born at a time of national reawakening. As with many others, membership of the Gaelic League, and of the Keating branch in particular, changed the whole pattern of his life. This branch was founded in 1901 by four Munster men: J.J. O'Kelly ('Sceilg'), a writer, teacher and journalist from Valentia Island; Shan Ó Cuív, a journalist and writer from Macroom; Tadhg Ó Donnchadha ('Torna'), future professor of Irish at University College Cork; and Risteard Ó Foghludha ('Fiachra Éilgeach'), a teacher and journalist from east Cork. The branch was notable for the number of female members and its vigorous promotion of the Munster rather than the Connacht dialect. Its meeting room was first in Parnell Square and later at 2 North Frederick Street. Brugha was a member of the Keating branch from its inception.[70] Keatingites were regular patrons of An Stad (discussed above). Over time, the Keating branch developed a more advanced nationalist position than the coiste gnótha (central executive of the Gaelic League) and became identified with separatism.[71]

The Keating branch was regularly at loggerheads with the coiste gnótha. Relations became strained in 1903 when Patrick Pearse rather than J.J. O'Kelly was selected as editor of *An Claidheamh Soluis*. They were soured further when members of the coiste gnótha, including Hyde, were involved in the dismissal of O'Kelly from the *Freeman's Journal*. A third controversy arose in 1908 around the payment of special fees for the teaching of Irish. This played out in bitter differences of opinion between Pearse and others in the pages of *An Claidheamh Soluis*. He accused the Keating branch of being 'moral thugs', 'cranks', 'traitors', and the 'wrecker party'.[72] Pearse maintained that if the teaching of the national language was the first duty of the teacher, a special payment was unnecessary. Béaslaí, a member of the coiste gnótha and the Keating branch, accused Pearse of acting without sanction. Brugha wrote an angry letter in which he argued that teachers needed to be induced not compelled. This was published by Pearse with a comment that the 'views of Gaels who disagree with us are just as sure of a place in our columns'.[73] Pearse was regularly needled by Fr Patrick Dinneen, the Irish language lexicographer and president of the Keating branch since 1904, who referred to him as 'Pee Haitch' and criticized his literary outputs and editorship of *An Claidheamh Soluis*.[74] The controversy around the payment of special fees was not the first sharp difference of opinion between Brugha and Pearse. In 1907 the Liberal government introduced the Irish Council bill which proposed to devolve to a 107-member council some administrative powers in areas such as education, agriculture and local government. Famously, it was described by the prime minister as 'a little, modest, shy humble effort to give administrative powers to the Irish people'. Nationalist Ireland condemned it as an inadequate substitute for home rule. J.J. O'Kelly recalled that when Pearse wrote an article strongly supporting the Irish Council bill Brugha 'felt very sore, and took him severely to task for it'.[75] When Dinneen resigned the presidency of the Keating branch in 1908, he was succeeded by Brugha who retained the position until his death in 1922.[76] As the next chapter will discuss, in 1908 Brugha also joined the IRB with which the Keating branch became synonymous.

It was inevitable that the politically neutral stance of the Gaelic League, championed by Hyde, would become unsustainable during the 1910s as the prospect of Irish home rule appeared to be within the grasp of the Irish Parliamentary Party (IPP) at Westminster. Sections of the League regarded the organization as part of a broader preparation for a home rule state.[77] By contrast, other factions such as the Keating branch had become increasingly separatist. Diarmuid Lynch, who represented New York on the coiste gnótha and was a member of the IRB, described the League's executive as divided into a left wing deemed separatist and a Redmondite right wing led by Hyde.[78] Attempts to commit the League to a political programme were initially repelled.[79] In November 1914 the Keating branch passed a resolution, strongly favoured by Brugha, calling on the coiste gnótha to adopt a 'political' structure.[80] In August 1915 an ard fheis in Dundalk, heavily influenced by the IRB, voted to make the League a specifically nationalist body committed to freeing Ireland from foreign rule.[81] Hyde resigned the presidency. In retrospect, MacNeill, who supported the change, believed that the 'Gaelic League had been severely damaged by linking its fortunes to a political movement' and that Hyde's stance was the correct one.[82] In their biography of Hyde, Janet and Gareth Dunleavy provide a tantalizing snippet on Brugha's position when the third home rule bill had been suspended for the duration of the First World War. Whereas Hyde counselled patience for the promise of home rule at the end of the conflict, Brugha maintained that 'only a fool or a dreamer' would believe in such promises 'which had no more substance behind them than those in Hyde's own Fairy talking to his Tinker' – a reference to Hyde's 1902 play, *An Tincéar agus an tSídheóg* ('The Tinker and the Fairy').[83]

The influence of the Gaelic League on Brugha was not only far-reaching in terms of his political outlook but it also shaped his career and personal life. In 1909 he resigned from his employment with Hayes & Finch, due, apparently, to a growing unease at working for an English firm. He formed a partnership with brothers Anthony and Vincent Lalor, who had also worked with Hayes & Finch. Messrs Lalor Ltd was incorporated on 14 June 1909; the

2 The factory of Lalor Ltd, *c.*1920s.

capital for the venture was provided by J.J. Lalor, father of Anthony and Vincent, who had a well-established business as a printer of memorial cards.[84] With premises at 14 Lower Ormond Quay, close to where Brugha's father had traded, and a branch office in Cork, the company specialized in the manufacture of church candles and the supply of allied products such as sanctuary oils, incense tapers, night lights and so forth. In 1911 *The Belvederian* (an annual Belvedere College magazine) praised the new company established by its alumni, Brugha and Vincent Lalor: 'In this age of Irish industrial revival, it is satisfactory to record that our old Belvederians are not wanting.'[85] Brugha worked as a director of Lalor Ltd until his death in 1922. As minister for defence in the underground Dáil Éireann from 1919, he managed his ministerial portfolio from Ormond Quay and the premises was regularly used from 1914 onward for receiving and dispatching arms and ammunition. The Derry city-born Joseph O'Doherty, a member of the IRB, the Irish Volunteers and a future Sinn Féin TD, worked as a travelling salesman for Lalor Ltd. Like Brugha, he used his employment as a cover for smuggling arms.[86] Robert Barton recalled the rather spartan conditions in Ormond Quay and suggested that Brugha must have been 'both economical and conservative for his business premises appeared to me to lack any modernising influence' (see plate 2).[87] In addition to his role as director,

3 Éamonn Ceannt in civilian attire, c.1914.

Brugha continued to travel, as he had done with Hayes & Finch, to various parts of the country to maintain and develop business contacts for the new company. As a businessman, he became a member of the council of the Dublin Industrial Development Association and shared the concerns of many Dublin businesses about the 'dislocation of trade in the city' caused by 'repeated strikes and lockouts which [had] inflicted serious injury' on industry.[88] In September 1911 Brugha, along with other businessmen, demanded new methods for settling trade disputes, including the establishment of courts of arbitration.[89]

The Gaelic League brought Brugha into contact with many like-minded individuals. One of the most significant was Éamonn Ceannt (see plate 3), with whom he shared the same passion for the language, cultural nationalism, sport and music. Like Brugha, Ceannt was also a devout Catholic and did not drink or smoke.[90] A close friendship soon developed, and this was reinforced by their involvement in the Irish Volunteers, discussed in the next chapter. By far the most important connection made through the League occurred in 1909 while on a visit to Birr, County Offaly. As was his wont, Brugha attended a local language class where he met Kathleen Kingston, his future wife. Several other future revolutionaries met their wives through the League, including Ceannt and de Valera. Born on 9 December 1879, Catherine (Kathleen) Mary was the youngest of six children of William Kingston and Catherine Roche, who owned a successful general provisions business on Main Street, Birr. Kathleen had a comfortable upbringing. She was educated at the Sacred Heart Convent, Roscrea, and one of her sisters joined that order.[91] For many years, her father had been a member of Birr Town Commissioners. On his death in 1904, he was described as belonging to one of the oldest and most respected families in the midlands.[92] Kathleen's mother continued to manage the family business with the assistance of her children, an example that Kathleen would follow in the 1920s.[93] As a local Gaelic League organizer, Kathleen, like many women of her generation, enjoyed the access to leadership roles and public life that it provided. Her enthusiasm for the Irish language and culture, her interest in public and political life, and her religious devotion ensured that a relationship with Brugha blossomed.[94] This was facilitated by Kathleen's relocation to Dublin in 1910. She lived at 5 Fitzwilliam Terrace, Upper Rathmines, with her mother and sister, Máire. Her older brother, John, was a member of the Congregation of the Holy Spirit (Spiritans) and on the staff in nearby St Mary's College, Rathmines (he was later bursar of Rockwell College).[95]

Kathleen and Cathal were married in the Church of the Three Patrons, Rathgar, on 8 February 1912. Friends and members of the Keating branch arranged a celebratory function in Wynn's Hotel, Lower Abbey Street, on 5 June 1912. The chairman of the event remarked that they had chosen the occasion of Brugha's marriage 'to mark in some slight way the esteem and respect in which they held him ... [and] ... his work for Ireland'.[96] Another claimed that Brugha's 'labours were an inspiration to every one of them'.[97] After her marriage, Kathleen became known as Caitlín Brugha and continued her own Gaelic League activities in Dublin.[98] Following the death of Caitlín's mother in January 1914, 5 Fitzwilliam Terrace became the Brugha home; it was shared with Caitlín's eldest sister Máire who helped rear Caitlín's young family after Brugha's death.[99] Between 1912 and 1922, the Brughas welcomed six children: Nollaig (1912), Nóinín (1913), Brenda (1916), Ruairí (1917),

4 The Brugha family, *c.* July 1921. *Left to right*: Brenda, Cathal, Nóinín, Nollaig,
Caitlín, Fidelma and Ruairí.

Fidelma (1919) and Nessa (1922) (see plate 4).[100] Brugha's nephew Liam
Ó Dochartaigh (and older brother of Tomás) recalled that his uncle was full
of fun among children, never visited them without bringing sweets, and was
generally quiet among adults. Brugha's sister emphasized his charitableness
and love of children.[101] As will be shown, family life was greatly disrupted by
Brugha's revolutionary career. While the word 'indomitable' is used in the
subtitle of this study, the term can be applied with equal facility to Caitlín who
shared her husband's ardent republicanism and supported his activities.

There were four significant constants in Brugha's life: his family, his
religion, the Irish language and republicanism. As this chapter has shown,
Burgess the sportsman became Brugha the Gaelic Leaguer. Writing in 1957,
Piaras Béaslaí described the League as 'one of the greatest forces ... in the
national resurgence that led to the events of 1916 and 1921' and stated that
many of those prominent in the 1916 Rising and War of Independence 'made
their first appearance as public men in the Irish language movement'.[102] While

that portrayal is true of Brugha and other members of the revolutionary elite, it is too simplistic to suggest a direct correlation between the Gaelic League and militant separatism. For Brugha the language movement became an essential underpinning and he later claimed that there would have been no 1916 Rising without it.[103] But the path towards the 1916 insurrection was less the product of the Gaelic League than of the IRB as the custodian of advanced republicanism with the Irish Volunteers as its instrument. To these we now turn.

CHAPTER 2

Republican: stalwart of the Irish Republican Brotherhood and Irish Volunteers

B RUGHA ADMIRED Owen Roe O'Neill (*c*.1580–1649), one of Ireland's greatest military commanders and a member of the famous O'Neill dynasty of Ulster. O'Neill's appeal for Brugha lay not simply in his reputation as a brilliant military strategist, much esteemed by the Spanish court, but also because O'Neill was the first prominent figure to pursue separatist plans for Ireland.[1] Three centuries later, Brugha was resolutely committed to the same cause. A decisive moment came in 1908 when Brugha joined the IRB, an oath-bound secret society committed to achieving an independent republic by force of arms. First established in 1858, it was one of the most influential of all Irish nationalist organizations. Through it, Brugha became invested in the Irish Volunteers as an officer in the 4th Battalion, Dublin Brigade, at a time when Irish politics was convulsed first by unionist opposition to home rule and then by the outbreak of the First World War. For Brugha and his ilk, volunteering was 'an act of reappropriation' and a liberation from an increasingly distant home rule campaign at Westminster.[2] It was a means of realizing the core principle of the IRB.

A semi-moribund IRB was revitalized in the early years of the twentieth century by younger adherents such as Denis McCullough, Bulmer Hobson and Seán Mac Diarmada, and by Tom Clarke, the veteran embodiment of militant separatism. Clarke's return to Dublin from the United States in 1907 was significant. Co-opted on to the supreme council of the IRB and appointed treasurer, he assisted younger radicals to gain control of the organization, most notably Mac Diarmada, who became national organizer in 1908, and Hobson who moved to Dublin in the same year. Clarke's tobacconist shop at 75a Parnell Street became a hub for IRB activity. His close links with Clan na Gael proved crucial in the realization of his dream of an Irish rising during his lifetime. The IRB was vampiric with its members infiltrating other nationalist organizations such as the Gaelic League and the GAA.[3]

The Keating branch of the Gaelic League was a manifestation of this phenomenon. It was closely associated with the Teeling circle of the IRB, named in honour of the United Irishman Bartholomew Teeling (1774–98), and chaired by Hobson. Biographies of Brugha are silent on who inducted him into the IRB but it was probably Clarke or Mac Diarmada. Brugha's unanimous election as president of the Keating branch in 1908 owed much to the brotherhood. It was an appointment that proved influential. Under Brugha's presidency, no other branch of the Gaelic League became so immersed in revolutionary politics and it became the 'branch of choice for Dublin IRB men and later revolutionaries'.[4] A list of those holding dual membership of the Keating branch and Teeling circle reads like a who's who of the leadership of advanced nationalism. It included, among others, Piaras Béaslaí, Diarmuid Lynch, Patrick McCartan, Richard Mulcahy, Seán T. O'Kelly, Diarmuid O'Hegarty, Seán Ó Murthuile and Gearóid O'Sullivan. All became prominent in either the Irish Volunteers, the Irish Republican Army (IRA) or Sinn Féin. O'Sullivan as adjutant-general, Ó Murthuile as quartermaster-general, Mulcahy as commander-in-chief and O'Hegarty as director of intelligence were 'four of the five brass hats' who on 16 December 1922 took over the British army's general headquarters building in Parkgate Street in Dublin – the final act in the evacuation of the British army.[5] Prior to the 1916 Rising, IRB meetings at 46 Parnell Square – headquarters of the Keating branch – were also attended by Mac Diarmada, Clarke, Thomas Ashe and the then largely unknown Michael Collins.[6] It was little wonder that J.J. O'Kelly later described the Keating branch as a 'mainspring' that made separatist nationalism 'a going concern in the full sense'.[7]

Many of the young Turks in the IRB using the front of the Dungannon Clubs flirted with Arthur Griffith's Cumann na nGaedheal organization and in 1907 the two bodies merged to form the Sinn Féin League. Griffith, an energetic, radical, and often pugnacious journalist, was useful to the IRB which supported his *Sinn Féin* newspaper. During the opening decade of the twentieth century Brugha does not appear to have been attracted to political activity. Although Florrie O'Donoghue claimed that Brugha took no active part in Sinn Féin other than providing some financial support for its eponymous newspaper, he did attend the convention that launched the organization in 1905.[8] The political impact of Sinn Féin before the 1916 Rising was at best marginal and, as Michael Laffan observes, 'even at the humble level of local politics its fortunes were mixed'.[9] As mentioned in chapter one, in 1909 Brugha contributed a long article to *Leabhar na hÉireann*, a yearbook published by Sinn Féin, on the Gaelic League and the language revival movement.

The coming together of republican separatism and Griffith's dual monarchist 'Hungarian policy' was brief and from 1908 there was a parting of ways. The internal power struggle within the IRB was also at this time reaching a climax. The older generation was content simply to keep the principles of the IRB alive and saw no prospect of a rising in their time.[10] Two developments in 1910 tilted the balance decisively in favour of the Clarke-Hobson-Mac Diarmada vanguard. The first was the expulsion of P.T. Daly, secretary of the IRB supreme council, for misappropriating IRB funds. The second was the publication in November 1910 of *Irish Freedom*, which 'marked the reassertion of the Fenian ideal'.[11] This monthly newspaper was financed, managed and written by the IRB with Hobson and P.S. O'Hegarty penning the editorials. Brugha was also involved in the management of *Irish Freedom*. The venture demonstrated the determination of the younger more radical members 'to reanimate Irish republicanism from within, while at the same time aggressively and openly propagating its message'.[12] An internal row about the newspaper in late 1911 prompted several resignations and cleared the way for the younger generation. 'So for the first time', wrote O'Hegarty, 'we had the men who meant business in complete control of things. It took us a year to get things smoothed down, and all the ropes in our hands.'[13] *Irish Freedom* was strongly critical of the IPP and partition. By the time of the newspaper's suppression in December 1914, the IRB was effectively preaching armed insurrection.[14]

Brugha's business role as a travelling salesman throughout the country and extensive Gaelic League connections provided an ideal cover to evangelize for the revamped IRB. Diarmuid Lynch, who served as provincial representative for Munster on the IRB supreme council from 1911 until 1916, recalled that Brugha had 'a sort of roving commission to do IRB organising', by keeping in contact with IRB centres in various towns while passing through on business, and enrolling new members as the occasion arose.[15] Perhaps the most prominent of Brugha's IRB recruits in 1908 was Austin Stack, the Kerry Volunteer leader and later minister for home affairs in the cabinet established by Dáil Éireann. In statements to the BMH, there are occasional references to Brugha inducting new members in Munster. John McKenna recalled how Brugha swore him in while representing Lalors Ltd in Listowel in 1910.[16] Brugha also visited other parts of Kerry and was a regular visitor to Caherciveen where he formed a warm personal friendship with Jeremiah O'Connell, a schoolteacher, who was sworn into the IRB by Brugha in 1914 and subsequently became the local centre.[17] The following October, O'Connell was dismissed from his position in Filemore National School, after a protracted dispute, due to his involvement in the Irish Volunteers.[18] In Kilrush, County Clare, Art O'Donnell, a future IRA commandant, recalled how Mac Diarmada and Brugha visited the town around 1910 and formally initiated an IRB circle there.[19]

Brugha also recruited for the IRB in Dublin and at times demurred when prospective members were mooted. A case in point was Patrick Pearse whose 'passage into the IRB was oddly long drawn-out', having been vetoed on a number of occasions by Brugha and Hobson, among others.[20] Brugha was critical of Pearse's financial affairs as he did not keep regular accounts, typically used one loan to pay off another, spent beyond his means on improvements at St Enda's and St Ita's, and constantly teetered on the brink of bankruptcy. At one point, Brugha had helped organize a Gaelic tournament to raise funds for Pearse to reduce his large debts.[21] Brugha's distaste for poor financial practice surfaced in a much more pronounced way during the War of Independence when he was sharply critical of Michael Collins's approach to underwriting IRA gun-running. As alluded to in the previous chapter, Brugha's insistence on probity and financial rectitude may have stemmed from the financial dishonesty that destroyed his father's business.

As a fellow Keatingite, Piaras Béaslaí's entry to the IRB was straight forward. He was inducted by Brugha in 1914. At that time Béaslaí was a producer with na hAisteoirí, a company of Gaelic amateur actors, and in due course all the male members joined the Teeling circle. Although they became bitterly estranged over the Anglo-Irish treaty in 1921, Béaslaí and Brugha enjoyed an intimate friendship in the 1910s and were closely associated in the Gaelic League, the IRB, the Irish Volunteers and Sinn Féin.[22] In his hagiographic biography of Michael Collins, Béaslaí produced a fascinating portrait of Brugha's character and qualities. He described him as 'of the highest character, ardently patriotic and devoted to the cause of Ireland … a man of the kindliest nature, a sincere friend, gentle in manner, but, as he was later to prove, as firm as steel, and as brave as a lion'.[23] Brugha's 'chief defect', according to Béaslaí and coloured by the passions of the Irish civil war, was an inaccessibility to new ideas 'outside a narrow and rigid list of formulas which he had prescribed for himself. His leonine courage was accompanied by an almost taurine obstinacy'.[24] Seán Ó Murthuile, a member of the Keating branch and a prominent Gaelic League organizer, was another sworn in by Brugha in 1912 and later became secretary of the IRB supreme council with close ties to Collins.[25]

As one might expect, the activities of the IRB were closely monitored by the authorities. Brugha first came to the attention of the Dublin Metropolitan Police (DMP) and Dublin Castle in 1911, following his involvement in a nationalist demonstration organized by the United National Societies at Beresford Place, Dublin on 22 June, the date of George V's coronation in Westminster Abbey. The *Freeman's Journal* described the event as an 'Irish independence demonstration' and 'a monster gathering representative of all sections of Dublin Nationalists'.[26] The rally, attended, by about 30,000, was presided over by Henry Dixon, who had been a leading member of the Parnellite wing of the IPP during the 'Split'. He claimed it was necessary to take action because 'efforts had been made to sap their Nationality by representing Ireland as a contented province of Britain'.[27] Brugha was joined on the platform by Laurence Ginnell, an agrarian radical, MP for Westmeath North from 1906 until 1918 and a bitter critic of the IPP; Arthur Griffith; Major John MacBride, founder and second in command of the Irish Transvaal Brigade of the Boer army and a member of the IRB supreme council until replaced by Mac Diarmada in late 1911; Dr Patrick McCartan, a member of the IRB and Clan na Gael's man in Ireland; and Countess Markievicz, founder in 1909 with Hobson of Fianna Éireann (the republican boy scouts) and by 1911 an executive member of Sinn Féin and Inghinidhe na hÉireann.[28] It was reported that after the demonstration had ended enormous crowds thronged the main streets of the city until midnight with many singing 'God Save Ireland'.[29]

In July 1911 Tom Clarke organized a pilgrimage to the grave of Theobald Wolfe Tone (1763–98), founder of the United Irishmen, in Bodenstown churchyard in County Kildare to counter the visit of George V to Dublin. During the visit he hung a large banner outside his shop which read: 'Damn your concessions, England, we want our country!'[30] Brugha was in agreement with such sentiments.[31] From the 1840s Tone's grave had been a place of pilgrimage, first for the Young Irelanders and subsequently for the Fenians who were inspired by his advocacy of physical force.[32] In 1912 Hobson and Brugha delivered graveside addresses in English and Irish respectively.[33] Bodenstown proved an important rite of passage for Pearse who was invited by Clarke to deliver the oration in June 1913, six months before his belated admission to the IRB. Brugha was an annual visitor to Bodenstown with a small group of friends, including Éamonn Ceannt, who was sworn into the IRB in 1912, and Páraig Ó Caoimh (Paudeen O'Keeffe). The occasion became an annual cycling expedition for Brugha and his friends. They generally assembled near Naas and after visiting Tone's grave returned to Dublin by way of Blessington, where Brugha generally insisted on buying the cycling party a 'tea meal'.[34] On these occasions, Ó Caoimh recalled Brugha's good spirits and entertaining manner.[35]

Despite notable advances in terms of its organizational structure and calibre of membership, the IRB remained a cadre of officers without an army. That situation was transformed by the third home rule crisis of 1912–14. In return for maintaining the Liberals in office, following the December 1910 general election, and for supporting the Parliament Act of 1911, which limited the veto powers of the House of Lords, John Redmond secured a commitment from Prime Minister H.H. Asquith to introduce the third home rule bill in April 1912. But the Irish question evolved in ways that were not foreseen due to the depth of Ulster unionist resistance. The signing of the Ulster covenant in September 1912 and the formation of the paramilitary Ulster Volunteer Force (UVF) in January 1913 emphasized that unionists were willing to adopt radical political defiance and militant action to defeat home rule. The implications were not lost on the IRB. At a quarterly meeting of the Sinn Féin executive in January 1913, Ceannt proposed a resolution that 'it is the duty of all Irishmen to possess a knowledge of arms'.[36] To this end, Ceannt, Brugha, Ó Caoimh and Michael Joseph O'Rahilly (The O'Rahilly), a journalist and nationalist but not a member of the IRB, began to practise their marksmanship at a rifle range set up at the Greenmount Oil Works in Harold's Cross. Brugha quickly developed a reputation as an excellent shot. At the end of August 1913, as protesting workers were attacked by police on Sackville Street during the lockout, Brugha claimed a prize of £5 presented by the manager of the Greenmount Oil Company. This was to the chagrin of Ó Caoimh, who declared: 'bloody bulls' eyes all the time'.[37]

The need for a nationalist response to the UVF was obvious to the IRB. Hobson claimed that the IRB began to drill in July 1913 and P.S. O'Hegarty recalled the acquisition of military textbooks and some rifles at that time.[38] As 1913 progressed, there was growing unease in wider nationalist circles with the accommodations of Redmondism at Westminster over mooted partition and the attenuation of the home rule bill. By October the starting of the Irish Volunteers could no longer be delayed and the Dublin Centres Board of the IRB, presided over by Hobson, decided to call a public meeting to this end with the approval of the supreme council.[39] However, this was overtaken on 1 November by the publication in *An Claidheamh Soluis* of an article – 'The North Began' by Eoin MacNeill which advocated a nationalist counterweight to the UVF. This led to a meeting at Wynn's Hotel on 11 November to discuss 'the extension of the Volunteer movement in Ireland'.[40] The objects of the Volunteers were drafted by The O'Rahilly, namely 'to secure and maintain the rights and liberties common to all the people of Ireland without distinction of class, creed or politics'.[41] This line subsequently featured in the manifesto of the Volunteers and on enrolment forms. It indicated not only a desire to exclude sectionalism of every kind but also for rapprochement with northern unionists. It echoed the principles of the Gaelic League and also article two of the pre-1917 IRB constitution that referred to the 'cultivation of union and brotherly love amongst Irishmen'.[42]

The Irish Volunteers were launched publicly on 25 November 1913 in the Rotunda Rink. Although the largest hall in Dublin, it could not accommodate the crowd of about 7,000 and two overflow meetings were held.[43] In his address to the main meeting, MacNeill declared that there was no hostility towards the UVF but that it was incumbent on nationalists to take 'a firm stand in defence of their liberties' against the machinations of the Conservatives in Britain to 'force upon this country some diminished and mutilated form of National self-government'.[44] Pearse was more provocative. He suggested that there would be no true freedom for Ireland within the British Empire, but an armed Ireland would at least make a better bargain.[45] In 1913 and early 1914 even the most dedicated IRB members wanted home rule to prevail. For instance, in December 1913 Mac Diarmada hoped that 'even in its rottenest form' home rule 'will get through' and the following month Pearse, speaking in Limerick, described the Volunteers as 'a weapon' that would enable Redmond to 'enforce the demand for home rule'.[46] From the outset, it was agreed that the Irish Volunteers should be non-party and representative of all shades of nationalist opinion. Predictably, the IPP did not welcome the establishment of a nationalist militia at such a delicate political juncture but did not openly condemn it. Prominent public supporters of the party held aloof because, as Matthew Kelly argues, 'adherence to the Volunteers inescapably bespoke a critique of Redmond's strategy and constitutional nationalism more generally'.[47]

Until June 1914, the direction of the Volunteers was entrusted to a provisional committee under the chairmanship of MacNeill. By design, its composition was 'widely representative' and by early 1914 was thirty strong.[48] Several members such as Pearse, O'Rahilly and MacNeill were Gaelic League veterans, five were members of Fianna Éireann, and many were moderate but not uncritical followers of the IPP. About half the committee were or later became members of the IRB. Although not a member of this committee, Brugha's zeal for volunteering and IRB membership ensured an officer role within the Volunteers. After the Rotunda meeting, Diarmuid Lynch recalled an IRB meeting at which it was emphasized that IRB men should 'cooperate to the fullest extent in the formation of Irish Volunteer companies and of choosing IRB men as officers where possible'.[49]

MacNeill professed himself astonished at the success of the Rotunda meeting when between three and four thousand enrolled, Brugha among them.[50] Despite this strong start, the Volunteers grew slowly thereafter. The force attracted little interest from the authorities who were far more concerned with the militancy of the UVF in the north and by Larkinism and labour disputes in Dublin. Augustine Birrell, Irish chief secretary, did not bring the Irish Volunteers to the cabinet's notice until April 1914.[51] This reflected the enormous challenges that confronted the Volunteers in the early months of its existence. Trained officers, funds, facilities and arms were scarce. In addition, the Irish Citizen Army was actively hostile until James Connolly took charge of that body in October 1914. Indeed, supporters of Larkin had attempted to disrupt the Rotunda meeting.[52]

To put the Volunteers on a firmer military footing, Colonel Maurice Moore from Mayo, a retired commander of the Connaught Rangers and a brother of novelist George Moore, joined the provisional committee as inspector general in January 1914. There was a unanimous desire to see the Volunteer movement take firm root throughout the country. This was aided by the publication from February 1914 of the *Irish Volunteer* newspaper, which provided a vital means of transmitting general orders and other communications. The first issue on 7 February carried instructions for forming companies and Volunteers were advised to secure the services of ex-British army men familiar with the *British Infantry Manual* (1911) which had been adopted by the provisional committee. Headquarters sent members of the provisional committee to address meetings but had no regular organizers or funds to cover expenses.

The initial development of the Volunteers was concentrated in Dublin, which was divided into four battalion areas – a configuration that remained until 1921. The 1st Battalion drilled at Colmcille hall on Blackhall Street; companies of the 1st and 2nd Battalions drilled at the Gaelic League hall at 25 Parnell Square; the 3rd Battalion drilled at York Street, and the 4th Battalion at Kimmage, where a rifle range was set up. At company and battalion levels, officers were chosen by election, subject to approval from headquarters. Brugha became a second lieutenant in D Company, 4th Battalion, under a Captain O'Donnell.[53]

Statements to the BMH and the *Irish Volunteer* offer little information on the early development of Brugha's 4th Battalion. However, George Walsh, a 44-year-old builder from Harold's Cross, provisional committee member and first lieutenant in D Company, kept a record of the initial activities at Larkfield in Kimmage.[54] Between forty and seventy men drilled in January and February 1914 with subscriptions amounting to an average of 15s. a week. Drilling took place initially on Fridays but from late January also on Mondays. The facilities were so rudimentary that Walsh had to supply a table and Ceannt a lamp. Brugha served on a company committee that assisted Walsh and Ceannt with organizational matters. D Company was also the first company to have a 'march out' in mid-January.[55] The training comprised mostly drilling – squad, section, company, close and open order – but later on also included musketry, bayonet fighting and elementary tactics.[56]

The interrelated issues of raising funds and acquiring arms were the most pressing for the provisional committee. Arms were crucial for sustaining interest and morale. As one instructor put it, 'I know what the rifle means to the holder: its touch is magnetic and obviously his real training only begins when he gets it'.[57] With three volunteer armies in existence – the UVF, the Irish Citizen Army and the Irish Volunteers – the British government signalled its unease by issuing two royal proclamations on 4 December 1913. One banned the importation of arms and ammunition; the second prohibited the carrying by sea of military stores. The timing, only days after the foundation of the Volunteers, outraged the provisional committee whose members saw it as blatant discrimination in favour of the already, as they imagined, armed UVF.[58] In mid-December the provisional committee issued an appeal at home and abroad for contributions to an Irish Volunteer fund to arm and equip the force; this was regularly renewed during 1914. In March headquarters purchased 100 practice rifles, which were distributed to the training centres of the four Dublin battalions.[59] Initially, funds came in slowly and in small amounts. This meant that only a few rifles could be purchased, even allowing for the large international trade in dated military technology.[60] MacNeill and The O'Rahilly formed a secret arms sub-committee that acted as a purchasing agent, selling on any weapons to corps across the country. Companies were instructed to open a rifle fund. As few individual Volunteers were able to buy rifles for cash, purchase was generally by instalment. By contrast, the UVF, backed by wealthy industrialists in Ulster and Britain, was flush with money and arms, having smuggled 25,000 rifles and three million rounds of ammunition into the ports of Larne, Bangor and Donaghadee on the night of 24–5 April 1914 in blatant defiance of the authorities. This facilitated the selling of UVF rifles for a nominal sum.[61] The lesson of the UVF activity for the Irish Volunteers was clear.

The development of the Volunteers in 1914 was intertwined with the fate of the third home rule bill. Many British figures, not least the monarch, believed that only the exclusion of Ulster would avert civil war. Redmond was forced to accept the principle of partition in early March ostensibly as 'the price of peace', though the area and duration of the exclusion was not specified.[62] In March 1914 the Royal Irish Constabulary (RIC) reported Volunteer corps in twenty-five counties, numbering an estimated 14,000.[63] By May this figure had almost doubled owing to the increasingly charged political atmosphere created by the Curragh incident, UVF gun-running and humiliating concessions by the IPP on some form of exclusion for Ulster.

The UVF gun-running alarmed Redmond as did the announcement by Asquith that the third reading of the Government of Ireland bill on 25 May

1914 would be accompanied by an amending bill with special provisions for the exclusion of Ulster. This forced an abrupt change of stance towards the Volunteers. The Ancient Order of Hibernians, a friendly society with close connections to the IPP, was authorized to cooperate fully with the Volunteers. Consequently, between May and June membership of the Volunteers jumped from 25,326 to 62,316.[64] Advanced nationalists naturally feared the capture of the Volunteers by the IPP. As Volunteer numbers increased, criticism by IPP politicians that the provisional committee was neither elected nor representative intensified. Redmond made his move in an open letter in the *Freeman's Journal* on 10 June, demanding that the committee accept twenty-five of his nominees 'so as to give confidence to all shades of National opinion'.[65] A long-expected moment of crisis had arrived.

Roger Casement played a pivotal role in convincing a majority on the provisional committee to accept Redmond's nominees. He won over MacNeill then Moore and then Hobson, and they carried the provisional committee meeting on 16 June by eighteen votes to nine.[66] There were IRB members on both sides of the vote. Those opposed to the admission of Redmond's nominees, including Ceannt, Pearse and Mac Diarmada, felt duty bound to continue their work and appealed to the rank and file in agreement with them 'to sink their personal feelings and persist in their efforts to make the Irish Volunteers an efficient armed force'.[67] Hobson did not want the IRB to return to a state of toiling in obscurity and believed that accepting Redmond's nominees 'saved the Volunteer movement from collapse' because it was 'too new and not sufficiently organised'.[68] For his actions Hobson paid a high personal price. He was 'assailed with extraordinary bitterness' by Clarke and Mac Diarmada, lost the editorship of *Irish Freedom* and was expelled from the IRB supreme council, though he retained the position of Dublin centre until after the Rising.[69] Hobson's action was crucial because it bought the Volunteers time to become more firmly established. It also allowed the IRB to exert greater control over the organization in terms of finance, arms and the appointment of reliable officers.

A nationalist riposte to Larne was suggested by Mary Spring-Rice, a member of the Monteagle family of Foynes, County Limerick, and enabled by a committee of friends of the Volunteers in London which raised £1,560 for the purchase of arms. Erskine Childers, author of the classic spy novel *Riddle of the Sands*, had made contact with the Volunteers in Dublin and was entrusted with the operation. Casement acted as liaison between the provisional and London committees. He told only Hobson who was tasked with making arrangements for the landing of arms at Howth in Dublin and Kilcoole in Wicklow. The London committee dispatched Darrel Figgis to

Germany to purchase 1,500 Mauser rifles of an old single-shot pattern and ammunition. The material was conveyed to Ireland on two yachts: *Asgard*, owned by Molly and Erskine Childers, was dangerously overloaded with 900 weapons and 26,000 rounds of ammunition, while *Kelpie*, owned by Conor O'Brien, transported 600 rifles and 20,000 rounds of ammunition. To reduce suspicion, *Kelpie*'s cargo was later transferred to *Chotah*, owned by Sir Thomas Myles, a prominent Dublin surgeon and regular yachtsman.

The deliberate landing of arms in broad daylight at 12:30 on Sunday 26 July 1914 was arguably the option least expected by the authorities. It also made possible the concentration of a large body of Volunteers as Sunday was their weekly training day for route marches. The propaganda value of such an audacious plan, even though a fraction of the scale of Larne, was significant. Hobson had prepared carefully. First, carpenter members of the IRB made 150 oak batons to deal, if necessary, with interfering coastguards or police. They were conveyed to Howth in a cart by the Fianna under the command of Pádraig Ó Riain, a member of the provisional committee and chief scout of the Fianna.[70] Second, about twenty members of the IRB under Brugha went to Howth on the morning of 26 July to prevent police interference in the event of *Asgard* reaching harbour before the main body of about 800 Volunteers arrived.[71] It was a measure of the esteem in which Brugha was held that he was entrusted with securing the pier. Third, a number of taxis were waiting to convey the heavy ammunition boxes. *Asgard* was unloaded smoothly in half an hour amid feverish general excitement. During the operation Childers and Figgis were introduced to Brugha. 'No one could look on that man [Brugha]', Figgis later vividly recalled, 'without perceiving his consuming, terrific, relentless courage. He was a born fighter … a sword … that would be shattered before it would bend'.[72] Brugha and Ceannt had dispatched couriers during the earlier part of the day to Clarke's house on Amiens Street to keep Mac Diarmada and Clarke abreast of developments before the pair took a taxi to Howth.[73]

Fearing the intervention of the authorities (or perhaps hoping for it), the Volunteers marched to Raheny before a halt was allowed. A brief scuffle occurred between Volunteers and a force of DMP and soldiers of the 2nd Battalion, The King's Own Scottish Borderers, under the command of William V. Harrel, DMP assistant commissioner, which tried to disarm the Volunteers. Two soldiers and a few Volunteers were injured. During the altercation, Hobson ordered the Volunteers to disperse with their weapons. According to one account, Brugha took over command of D Company and ordered the men to stand two deep across the road to prevent the military from advancing and thereby allowing Volunteers at the rear to get their arms away safely.[74] The military was reinforced by an additional sixty men and at around 17:30 were ordered to return to the Royal Barracks. The column was heckled by a crowd described in the regimental diary as 'a savage mob'. In Sackville Street the situation became tense when stones and other missiles were hurled at the military. Near the Ha'penny Bridge, the soldiers discharged a volley without warning.[75] Three civilians were killed, a fourth later died of his injuries, and twenty-six others were injured.[76] The incident became known as the 'Bachelor's Walk Massacre'. The funeral of the three victims on 29 July was one of the largest seen in Dublin. Archbishop William Walsh of Dublin presided at a solemn high Mass in the pro-cathedral and 3,000 Volunteers lined the funeral route to Glasnevin cemetery.

With none of the publicity of Howth, the second consignment of arms was landed at Kilcoole on 1–2 August and once again Brugha, Ceannt and Hobson were involved, and Seán T. O'Kelly played a supervisory role. Though not in the IRB, Seán Fitzgibbon carried out the arrangements in conjunction with Mac Diarmada. The plan was to bring a motor charabanc to Kilcoole on a Saturday afternoon under the pretence of an excursion and remain in seclusion until Myles's yacht arrived.[77] It was intended to take the cargo by charabanc to Pearse's school at St Enda's from where it would be dispersed by motor car. The material was landed by rowboat between 01:00 and 03:00. During this part of the operation two RIC men on patrol were taken prisoner. When they attempted to escape they were apprehended by Brugha and a few other Volunteers.[78] All went smoothly until the axle of the heavily loaded charabanc broke when passing through Bray. Fortunately, the driver knew a local resident and Liam Mellows went by borrowed motorcycle to St Enda's to have the motor cars that had assembled there collect the weapons.[79]

The successful landing of arms at Howth and the outrage occasioned by the Bachelor's Walk shootings had a number of consequences. First, the government was widely condemned. The contrasting treatment of the Ulster and Irish Volunteers was seized on by contemporaries and widely reported in the press. A commission of enquiry found that the circumstances did not warrant military intervention or the use of firearms and that the Dublin victims were innocent. The commissioners then fudged the verdict by suggesting that the soldiers believed that an order had been given and that Major Haig, the commanding officer, was not aware that the rifles were loaded.[80] Second, Bachelor's Walk occasioned an influx of Volunteers. Pearse suggested the loss of life had

> given public sentiment just that turn that was desirable. The army is an object of odium and derision, and the Volunteers are the heroes of the hour. The whole movement, the whole country, has been re-baptised by bloodshed for Ireland.[81]

The improved but still inadequate availability of weapons was a further incentive for new members. Numbers peaked in September 1914 when the authorities estimated that there were 1,618 branches and 182,822 members.[82] Third, the financial difficulties of the Volunteers were eased. Following the *coup de theatre* of Howth, Hobson recalled how 'money poured in for arms from every part of Ireland, and American subscriptions came in at the rate of £1,000 a month'.[83] Fourth, tensions on the provisional committee increased. Lastly, gun-running by both the UVF and the Irish Volunteers represented another lurch towards civil war.

The impact of the First World War on Ireland and on the Volunteers was profound. The seemingly inevitable conflict between nationalists and unionists was neutralized by the outbreak of war in Europe. 'For Redmond, Irish involvement in the war promised the reward of early Home Rule; while [Edward] Carson saw an opportunity to strengthen Ulster's case for exclusion by demonstrating that its loyalism was more than a rhetorical figment.'[84] Accordingly, on 3 August the IPP leader committed himself to the war effort by offering the services of the Volunteers to defend Ireland. Redmond envisaged the Volunteers being equipped and instructed for home defence without altering the character of the organization. He maintained that this would release about 20,000 regular troops for foreign service and, inculcate a sense of patriotism and enthusiasm which might lead Volunteers to enlist in due course. To Redmond's dismay, Herbert Kitchener, the newly appointed secretary of state for war, was hostile to the idea of regularizing and arming the Volunteers. Second, the war swiftly extinguished the novelty of playing soldiers as many Volunteers feared being called to the front. Third, the war created the immediate difficulty of how to sustain momentum as drill instructors, typically reservists or ex-servicemen, were recalled to their regiments at precisely the time the Volunteers needed them most. In many locations the existence of companies on paper was not matched by any practical martial preparation. Even in Dublin a large-scale training exercise on Three Rock Mountain on 6 September, involving the city battalions, demonstrated weak organization and a sham battle ended in confusion.[85]

The question of whether the Volunteers should serve Ireland or the British Empire inflamed tensions on the provisional committee. On 7 August three out of five Dublin battalions unanimously adopted a resolution to cooperate with Ulster for the defence of Ireland but not to support the British government against foreign nations with which Ireland had no quarrel; an *Irish Volunteer* editorial at the end of August declared: 'England's war is not our war'.[86] The last meeting of the full committee took place on 10 September and was an extraordinary affair. The Redmondite faction repudiated the anti-war position of the *Irish Volunteer*. The IRB position was exemplified by Ceannt who proposed that no form of compulsory service be applied to Ireland and that control of the Volunteers remain with the Volunteers or an Irish parliament.[87] Pearse was interrupted mid speech and called a 'contemptible cur' before blows were exchanged. Séamus O'Connor recalled that Father O'Hare, one of Redmond's nominees on the committee, drew a small automatic pistol and challenged Ceannt to draw his revolver![88]

Home rule was placed on the statute book on 18 September 1914 but was immediately suspended for the duration of the war and accompanied by an unspecified provision for the special treatment of Ulster. Two days later, at Woodenbridge in County Wicklow, in his first public address since the passage of home rule, Redmond exhorted those present to serve 'wherever the firing line extends, in defence of right, freedom and religion'.[89] This fractured the Volunteers. Three days later, twenty members of the original provisional committee issued a statement denouncing Redmond's departure from the 'published and accepted aims and pledges' of the Volunteers and repudiating 'the claim of any man to offer up the blood and lives of the sons of Irishmen and Irishwomen to the services of the British Empire while no National Government which could speak and act for the people of Ireland is allowed to exist'.[90] This group pledged to carry on the Volunteers without the Redmondites, retained the name Irish Volunteers but only numbered between 11,000 and 13,000. The overwhelming majority supported the position of the IPP and formed a rival organization, the Irish National Volunteers.

Dublin was the pivotal battleground following the split. Only the 1st and 3rd Battalions returned a majority against affiliation with the Redmondites. Two of six companies in the 2nd Battalion and two of seven in the 4th sided with the Irish Volunteers. One member of Brugha's D Company recalled about 55 in favour of the Volunteers and just over forty for Redmond.[91] According to one source, sixteen battalion meetings were held in the DMP district between 24 September and 31 October after which it was estimated that 4,850 Volunteers sided with Redmond and 1,900 with MacNeill.[92] The split did not cause despondency among the minority. A jubilant Pearse believed that the secessionists had 'pulled the Volunteers straight'.[93] The following year the executive of the Irish Volunteers made clear that its commitment to the original pledge 'to secure and maintain the rights and liberties common to all the people of Ireland' implied 'the attainment of a National Government, free from external political interference', opposition to any partition of Ireland, and resistance to any scheme of compulsory military service or taxation imposed without the consent of the Irish people.[94] Notably, the Irish Volunteers were labelled Sinn Féiners from September 1914 and increasingly characterized in official discourse as fomenters of disloyalty. However, declining numbers of Volunteers of both kinds was a recurring theme in police reports at the end of 1914 when it was estimated that there were just under 10,000 Irish Volunteers.[95]

Although the Irish Volunteers did not have the backing of a major political party, ready access to a national newspaper, significant financial resources, or arms, they were, nevertheless, better placed than their rivals to survive. First, a smaller more compact body was, to quote Pearse, 'infinitely more valuable than the unwieldy loosely held together mixum-gatherum force we had before the split'.[96] This reduced body included a number of committed ideological zealots imbued with a deep sense of mission. Brugha was a case in point. Second, despite his subsequent historical marginalization, Hobson was an organizer *par excellence* and played a vital role as honorary secretary in sustaining the Volunteers. Third, by opposing conscription the Irish Volunteers exploited a potent mobilizing asset and one that increased to their benefit as the war inexorably continued.

One of Hobson's first tasks was to organize a Volunteer convention in the Abbey Theatre on 25 October 1914. That it took place so promptly was a statement of intent. Members of the original provisional committee were re-elected *en masse* as a central executive. A motion by Ceannt pledged resistance to compulsory military service.[97] In December 1914 a headquarters staff of six was appointed with MacNeill as chief of staff, Pearse as director of military organization, Joseph Plunkett as director of military operations, Thomas MacDonagh as director of training, Hobson as quartermaster, and The O'Rahilly as director of arms. In 1915 a seventh member was added when Ceannt became director of communications. A quartet of full-time organizers was appointed in January 1915: Ernest Blythe, Liam Mellows, Robert Monteith and J.J. O'Connell, who had been in the US army. The latter became chief of inspection in November 1915 when the headquarters staff were reappointed.[98] Until reinforced by American funds, the Irish Volunteers were not financially strong enough to undertake a nationwide campaign of organization. The challenge was captured by the *Irish Volunteer*: 'In 1914 we needed only courage: in 1915 we shall need the rarer and more valuable thing, grit. It was easy to start the Irish Volunteers; it will be difficult to make them a really effective military force.'[99]

The need for 'grit' in the face of popular indifference and at times outright hostility was demonstrated at various Volunteer parades in the opening months of 1915. For instance, on Whit Sunday, 23 May 1915 Volunteer companies from Dublin, Tipperary, Cork and Limerick were aggressively scorned as they marched through the streets of Limerick. They encountered particular antagonism from soldiers' wives and families. James Gubbins recalled how at Mungret Street the Volunteers were 'met by a fusillade of stones, jampots, bits of lead etc. ... and all along the way the women from the windows of the houses kept peppering away at them with various sorts of missiles'.[100] Dan Breen of Tipperary later wrote that he had been 'sorely tempted to open fire on the hostile crowd'.[101] Brugha witnessed this first hand as he attended with Pearse, Clarke and Ned Daly – an indication of his alignment with the insurrectionist wing of the Volunteers. Pearse maintained that the 'hostile element was small' and that the Volunteers had largely maintained their discipline despite significant provocation offered at least some consolation.[102]

As the year progressed, the tide began slowly to turn and the work of organization was aided by several factors. The first was the formation in May of a coalition government that included Edward Carson, Ulster Unionist leader, and Bonar Law, leader of the Conservative Party, but not Redmond, who though offered a position refused to join in line with IPP policy. The Conservatives in the coalition strongly favoured conscription. Second, conscription was a real concern in Ireland from autumn 1914 which worked to the advantage of the Irish Volunteers. Fears intensified in summer 1915 when the registration bill, intended to establish the numbers employed in each industry, was regarded as a precursor to conscription. There was a further panic in November 1915 occasioned by the lord lieutenant's recruitment conference. This was a boon for the Irish Volunteers, who organized an anti-conscription meeting in Dublin City Hall on 6 December 1915, only weeks before conscription was introduced in Britain. A third factor was the publicity generated by the carefully staged public funeral of the Fenian Jeremiah O'Donovan Rossa in August 1915 at which Pearse delivered his classic graveside declaration that Ireland unfree shall never be at peace. All military guard duties were carried out by the Dublin Brigade. Fourth, was the increasing dissatisfaction with the IPP among moderate nationalists. Robbed of home rule, Redmond increasingly bore responsibility for a British war effort that imposed heavy burdens on Ireland without any facility to shape that policy. A fifth factor was that the authorities displayed a curious reluctance, partly due to legal technicalities and partly due to concern about the vulnerability of the IPP, to take decisive action against Volunteer organizers. When deportation orders were eventually issued against Blythe, Mellows and Denis McCullough, they became a source of protest and publicity for the Volunteers.

At the second Volunteer convention on 31 October 1915, Hobson emphasized the progress that the Volunteers had made and claimed there were 200 corps 'in active existence'.[103] Brugha was not listed as a delegate but D Company, 4th Battalion, proposed a number of motions that reflected

Brugha's stance. These concerned the training and certification of officers, the provision of arms by headquarters to country units lest men fall away from the Volunteers, that measures be taken to secure the country's food supply, and that measures be taken to end the victimization of Volunteers by the authorities.[104] A report on the four Dublin battalions for the second half of 1915 found that although there were 1,786 on the rolls, the average attendance at company drill was forty-four per cent. Furthermore, for every two recruits who joined, one fell away.[105] In Dublin in March 1915 all company officers were directed to attend Saturday night military lectures at 41 Kildare Street and fieldwork on Wednesday afternoons in Father Mathew Park, Fairview.[106] Among Ceannt's papers was a set of notes from a lecture on street fighting in May 1915 where subjects such as preparing a house, a street, artillery, fire control and the height of buildings were addressed.[107] Within the Dublin battalions training was intensified with special classes for new recruits, signallers and engineers; shooting competitions; special parades for NCOs under Eimar O'Duffy; and some large-scale manoeuvres such as at Finglas at Easter 1915.[108] Members of the 4th Battalion began a rifle fund and Séamus Murphy recalled how 'some men gave up their little luxury of a "pint" or some other amenity in order to help to acquire arms'.[109] To this end, in October 1915 companies were instructed to form collection committees for the Defence of Ireland fund. Arms were also acquired in more clandestine fashion from serving soldiers and from those with access to barracks stores.[110]

Several significant appointments were made in March 1915. Captains Pearse, O'Rahilly, Plunkett and Hobson were promoted to commandants unattached; Edward Daly to commandant 1st Battalion; MacDonagh to commandant 2nd Battalion; de Valera to commandant 3rd Battalion; and Ceannt to commandant 4th Battalion with Lieutenant Brugha becoming his vice-commandant.[111] In this capacity, Brugha was regularly present at various parades within the battalion. In his BMH statement Henry Murray recalled Brugha as 'a fearless fighter and a hard hater of everything British but that he did not possess the personal qualities that inspired the respect and regard shown to Patrick Pearse, Éamonn Ceannt, Seán McDermott and Con Colbert'.[112] As dedicated Volunteers, Ceannt and Brugha led by example. It is hardly surprising that Brugha did not occupy a more prominent position within the Volunteer leadership before 1916 given the many demands on his time as the father of two young daughters – Nollaig and Nóinín (who was born two weeks after the inaugural meeting of the Volunteers in 1913) – and a commercial traveller, not to mention his Gaelic League responsibilities, attendance at IRB meetings, and inspections of Volunteer companies in his battalion.[113]

5 Cathal Brugha in his Irish Volunteer uniform, the best-known image of him.

A fundamental fault line divided the leadership of the Volunteers. An advanced section, which included Brugha, favoured a pre-emptive insurrection before the end of the First World War and from May 1915 a secret military committee (later styled council) conspired to this end. It was composed of

Pearse, Plunkett and Ceannt, and in September was augmented by Clarke and Mac Diarmada. By contrast, Hobson, MacNeill and O'Connell favoured a longer term strategy of building up a force of armed Volunteers prepared for defensive resistance in the event of an attempt at their suppression, if conscription was imposed on Ireland, or if the food supply was endangered. Such circumstances would, they held, rally the public and consequently have a reasonable prospect of success. O'Connell regarded the Volunteers as a military body not a revolutionary one and was firmly of the view that the Volunteers should not engage in a state of war unless it was forced on them. In his memoir of the Volunteers, O'Connell revealed his frustration with some of the amateur generals on the headquarters staff and their lack of real military knowledge and his fears of a pre-emptive insurrection.[114] He also emphasized the proficiency of the subordinate ranks in Dublin, who were better officered, better resourced in terms of arms and equipment, and exhibited a stronger *esprit de corps* than anywhere else in the country.

One of the most enduring images of Brugha is a head and shoulders portrait of him in military uniform (see plate 5), 'a hard-featured little soldier with a firmly-set mouth [and] piercing eyes', as an unnamed contemporary recalled.[115] In many respects, Brugha embodied the application and dedication of the well-trained Dublin Volunteer officers noted by O'Connell. But as the next chapter will illustrate his republicanism also exemplified the first editorial of the *Irish Volunteer* in 1914: 'Belief must always translate itself into action or that belief will die.'[116]

CHAPTER 3

Rebel: the 1916 Rising

THE 1916 RISING WOULD have been inconceivable without Britain's involvement in a major international conflict and the IRB supreme council resolved to act before the First World War ended. On 22 February 1916, Matthew Nathan, the Irish under-secretary, informed the prime minister that while he did not 'consider that there was any likelihood at the present time of a serious rising', he believed that 'the Sinn Féiners were increasing in strength and that side by side with the Irish Volunteer organisation the remnants and disciples of the old Fenians were planning outrages and violent measures'.[1] As events transpired two months later, he could scarcely have been more accurate when a general call for manoeuvres on Easter Sunday, 23 April 1916 was in fact a cover for a surprise insurrection. Even though the preparations miscarried due to the interception of the *Aud* with its cargo of arms from Germany and an eleventh-hour countermanding order by Eoin MacNeill, the 1916 Rising was the most serious and sustained rebellion in Ireland for more than half a century, despite being predominantly a Dublin affair. The story of the 1916 Rising has been much written about and will not be recounted here.[2] This chapter focuses on Brugha's involvement.

From January 1916 secret meetings of the military council were usually held in Éamonn Ceannt's house in Dolphin's Barn. The membership of the council increased from five to seven through the addition of the socialist leader James Connolly and Thomas MacDonagh, commandant 2nd Dublin Battalion. In the wake of the defeated 1913 lockout and James Larkin's departure for the United States, Connolly became acting general secretary of the transport union and commander of the Irish Citizen Army. This had been established in November 1913 as a worker's defence militia. In early 1916 the IRB was forced to dissuade Connolly from leading an independent insurrection in favour of a joint uprising. MacDonagh was co-opted in April. From early 1916 a growing number of IRB members and Volunteers were aware that something would occur at Easter, though they had no knowledge of the precise details. To this end, St Patrick's Day parades in 1916 were in fact a trial mobilization.

Brugha was not a member of the military council. A close inspection of DMP intelligence reports in the twelve months prior to the Rising reveals that he did not come to their beady attention as a 'suspect' or 'extremist' in police parlance, despite his role as vice-commandant of the 4th Battalion. If this suggests that Brugha was on the margins such an impression is misleading as he was one of a select few taken into the confidence of the military council. He was entrusted on oath with a copy of Connolly's plans for the Rising and given instructions to put them into effect should the leaders be arrested.[3] Taking no chances, Brugha stored the plans for the Rising in a canister, which was then buried in a small greenhouse at the end of his garden at 5 Fitzwilliam Terrace; the interment was witnessed only by Caitlín.[4] It was a measure of the bond between them and their shared uncompromising republicanism.

Brugha was also tasked with conveying instructions to Volunteers in Kilkenny, about two weeks before the Rising. Outside the Volunteer hall on King (now St Kieran) Street, he met Thomas Treacy, captain of A Company in Kilkenny, who knew Brugha by sight as a commercial traveller. Brugha informed him that general manoeuvres were to be arranged for Easter Sunday and that A Company, with whatever arms they possessed, was to proceed via Borris to the Scullogue Gap on the county border with Wexford to link up with Wexford Volunteers. No operations were to be carried out until both contingents came together. Captain J.J. O'Connell would command all units in Kilkenny city and county, and the combined force on the Wexford border.[5] When Treacy objected that his company only had about twenty-five guns (including pistols) for some sixty men, Brugha told him that they would be able to acquire 'sufficient arms and ammunition for all the available men' from Dr Dundon in Borris. After Brugha's visit the Kilkenny Volunteers held a meeting and decided to seek clarification. Peter Deloughry and Pat Corcoran, Kilkenny Volunteers who had contact with general headquarters, were dispatched to Dublin to consult MacNeill about the planned rising. It was agreed that Kilkenny would not rise without a direct order from MacNeill and the advice brought back to Kilkenny was that 'everything was off'.[6]

The military council had successfully kept MacNeill and Hobson in the dark about their plans as both were opposed to a pre-emptive insurrection without popular support. The conspirators went to significant lengths to convince MacNeill that the authorities aimed to suppress and disarm the Volunteers by concocting the 'Castle document' – possibly based on actual contingency plans – the details of which were dramatically revealed on Wednesday 19 April. This prompted MacNeill to issue an 'urgent' circular advising officers 'to preserve the arms and the organisation of the Irish Volunteers'.[7] The military council also took the extraordinary step of involving J.J. O'Connell and Seán Fitzgibbon in its plans, even though neither was in the IRB, and both were aligned with Hobson and MacNeill. Fitzgibbon, who had successfully organized the Kilcoole gun-running in August 1914, was asked by Ceannt to reprise this role by landing German arms in Kerry. O'Connell was ordered to lead the Volunteers in south-east Leinster. This may simply have been designed to ensure his absence from Dublin at Easter.

The plans of the military council unravelled in the days before Easter Sunday due to incompetence, misfortune and excessive secrecy. Having waited two days off the Kerry coast, the *Aud* was intercepted by the British Navy and scuttled by its crew off Queenstown (now Cobh). On Holy Thursday 20 April Hobson received 'an urgent note' from O'Connell to see him at headquarters that evening.[8] Satisfied that the general mobilization planned for Easter Sunday was really a cover for insurrection, they went to see MacNeill. When the three confronted Pearse in St Enda's, he admitted for the first time that a rising was planned. In the early hours of 21 April, MacNeill drafted three orders: one cancelling all orders issued by Pearse, a second empowering Hobson to issue orders in MacNeill's name, and a third giving O'Connell authority over the Volunteers in Munster.[9] Later that day Roger Casement was arrested in Kerry. He had travelled to Ireland on a German submarine to prevent the rebellion as he feared it would be crushed without substantial German assistance. That evening Hobson was detained by the military council. It finally became clear to MacNeill that he had been deceived: the arms ship sent from Germany had been sunk and the Castle Document had been a ruse.

On Saturday evening 22 April MacNeill again confronted Pearse, reminding him that he was still chief of staff and signalling his intention to dispatch orders around the country for a general demobilization. MacNeill then went to the house of his family doctor Séamus O'Kelly at 53 Rathgar Road, where he had arranged to meet members of the Volunteer central executive and headquarters staff.[10] Some prominent figures were absent. Ceannt and his wife, Áine, had spent the day in Dalkey with friends and did not know about the meeting in Rathgar.[11] Brugha was also unaware of it until Paudeen O'Keeffe fetched him from his bed in Rathmines. The various meetings in O'Kelly's house continued into the early hours of the morning and the visitors included Plunkett, MacDonagh and Pearse of the military council. MacNeill's interview with Brugha was stormy. Mary ('Min') Ryan, a member of Cumann na mBan and future wife of Richard Mulcahy, recalled the tension in O'Kelly's house: 'we were all waiting, and getting into an awful state' and that an angry Brugha 'fought against issuing anything'.[12] Another account suggests Brugha threatened his chief of staff with violence if he persisted with the demobilization order.[13] But persist MacNeill did. Ryan was one of a number of couriers sent around the country with a countermanding order with the telling line 'Volunteers completely deceived'. MacNeill also placed a notice in the *Sunday Independent* on 23 April. It rescinded all previous orders and 'owing to the very critical position' forbade any marches, parades or other manoeuvres on Easter Sunday. MacNeill subsequently sent a note to officers authenticating the newspaper notice and stating that 'every influence should be used immediately and through the day to secure faithful execution of this order as any failure to obey it may result in a very grave catastrophe'.[14] On leaving O'Kelly's house in the early hours of Easter Sunday, Brugha went to Ceannt's home in Dolphin's Barn, where he was informed by Áine Ceannt that for security reasons her husband had opted to spend the night at the home of John Doherty in nearby St James's Terrace.[15] Brugha eventually located his commanding officer, who, after hearing about the Rathgar meeting, returned home 'with all his equipment, guns, ammunition', declaring to his wife: 'MacNeill has ruined us – he has stopped the Rising'.[16] Brugha and Ceannt were dismayed, 'fiercely denunciatory' of MacNeill's conduct, and wondered if he should be shot as a traitor.[17]

Remarkably, the authorities drew all the wrong conclusions from the dramatic events of the previous days, believing that Casement had arrived to lead a rising, that there were insufficient weapons, and that the countermand had cancelled the Rising. Furthermore, large-scale arrests were postponed until Tuesday, the day after the bank holiday. Only Tom Clarke argued that the Rising should proceed as planned. Disagreeing, the other members of the military council postponed the insurrection until Easter Monday 24 April. MacNeill's countermand effectively confined the Rising to Dublin where frantic efforts were made to salvage the planned outbreak and communicate with companies of the Dublin Brigade. About 1,500 took part during the course of Easter Week in six rebel garrisons. These were the General Post Office on Sackville (now O'Connell) Street which served as headquarters and from where Pearse read the proclamation of the Irish Republic; the Four Courts was seized by the 1st Battalion commanded by Edward Daly; Jacob's biscuit factory was occupied by the 2nd Battalion under Thomas MacDonagh; Boland's Mills was the garrison of the 3rd Battalion under Éamon de Valera; St Stephen's Green was taken by the Irish Citizen Army under Michael Mallin; and the South Dublin Union was held by the 4th Battalion under Ceannt. Most of the insurgents were Irish Volunteers but some were members of Cumann na mBan and the Irish Citizen Army. The rebels held out for six days until Pearse surrendered to avoid further civilian fatalities. There was no fighting retreat as had originally been planned.

From the beginning of 1916 Ceannt had contemplated making the ultimate sacrifice in pursuit of a republic. Revealingly, in a jotter, among notes

6 Áine Ceannt and her son Rónán who stayed in the Brugha home during
Easter Week 1916.

about company drill and route marches, he penned a will on 7 January that left
all his possessions to his wife in the event of his death.[18] As a married man
with two young daughters and with Caitlín heavily pregnant with a third
daughter, Brenda, it was surprising that Brugha had not made a will, even
though it was clear that the chances of death were all too real. It was
inconceivable that he acted without his wife's blessing. While Brugha left no
trace of his interior standpoint, it is probable that in addition to his avowed
republicanism he shared the conviction articulated by de Valera on joining the

Volunteers that the contribution of the married man was necessary given the small size of the force.[19] One further point should be stated. The extraordinary commitment displayed by Brugha – literally putting his life in the firing line – despite his family responsibilities intensified his dismay at the botched planning of the Rising and the IRB's role in this. As will be discussed in the next chapter, it transformed his attitude towards the brotherhood in the post-Rising period. The bond between Ceannt and Brugha was illustrated by arrangements being made in advance for Áine Ceannt, her son Rónán, and her mother to stay in the Brugha home during the fighting (see plate 6). Ceannt feared that his house 'would be in the line of fire'.[20] His final letter to his wife was addressed to the Brugha home. As soon as her husband had departed Dolphin's Barn on Easter Monday, Áine Ceannt went to Caitlín Brugha. Máire Kingston, Caitlín's sister, was also present. She had travelled across the city and spoke of hearing shots. Áine Ceannt later remarked how this 'brought home vividly to us that the die was now cast'.[21]

Members of the 4th Battalion of the Dublin Brigade received orders to mobilize at Emerald Square, Dolphin's Barn at 10 a.m. with full equipment. Turnout was poor due to the confusion caused by MacNeill's countermand and the fact that Ceannt's new mobilization order had been issued at short notice early that morning.[22] According to one estimate, just 125 had reported for duty from a nominal battalion strength of 700.[23] The sense of depletion was captured in a message from Brugha to Ceannt at 10:22 a.m. on Easter Monday. He reported that 'only 4 more has [sic] turned up in addition to the messenger' and asked what time they should leave.[24] John V. Joyce, a section commander in C Company, recalled: 'One had little time to think on Easter Monday morning: it was all hustle'.[25] After inspecting the men and giving orders for the occupation of various posts, Ceannt and Brugha set off from Emerald Square at about 11:30 a.m. for the South Dublin Union. The march was 'uneventful' as the stark reality of what lay ahead dawned on many Volunteers.[26]

Comprising fifty-two acres and extending from Rialto on the south to James's Street on the north, the South Dublin Union was the largest site occupied by the Irish Volunteers on 24 April and an important link in the chain of insurgent positions. Ceannt was greatly handicapped by the numerical weakness of his force which was expected to hold the largest poorhouse in the country with 3,000 destitute inmates and a rambling collection of buildings. The complex had its own churches, stores, refectories, two hospitals with their own medical staff, staff residences and workshops. Little effort was made to evacuate the inmates and staff, who became embroiled in the conflict. The nursing staff were given the option of leaving but in the main opted to stay and to care for their patients.[27] The garrison's principal objective was to prevent British troops moving via the south-western suburbs into the centre of Dublin. Three detachments, each of about twenty men, were assigned to strategic outposts at Jameson's Distillery on Marrowbone Lane commanded by Captain Séamus Murphy, Watkins Brewery on Ardee Street under Captain Con Colbert, and Roe's Distillery on James's Street led by Captain Thomas MacCarthy. Between sixty and seventy Volunteers occupied the Union. Ceannt led one group along the banks of the Royal Canal to the Rialto entrance where the telephone wires were cut, and an astonished porter was overpowered and relieved of his keys. Ceannt then proceeded through the complex to rendezvous with Brugha who headed a second group at the James's Street entrance.[28] The main Volunteer stronghold was in the James's Street block of buildings which was occupied at about midday. Brugha ordered his men to barricade the main entrance and to ensure that the buildings were put in a state of defence. On the advice of Lieutenant William T. Cosgrave, future president of the executive council of the Irish Free State, the battalion headquarters were established in the night nurses' home, a three-story solid stone building on the west side of the main entrance.[29] Cosgrave was familiar with the South Dublin Union as his home and family's public house were located directly opposite the main entrance. After the night nurses were woken from their sleep and evacuated to another building, a republican flag was unfurled from an upper window. It was here that the most intense action took place.[30] Ceannt placed a detachment at the southern Rialto entrance and another section of five men in McCaffrey's Estate, an area of open fields at the junction of Mount Brown and Brookfield Road. This group was so placed to prevent a possible military advance from nearby Richmond Barracks via Old Kilmainham and Mount Brown. Other detachments covered the canal wall at the rear of the Union, the eastern boundary wall facing the city, and various strategically placed buildings within the complex such as the acute hospital.

At about 12:40 members of the Royal Irish Regiment in Richmond Barracks were ordered to proceed at once fully armed to Dublin Castle. An inlying picket of 100 men, commanded by Major Holmes, attempted to reach the castle via Kilmainham. A 20-member section was ordered to proceed along Brookfield Road but came under fire from the Irish Volunteers and suffered three casualties. When Holmes' picket was reinforced by the main body from Richmond Barracks, two companies were sent along Brookfield Road to outflank the rebels. One attacked the rear of the complex, while the other company attempted to take the James's Street entrance. In addition, a machine-gun was mounted in the nearby Royal Hospital, Kilmainham (where the British commander-in-chief resided).[31] This was the beginning of an unremitting fight that persisted for several hours with fatalities on both sides. Seán Owens of B Company was the first rebel fatality. The Volunteer section at the Rialto gate, under George Irvine, occupied a long, corrugated iron shed easily perforated by British fire.[32] A small gate was forced open by the British military and some soldiers scaled the nine-foot walls. The Volunteers were severely outnumbered. Only fourteen men held the line of communication between Rialto and James's Street and their positions were quickly over-whelmed. Irvine's section was forced to surrender; the southern portion of the Union complex was overrun by 15:30. The Volunteers in the fields at Mount Brown were the most vulnerable, coming under machine-gun fire from the Royal Hospital. Three Volunteers were killed as they attempted to retreat to the acute hospital. In his BMH statement, James Coughlan recalled that two men were sought for special duty. He and William McDowell volunteered and were ordered to report to Brugha, who instructed them to help bring in the wounded from the field to the west of the nurses' home. Assisted by two inmates, McDowell and Coughlan came under heavy fire and McDowell was shot dead.[33]

The British military came under fire from six Volunteer snipers at the upper windows of the acute hospital but managed to reach the building in a series of short dashes forward. During this siege, Nurse Margaret Kehoe, who was on duty and in uniform, was killed at about 13:30 by two soldiers at the bottom of the stone staircase.[34] A report by the master of the South Dublin Union later stated that she was shot, possibly by a stray bullet, as soldiers pursued insurgents within the building.[35] By dusk the military had driven the insurgents from the female chronic hospital to the rebel headquarters in the night nurses' home and the buildings surrounding the main entrance on James's Street. But instead of pressing home its advantage, the Royal Irish Regiment was surprisingly withdrawn to nearby Kingsbridge railway terminus. The regimental history recorded two officers and five men killed, and one officer and six men wounded.[36] When Ceannt proposed a temporary truce to allow both sides collect their dead and wounded a brief reply from a British NCO stated that negotiations were impossible as all their officers were dead.[37]

Whereas rebel garrisons elsewhere in the city waited to be attacked as British troops flooded into Dublin and created cordons around Volunteer strongholds, members of the 4th Battalion had been immediately plunged into fierce fighting and their first experience of real combat. As McGarry has observed, Ceannt, Brugha and Con Colbert in Jameson's distillery 'demonstrated remarkable resilience and courage', whereas de Valera and MacDonagh 'appeared unable to cope with the pressure'.[38] The morale of the

Volunteers in the South Dublin Union remained high despite their manifest vulnerability. It was sustained by the inspirational leadership provided by Ceannt and Brugha, who repeatedly risked their lives to check on their men or monitor enemy activity. Brugha was described as 'a first rate sniper' who always 'had the effect of silencing the enemy's guns', and whose 'bravery in action … encouraged the most timid'.[39] James Coughlan recalled that Ceannt was 'always cool and cheerful', whereas Brugha, who 'seemed the most silent member of the garrison', spent whatever time he could cleaning his automatic pistol but 'always appeared composed and contented'.[40] Each night Ceannt and Brugha called the Volunteers together for a short review of the day after which the rosary was recited.[41] Joseph Doolan recalled that in addition to the nightly rosary, Brugha 'never forgot to call down God's blessing, by having prayers recited in public each morning … [and] looked after the spiritual interests of his men by having a priest in attendance almost daily'.[42]

By Wednesday the Volunteers were well entrenched in the night nurses' home and the boardroom over the main gate. Significant effort was expended on improving their defences: sandbagging windows, barricading doors and boring through walls between the two rebel positions. Although contact had been lost with the three outposts, a transitory sense of calm prevailed. This ended on Thursday with the arrival of two battalions of the Sherwood Foresters and a determined attack to dislodge the rebels. Lieutenant-Colonel W.C. Oates, the commanding officer, ordered an advance guard to occupy as much of the grounds as possible and to divert the insurgents' attention away from a wagon load of ammunition that was being escorted by soldiers across Rialto bridge to the Royal Hospital. By this time, the Volunteer garrison had been reduced to just forty-three men, many of whom had not slept for days. Eight had been killed, twelve wounded and over a dozen were captured.[43] Food was less of a concern. Annie Mannion, assistant matron, recalled that the storekeeper provided provisions to the opposing forces and that the union's bakehouse operated throughout the week.[44] The British army had little sense of the strength of the rebel forces in the South Dublin Union. Based on information received from union officials, they estimated that 200 rebels were holding out either in or around the night nurses' home.[45] That building was pounded by hand grenades and rifle and machine-gun fire. The fighting lasted between five and seven hours, and, as noted by Charles Townshend, was 'grim enough to satisfy the goriest fantasies of hand-to-hand combat'.[46]

The progress of the military was stopped by an eight-foot barricade erected directly behind the hall door of the nurses' home. It was defended by Volunteers behind it and on the stairs and first landing.[47] This forced the military to lob grenades over the barrier. Believing that troops were about to enter their headquarters and amid confusion about orders, the insurgents started to abandon the building. Brugha, apparently the last of the party to descend the stairs, was severely wounded by a grenade and also by rifle fire. Despite his injuries, he managed to drag himself to the ground floor and into a kitchen off the main hall. John Joyce, who left his post in the nurses' home to replenish his ammunition, was surprised to find the upper floors of the building abandoned on his return. Shortly after, he discovered Brugha in a pool of blood. He asked for a drink and told Joyce that the others had retreated towards the boardroom.[48] Brugha extracted a watch from his pocket which he gave to Joyce with the instruction: 'If you ever get out of here alive, will you give this to my wife?'[49] He then ordered Joyce to join the rest of the men and to inform Ceannt: 'I'll hang on here as long as I'm able'.[50] On hearing the extent of their vice-commandant's injuries and believing that the British had taken control of the nurses' home, it was assumed that Brugha was either dead or had been captured. Suddenly, the depleted garrison not only heard the sound of gunfire from the nurses' home, but Brugha singing *God Save Ireland*, the Irish rebel song celebrating the Manchester Martyrs of 1867 which served as an unofficial national anthem.[51] According to Joyce, the effect of such defiance 'was electric'.[52] Some Volunteers also heard Brugha taunting soldiers within earshot: 'Come on you cowards, till I get one shot before I die'.[53] When Ceannt and his men returned to the nurses' home from the James's Street post they were surprised to find it empty and Brugha in the yard off the kitchen firing his 'Peter the Painter' revolver at the barricade, which he was able to enfilade at an angle of forty-five degrees despite being gravely wounded. Brugha's actions led to the withdrawal of the attacking British soldiers who assumed there was a strong rebel presence.[54]

Captain John Oates, son of Lieutenant-Colonel Oates, admitted 'none of us felt brave enough to storm the barricade' protecting the rebels' headquarters and defended by Brugha.[55] Joyce later wrote of Brugha: 'It was typical of this brave man, who was absolutely fearless, and who would – and ultimately did – prefer to die rather than to surrender'.[56] William Cosgrave later paid tribute to Brugha's valour: 'even when the spark of life was practically gone out of him, he was as full of fight as when he was going into it'.[57]

On re-entering the nurses' home, Ceannt quickly surveyed the building before poignantly embracing Brugha and speaking with him in Irish. He then directed some of his men to occupy specific positions. Others brought Brugha into a back room and attended to his extensive wounds. Joseph Doolan, the first aid officer, assisted by Cosgrave provided aid over the course of a number of hours, but this was limited by the difficult circumstances and their exhaustion. While trying to staunch the blood from Brugha's many wounds it was also necessary to move him from one position to another as the British re-launched their attack on the building. In addition, Brugha's clothing was embedded into some of the wounds which made treatment more difficult. Although continually asking for cold drinks, which were given to him along with sips of hot coffee, by early morning he had become delirious and was in urgent need of professional medical intervention.[58] Brugha apparently related to his brother, Alfred, and sister, Eveleen, that he drank a small bottle of holy water from Lourdes to help stop the bleeding.[59]

By nightfall, the British troops had withdrawn, 'leaving behind a number of dead, dying and wounded'.[60] That the night nurses' home had been reduced to 'a deplorable condition' with pulverized walls, floors and ceilings occasioned pride. As one Volunteer recalled, 'we had held on to it, and it gave us intense satisfaction to think that we had repelled such an overwhelming force … it was a remarkable achievement'.[61] After guards were posted, the insurgents settled in for the night. Sleep was impossible due to the difficult conditions and anticipation of a further attack. Joyce vividly remembered the quietness and the 'wonderful glow' that had settled over the city skyline, turning the night sky a blood-red.[62]

Brugha's deterioration now became the focus of attention. On Friday afternoon he was removed under a Red Cross banner to the nearby South Dublin Union hospital with the assistance of the hospital chaplain, Fr Gerhard, and some union officials.[63] By this time peaceful conditions prevailed as Joyce recounted: 'We all got a good rest on Friday night, and Saturday was more or less a lazy day. Beyond having an occasional shot at the enemy … everything appeared peaceful'.[64] The withdrawal of the British troops from the South Dublin Union was unexpected. Captain John Oates of the Sherwood Foresters later stated: 'Orders now are to withdraw … [I] re-joined the other men in the yard and [we] made our way … back to Rialto Bridge and from there to the Royal Hospital … [where] we dossed down in front of the altar of the Chapel and fell asleep'.[65]

While most of the rebel garrisons across the city remained relatively optimistic of continuing their tenacious resistance, the GPO was in a perilous situation. After coming under direct artillery bombardment, Pearse was forced to evacuate the blazing ruins and retreat to Moore Street. By Saturday the surviving forces were at the end of their endurance, compelling Pearse to surrender to save the lives of rank and file and members of the public.[66] A general surrender was completed over the following twenty-eight hours as each garrison commander surrendered. On Sunday morning Thomas MacDonagh, accompanied by Frs Augustine Hayden and Aloysius Travers, members of the Church Street Capuchin community, informed Ceannt of

Pearse's decision. Ceannt called his men together to outline the situation. He stated that he would not order them to surrender, allowing any man who wished to make his getaway, but that having fought as soldiers they should surrender as soldiers.[67] A reluctant Ceannt offered his surrender to Brigadier-General W.H.M. Lowe, commander of the 3rd Reserve Cavalry Brigade, at 7 p.m. on Sunday evening.[68] Fr Augustine recalled that the South Dublin Union garrison 'wore no look of defeat, but rather of victory'.[69] Indeed the following day General Sir John Maxwell, the newly appointed military governor, privately complimented the insurgents: 'The fighting qualities so far displayed by rebels give evidence of better training and discipline than they have been credited with'.[70] Proud of the achievements of the 4th Battalion, which was involved in some of the most intensive fighting of Easter Week, Ceannt wrote of their 'magnificent gallantry and fearless, calm determination'.[71] After the surrender the men were marched to the nearby Richmond Barracks where a temporary prison compound had been erected on the barrack square. There they were screened by police and military for court-martial or for internment in England.

Both Caitlín Brugha and Áine Ceannt had waited anxiously all week for news of the Rising and, in particular, the fate of their husbands. Throughout Easter Week they observed flames rising in the distance and heard the sound of battle. Early on the morning of Friday 28 April, Caitlín's home was searched by the military who questioned her on why the house was only occupied by women and children. She convinced them that her husband was a commercial traveller who had been stranded outside Dublin.[72] That evening Caitlín was informed by her brother, Fr John Kingston, that her husband had been injured in the fighting at the South Dublin Union. Caitlín was expecting her third child and it was perhaps for this reason that the priest deliberately made light of Brugha's injuries. Áine Ceannt recalled that though anxious, Caitlín was 'reassured'.[73] In a bid to hear news of the Rising on Sunday, the women ventured into Rathmines and although fires were still burning across the city, 'there was very little shooting'. They learned 'there was a truce but nothing more'.[74]

Following initial treatment for his injuries at the union hospital, five of Brugha's twenty-five bullet and shrapnel wounds were described as dangerous, while nine were serious and eleven deemed slight. His left foot, hip and leg were 'practically one mass of wounds'.[75] During the following week, an apprehensive Caitlín made a number of unsuccessful attempts to visit her husband but was prevented from doing so due to the havoc engulfing the city and the imposition of martial law. Finally, on Friday, 5 May she made her way to the South Dublin Union to see her seriously ill husband.[76] Despite the severity of his injuries, Brugha's main concern was that the plans for the Rising deposited in his back garden should be destroyed. He privately conveyed those concerns to Caitlín who, on returning to Fitzwilliam Terrace, took them up and burned them.[77] The anxiety caused to Caitlín must have been immense as she wondered if her husband would survive, and even if he did whether he would face execution or imprisonment. The stress contributed to the early arrival on 18 May of a third daughter, Brenda, who had been due in July. Brugha was too ill to stand trial, and this spared him the death penalty or incarceration. Fittingly, Brenda was known to her parents as 'our 1916 baby'.[78]

The 1916 Easter Rising ended after six days, leaving almost 500 (the majority civilians) dead and much of the centre of Dublin in ruins. Writing to Herbert Kitchener, Maxwell was incredulous at how the Volunteers had been 'allowed to parade openly and march about the streets of Dublin and elsewhere armed and defiant. They have been allowed to train, drill, practice street fighting etc with police and Irish constabulary looking on, taking notes and reporting, yet nothing was done!'[79] He was determined to inflict severe punishment on the fomenters of the outbreak and set down an example to deter any other putative rebels. The execution of fourteen men in Dublin, some only minor figures, after secret courts martial over a ten-day period between 3 and 12 May shocked Ireland. John Dillon, the deputy leader of the IPP who had been in Dublin during the outbreak, warned Maxwell that even those opposed to the Rising were becoming 'intensely bitter' at the execution policy.[80] Famously, in the House of Commons on 11 May Dillon denounced the executions and praised the bravery of the insurgents. The executions were paralleled by widespread arrests and the deportation to British jails and prison camps of 2,000 men and six women. These responses by the authorities ensured that initial public hostility towards the rebels soon gave way to popular sympathy for them. Brugha's commandant and close friend, Éamonn Ceannt, went before a firing squad at Kilmainham Jail on 8 May. In one of his final letters, addressed to the Irish people, he expressed regret for surrendering:

> I leave for the guidance of other Irish Revolutionaries who may tread the path which I have trod this advice, never to treat with the enemy, never to surrender at *his* mercy, but to fight to a finish. I see nothing gained but grave disaster caused, by the surrender which has marked the end of the Irish Insurrection of 1916.[81]

Two days before his death, Ceannt was allowed a brief visit from his wife. He had held Brugha's watch for safekeeping and asked Áine to give it to Caitlín Brugha.[82]

Sometime after the emergency phase of his medical treatment, Brugha was transferred as a patient and prisoner to the Dublin Castle hospital where he was in a ward surrounded by other wounded members of the Volunteers. It is unclear how many weeks Brugha spent there but a note to Fr Albert Bibby, a Capuchin based in Church Street, on 14 June asked him to visit to hear Brugha's confession.[83] One of Brugha's many visitors in Dublin Castle was Brian Cusack. He had joined the IRB while working as a civil servant in London and enrolled in the Volunteers while studying medicine at Galway University from where he graduated in 1915. Brugha was the godfather of Cusack's first child. Cusack took it on himself to visit and assess the condition of all wounded Volunteers who had been hospitalized due to injuries sustained during the Rising. His account of Brugha's condition is brief but illuminating: 'He was shattered with wounds, but he showed no fear. He was possessed with an indomitable spirit … No sooner had he got out of hospital than he was off organising again'.[84]

Brugha was subsequently transferred to King George V Hospital (later St Bricin's) on Infirmary Road in Dublin along with other severely wounded Volunteers. These included Liam Staines, Dick Balfe and James Purfield. Staines's mother maintained that her son, who died in November 1918, never fully recovered from the effects of his wounds and a subsequent period of internment. Nevertheless, her application under the Army Pension Act (1932) was denied.[85] One unidentified fellow patient recalled that although they were all 'helpless … shot, riddled, and disabled', they were in a 'detention ward' where windows 'were barred and a sentry, with bayonet fixed, stood inside the door'. Otherwise, they were well treated.[86] After months of hospital treatment, clinicians regarded Brugha as incurable, permanently incapacitated due to his injuries, and unlikely to benefit from any further form of treatment. He was discharged, unconditionally, from hospital in August 1916, by which time his detention order had expired.[87] He was transported home by ambulance and two soldiers had to carry him in. Their efforts were rewarded with a glass of whiskey.[88]

A long period of recuperation commenced under the tender care of Caitlín. Brugha's wounds healed slowly but his mobility was seriously hampered by a lacerated nerve and other irreversible damage to his left leg. This required him to wear a silk bandage for protection and a special shoe with a raised heel. At private meetings and at his desk, he generally removed his shoe as he could not wear it for long. The nerve damage required electrotherapy by means of a medical battery, a popular form of treatment for a variety of ailments in the late nineteenth and early twentieth centuries.[89] He never recovered full use of his injured limb, which 'pained him sorely' for the remainder of his life, and he generally moved about on a bicycle, being unable to walk much. However, he soon found that cycling against a hill was also too much of a challenge for his injured leg, forcing him to dismount.[90] After regaining a moderate level of mobility, Brugha, still on crutches, spent six weeks in the cottage of Mary Ellen Vaughan at Cream Point near Milltown Malbay, County Clare, where he rested and bathed in the sea.[91] On the way to Clare, Brugha met Frank McGrath, a member of the Volunteers in Nenagh and later commandant Tipperary No. 1 Brigade, by appointment at Limerick railway station. Brugha knew him well and in 1915 McGrath had sourced ammunition for the German pistol used by Brugha during Easter Week. They discussed the re-organization of the Volunteers 'at some length'.[92] Brugha was visited in Clare by his Caherciveen friend Jeremiah O'Connell, who was anxious to establish if there were any plans 'about continuing the Rising'.[93]

Although the immediate prospects of another insurrection were remote, Irish public opinion was undergoing a steady transformation. The impact of the executions and internment was reinforced by three other developments. The first was the failure of David Lloyd George's home rule negotiations in the summer of 1916. While not immediately clear until an electoral alternative in the shape of Sinn Féin emerged in 1917, home rule was the chief casualty of the Rising. The IPP had little to offer the Irish electorate beyond calls to support the war. In his report for June 1916, the RIC inspector general commented on the 'unsettled condition' of the country 'due in great measure to sympathy with the Sinn Féin insurgents, and divergence of opinion with regard to the Home Rule proposals … a wave of resentment sprung up and spread rapidly through the Nationalist population'.[94] Second, the drawn-out British response to the insurrection offered regular reminders that had a corrosive effect on public opinion. The discipline of the army was brought into question during inquests on civilians killed in North King Street and a royal commission into the circumstances of the shooting of Francis Sheehy-Skeffington and two other journalists in Portobello Barracks. The commission on the Rising reported in July; Roger Casement was hanged in August. A campaign to have the British government provide compensation for damage caused to property by bombardment, fire or looting, estimated at £2.5 million, was a further irritant. In June 1916 the Property Losses (Ireland) Committee was established and awarded £1.84 million for 6,236 admitted compensation claims.[95] One of those claims was made by Lalor Ltd for beeswax lost during the looting of the British and Irish Steam Packet Company Stores on Sir John Rogerson's Quay. Brugha himself corresponded with the assessors in October 1916 and the company's claim for £9 12s. 10d. was granted in full the following month.[96] Although lists of claims were scrutinized by the DMP for any links with the insurgents, Brugha's connection with Lalor's was not noticed.

Lastly, there was an increasing re-evaluation of the rebels as men 'who willed no evil' in the words of writer James Stephens, and as good Catholics. Over time they became the most potent of martyrs. J.J. O'Kelly was instrumental in this. In 1911 he became editor of the *Catholic Bulletin*, a monthly magazine with a large circulation of 10,000–15,000. Although he did not take part in the Rising, O'Kelly strongly supported it and adeptly steered the *Catholic Bulletin*'s stance around the censorship and Defence of the Realm regulations. That the wounded Brugha's single-handed defence of his position in the South Dublin Union became one of the most celebrated acts of bravery and defiance of the Rising was due in no small way to the *Catholic Bulletin*. From July 1916, it ran a series of articles called 'Events of Easter Week' that included tributes to participants, obituaries, photographs and a focus on the families of those killed or interned; O'Kelly was also conscious that the *Bulletin* would serve as a source for the motives of the Easter rebels.[97] Half a century later, to mark the fiftieth anniversary of the Rising in 1966, RTÉ produced *Insurrection*, an ambitious eight-part dramatic reconstruction of the events of Easter 1916. In a novel approach, on the spot news reportage was interspersed with dramatized re-enactments. Joe Lynch gave a moving portrayal of Brugha.

As Townshend has written, the rebellion shifted 'the horizons of possibility, both at the subliminal and the practical level'.[98] Brugha's gallant contribution in the South Dublin Union, his martial skills and tactical ability, his fearlessness in the face of death, and the wounds borne for the republic generated a formidable aura around him. This profoundly altered the course of his life. Although certainly more comfortable in the background away from the public spotlight, Brugha was thrust into a new leadership role. In the aftermath of the Rising, with significant rebel leaders either dead or in detention, many looked to him to continue the struggle. Typically, he embraced this challenge with unswerving singularity of purpose.

CHAPTER 4

Facilitator: Brugha and the reorganization of separatism, 1917–18

THE PERIOD BETWEEN THE 1916 Rising and the 1918 general election witnessed the steady radicalization of Irish public opinion and saw home rule, a pole around which Irish politics had revolved since the 1870s, jettisoned in favour of a demand for an Irish republic. To this end, three significant organizations were rebuilt: the Irish Volunteers, Sinn Féin and the IRB. Having eluded death in 1916, Brugha defied his injuries in 1917 and the constant pain which he must have endured to play a galvanizing role in two of the three reorganization efforts. Conferred with the prestige of being a Rising veteran, his primary concern was the re-establishment of the Volunteers throughout the country, in 'gathering together the broken threads' as one Volunteer expressed it.[1] Brugha remained a significant figure within the Volunteers until the establishment of a general headquarters staff in March 1918 after which his influence waned. That decline was also due to his absence from Ireland for five months from May until October 1918 on a fearless but madcap plan to assassinate the British cabinet if conscription, the threat of which convulsed Ireland, was imposed. Ultimately, it was not. Brugha was also engaged in the reinvention of Sinn Féin from a tiny and marginal party in the immediate aftermath of the Rising to the dominant political force it became by the end of 1918. A member of its national executive, he won a parliamentary seat for Waterford County in the seismic 1918 general election. Brugha did not participate in the third reorganization, emerging from the Rising as a vehement critic of the IRB and its secretive influence. This opposition became deeply entrenched.

Between the aftermath of the Rising and Christmas 1916, the separatist cause was sustained by two types of activity. The first was the promotion of the welfare of those who had been interned without trial or imprisoned and their dependants: about 140 were sentenced to penal servitude and just over 2,000 were initially interned, the majority in Frongoch in north Wales.[2] Until August 1916, two organizations – the Irish National Aid Association and the Volunteer Dependents' Fund – vied with one another to coordinate relief efforts.[3] The former was cross-party, whereas the latter was largely controlled by Cumann na mBan and, in particular, by Katheen Clarke, Tom Clarke's widow. At the time of the Rising, the military council of the IRB had entrusted her with £3,100 to relieve the families of those killed, injured or imprisoned as a result of the outbreak.[4] The intervention of Clan na Gael, with sizeable funds raised in the United States, forced the amalgamation of the two relief bodies in August and the creation of the Irish National Aid and Volunteer Dependents' Fund. The RIC inspector general estimated that the fund had £28,000 at its disposal.[5] Cumann na mBan and the female relatives of several of those executed remained prominent. They included Kathleen Clarke as president; Áine Ceannt as vice-president; Margaret Pearse, mother of Patrick; and Muriel MacDonagh, widow of Thomas MacDonagh. The Irish National Aid and Volunteer Dependents' Fund reinforced the morale of those incarcerated, maintained a vital link between the old and new phases of Irish separatism, and reinforced a growing public sympathy with the objects of the Rising.[6] During the treaty debates, Brugha delivered a strong tribute to the role played by women in the aftermath of the Rising for keeping 'the spirit alive ... the flame alive, and the flag flying'.[7]

The second type of activity involved discreet efforts to reorganize the Irish Volunteers. This was, of necessity, covert because martial law remained in operation until the end of 1916. The release of the first batch of internees in July 1916 gave the rebuilding efforts a major fillip. Neville Chamberlain, the RIC inspector general, observed astutely that their 'rebellious spirit' had in no way been subdued by their temporary loss of liberty.[8] The experience of internment proved important in the militarization of the Volunteers. First, force of association led many men from all parts of the country, who had no previous association with the Volunteers, to join and become radicalized. Second, internment facilitated training. For many Volunteers, especially those outside Dublin, this was rudimentary before the Rising. The military atmosphere ensured, as J.J. O'Connell suggests in his memoir, that when released from Frongoch the former internees were soldiers rather than the enthusiastic nationalists who had turned out during Easter 1916.[9]

Two members of the 4th Battalion, rendered lame due to injuries incurred during the Rising but who avoided arrest, played a central role in the reanimation of the Volunteers: Brugha and Liam Clarke. From June 1916, the unheralded Clarke gathered together trusty men in Dublin. He made contact with Kathleen Clarke and using the Irish National Aid and Volunteer Dependents' Fund as cover began to reorganize outside Dublin. On 7 August 1916 a meeting of the survivors of various units was held in the Minerva Hotel on Parnell Square at which a provisional executive was formed. Chaired by Clarke, it included Diarmuid O'Hegarty, Gregory Murphy, Luke Kennedy and Séamus O'Doherty. Brugha was co-opted on his release from hospital.[10] Several statements to the BMH emphasized Brugha's determination to rebuild the Volunteers to continue the struggle. Gerald Byrne recalled how Brugha made indirect contact from his hospital bed with members of the four companies of the 4th Battalion about reviving their units.[11] Of the four battalions of the Dublin Brigade, Brugha was the sole surviving senior officer then at liberty. With the exception of de Valera, who was eight years younger than Brugha, all other battalion commandants – Daly, MacDonagh and Ceannt – had been executed and their deputies Béaslaí and Thomas Hunter were penal servitude prisoners until June 1917.[12]

Following his release from hospital and still suffering from his wounds, Brugha played an enabling role in the reconstitution of the Volunteers. This dominated his energies in the closing months of 1916 and all of the following year. He and Clarke worked closely together until Brugha's death in 1922. A steady stream of Volunteer officers, who had either escaped arrest after the Rising or were released early, visited Brugha at home in Fitzwilliam Terrace, Rathmines. Nicholas Laffan, a captain of G Company, 1st Battalion, was one of many who recalled Brugha's advice to get in contact with members of companies or battalions and to keep them together until the main body of internees and political prisoners was released. To conceal this reorganization work, Brugha suggested that Irish classes be used and one was duly formed in Columcille hall on Blackhall Street, headquarters of Laffan's company.[13] When Henry Murray of A Company, 4th Battalion, visited Brugha at home he found him 'by no means recovered from his wounds' but 'in very good spirits and full of enthusiasm for the work in hand … never even hinted at the discomfort and suffering which he had endured and discussed the position and prospects with me in a cheerful, even boisterous, manner'.[14] Murray was directed to cooperate with Douglas Ffrench-Mullen, captain of D Company and acting battalion commandant, to resurrect the dormant Thomas Davis branch of the Gaelic League as a cover for reviving the 4th Battalion. Some companies such as C Company, 2nd Battalion, had been run as a Sinn Féin club until instructed by Brugha to resume on a military basis.[15] Brugha also ordered the holding of elections to fill any vacant officer roles within companies. In this way, for example, Michael Lynch was elected captain of B Company, 4th Battalion.[16]

The work of reorganization had sufficiently advanced that a convention of Volunteer officers was held in November 1916 in Fleming's Hotel on Gardiner Place. Seán O'Mahony, the proprietor, had been active in the Rising and was a friend of Brugha who, still on crutches, presided at the meeting.[17] A national executive was established to direct the military organization of the Volunteers throughout the country. But the real locus of power lay in the smaller resident executive which consisted of those living in Dublin. Brugha was unanimously chosen as chairman. From December 1916 until the October 1917 national Volunteer convention, the resident executive met weekly and mostly in Brugha's house, which became an interim quasi-headquarters for the Volunteers.[18] As Richard Mulcahy subsequently recalled, this body 'brought increasing life and cohesion into the Volunteer movement'.[19] For example, in January 1917 an instruction was issued to the Dublin battalions to resume musketry classes.[20] Furthermore, it should be mentioned briefly that Brugha entered into discussions with James O'Neill, commandant of the Irish Citizen Army, towards the end of 1916. On grounds of practicality, a fusion with the Volunteers was not deemed possible but there was an undertaking to cooperate.[21]

During the second half of 1916 the British government was consumed by the war effort and Ireland was raised in the House of Commons on just six occasions. On 5 December Asquith resigned and was succeeded as prime minister by David Lloyd George. He formed a second coalition government but one that was dominated by the Conservative Party. This had fateful implications for Ireland. In an effort to mollify Irish public opinion, the new government announced an unconditional Christmas amnesty for Irish internees on 21 December. This gesture elicited little gratitude and, if anything, hastened the steady transformation of Irish public opinion occasioned by the government's ill-conceived responses to the Rising and the failure of Lloyd George's attempt to arrive at an agreed solution of the Irish question in July 1916. Feted as heroes on their return home, the newly released men backboned the reorganization of the Volunteers. In a sharp break with the strategy pursued before Rising, the military wing was linked to a revamped Sinn Féin party with a broad political platform and appeal.

Given Brugha's seniority, he was involved in several inquiries pertaining to the Volunteers during the Rising. One of those concerned the circumstances of the evacuation of Roe's Distillery where the small rebel garrison was quickly overwhelmed with some men, including officers, appearing to abandon their post.[22] Brugha and Liam Clarke, who had succeeded Ceannt as commandant for the first quarter of 1917, exonerated the garrison from all blame.[23] More generally, Brugha indicated that no action should be taken against men who did not turn out during the Rising other than to remove their names from company rolls.[24] Along with Diarmuid Lynch and Con Collins, Brugha sat on a court of inquiry in 1917 that investigated the activities of Cork, Kerry and Limerick Volunteers during Easter Week. The IRB also held its own inquiry. The Cork men were widely criticized for barricading themselves inside their headquarters rather than rousing the countryside and for agreeing to the surrender of their weapons. It had been arranged that the weapons would be held in safekeeping by the lord mayor but they were seized by the authorities and the Cork Volunteers were arrested. Tomás MacCurtain and Terence MacSwiney, the Volunteer leaders, regarded this as a breach of promise. Although no blame was attached to them for the inaction, MacCurtain and MacSwiney found the investigation humiliating.[25] Notably, during his seventy-three-day hunger strike in 1920 MacSwiney wished to atone for the failures of 1916 in Cork. He wrote poignantly to Brugha: 'ah, Cathal, the pain of Easter Week is properly dead at last'.[26]

The reorganization of the Volunteers brought into question the role of the IRB which had been revealed publicly in the 1916 proclamation of independence. Brugha had lost faith in the IRB and no longer saw any justification for its continuation. This view was not peculiar to him, and it was also shared by other veteran members such as Denis McCullough, Éamon de Valera, Rory O'Connor and Tomás MacCurtain, all of whom relinquished their membership. That position was opposed by brotherhood stalwarts such as Diarmuid Lynch, Michael Collins, Diarmuid O'Hegarty and Seán Ó Murthuile, among others, who reconstituted the organization.[27] The central spine of the rekindled IRB had experienced internment or imprisonment after the Rising which afforded them considerable time to bond and to plot. By not being captured after the Rising, Brugha in a sense missed out on this formative experience. Ó Dochartaigh suggests that Brugha's religious convictions (the Catholic Church opposed secret societies) and the profound issues of conscience raised by the deaths of comrades killed during the Rising influenced his anti-IRB stance.[28] O'Hegarty and Ó Murthuile had been released early and were centrally involved in the reanimation of the Volunteers. Both had been involved in the Rising. O'Hegarty served a short sentence in Knutsford Prison in May 1916 before being released in error and returning to his civil service position in the Department of Agriculture and Technical Instruction.[29] Ó Murthuile had been interned in Frongoch in north Wales, where he associated with Collins and Gearóid O'Sullivan, fellow west Cork members of the IRB.[30] Collins exploited his appointment as secretary of the Irish National Aid and Volunteer Dependents' Fund in February 1917, facilitated by Kathleen Clarke, to rebuild the IRB. The influence of this secret cabal perturbed Brugha for the remainder of his life. As Brian Murphy has observed, 'the renewal of the IRB and the Irish Volunteers contained within itself the seeds of discord and the grounds for the personal animosity that developed between Brugha and Collins'.[31]

Initial efforts to revive the IRB were made by Kathleen Clarke with Ó Murthuile becoming the secretary of a new provisional council. In her autobiography, she recalled getting in touch with Brugha. She had only met him once before and the pair had 'clashed over his arrogant attitude on the Irish language'. However, his involvement in the Rising softened her stance and she attended a Sunday dinner in Fitzwilliam Terrace to discuss various matters with him. The encounter was tempestuous. Clarke later wrote that her host 'paid very little attention to what I had to tell him; he was full of himself. He started off by saying that divided counsels had caused the failure of the Rising ... In future there would be only one organisation, the Irish Volunteers'.[32] They clashed over the effectiveness of the IRB in bringing about the Rising. Clarke 'put every argument I could think of before him but ... failed to make an impression on him'. At about 9 p.m. when Brugha banged the table and proclaimed that the IRB must go, she replied acidly that he 'was a very small man to make such a big decision'.[33] This disagreement should not be regarded as tantamount to a loss of esteem by Brugha for Tom Clarke or Seán Mac Diarmada. As Brugha later revealed to Seán Matthews, a Waterford member of the IRB and IRA commandant, while they were alive only Clarke and Mac Diarmada had been able to keep the IRB 'free from graft and corruption'. All the Dublin IRB wanted, Brugha claimed, 'was to pull their caps over their eyes, pull up the collars of their coats and be shadowed by detectives'.[34] His preference was for soldiers rather than conspirators.

There was further histrionic table thumping over the IRB. In summer 1917 Éamon Dore, a Limerick Volunteer and IRB member, met Brugha who was in Limerick on business for Lalor Ltd and stayed overnight on Barrington Street. When asked why he had withdrawn from the brotherhood, Brugha 'got very excited' and maintained that it was unnecessary and even dangerous if in the hands of 'the wrong people'. When Dore suggested that Brugha's opposition might push the brotherhood in that very direction, he got even more excited, striking the table with his fist and exclaiming: 'I don't care. If it is the last act of my life, I will lead a crusade to destroy it'.[35] Richard Walsh, a Mayo Volunteer and future brigade adjutant, recalled Collins speaking to him at the end of 1917 about reorganizing the IRB in Mayo. Walsh was subsequently sent for by Brugha who advised him to leave the IRB because the Volunteers was an open military organization that obviated the necessity for a secret body. Brugha contended that if the IRB continued it would 'only create trouble and do harm ... a case of "too many cooks spoiling the broth"'.[36] In the event, Walsh did not leave the IRB, considering it better to remain inside rather than outside the brotherhood. Brugha did not raise the issue with him again.

After the 1918 general election, Brugha and de Valera maintained that the separatist movement should be an open one and that elected representatives should not be 'subject to secret control'.[37] This point was further elaborated in discussions between Brugha and James McGuill, commandant of the Volunteers in Dundalk and an IRB centre. Brugha was adamant that 'dual command would always lead to ultimate confusion' and that the supreme council 'could not realistically function as the Government of the Republic whilst Dáil Éireann remained in existence'.[38] Brugha initially advised McGuill to sever his ties with the IRB but then recommended that he remain as head centre lest someone untrustworthy succeed him. McGuill largely refrained from recruiting new members.[39]

The influx of activists after December 1916 necessitated another Volunteer convention in March 1917 in Barry's Hotel on Gardiner Row.[40] Richard Walsh recalled the attendance of Volunteer officers from different parts of the country who were determined to expedite reorganization in their localities, and, as an order subsequently indicated, to put the Volunteers 'in a position to complete by force of arms the work begun by the men of Easter Week'.[41] The meeting reappointed the executive and made a commitment to hold a national convention of Volunteers later that year. Brugha's determination to resist any secret influence over the Volunteers was sharply evident. An executive order in May 1917 stated explicitly:

> In order that we may not be hampered in our next effort by any misunderstanding such as occurred on the last occasion, as a result of conflicting orders, Volunteers are notified that the only orders that they are to obey are those of their own Executive.[42]

The same order was equally clear (and perhaps tacitly critical of 1916) that the Volunteers would not take to the field until sufficiently trained, that they could 'rest assured that they will not be called upon to take part in any forlorn hope', but that when the moment came to strike they would do so 'relentlessly'.[43] Brugha's reorganization work was broad ranging. Geraldine Plunkett Dillon wrote in her memoir that he had begun to gather arms, ammunition and explosives and that her husband, Thomas, professor of chemistry in University College Galway, was summoned by Brugha in early February 1917 to go to Limerick to advise on explosives.[44] Dillon had been in Roscommon awaiting the result of the by-election contested by his father-in-law George Plunkett and had acted as a chemical adviser to the Volunteers before the Rising; he married Geraldine Plunkett on Easter Sunday 1916.[45] In 1917 arms and ammunition from Liverpool were smuggled into Dublin port and stored in a warehouse belonging to Lalors Ltd, close to Ormond Quay. As many as 200 rifles and 90,000 rounds of ammunition were stored there at any one time and were gradually dispatched to other locations in co-operative creamery vans.[46] By August 1917 specific training orders were being issued and provided tangible proof of the progress and rising confidence of the Volunteers. Open company training was to resume on 9 September, but public parades were to be avoided; special attention was to be given to scouting (particularly of any police monitoring training), field work, cycling, and the training of section leaders and lieutenants; and arrests should not lead training to stop.[47] Those arrested were instructed not to recognize English law in the matter.

The remoulding of the Volunteers absorbed most of Brugha's energies, but some were reserved for the concurrent and interlinked reconstitution of Sinn Féin. Although not immediately apparent, one of the chief casualties of the 1916 Rising was the IPP. The transformation of the post-1916 Sinn Féin party, which apart from its name bore little resemblance to Griffith's original organization, from a loose coalition into the dominant political force took about eighteen months from the beginning of 1917. The first opportunity to test the IPP came in the Roscommon North by-election in early February 1917, a watershed moment in twentieth-century Irish history. When Michael Davitt junior declined to stand, Fr Michael O'Flanagan and a group in Dublin proposed George Plunkett, a papal count, former director of the National Museum, and father of the 1916 martyr Joseph (two other sons were imprisoned after the Rising). His opponents were Jasper Tully, owner of the *Roscommon Herald* who ran as an independent, and Thomas Devine for the IPP. The campaign saw disparate separatist elements work in unison to secure a comfortable victory for Plunkett in a staggering upset for the IPP.[48] But worse followed for Redmond's party. In May Joseph McGuinness won the Longford South by-election for Sinn Féin by a slender thirty-seven votes. This victory with the famous slogan – 'put him in to get him out' – was significant for several reasons. First, whereas Plunkett attracted a sympathy vote as the father of a rebel, McGuinness was a serving penal servitude prisoner in Lewes Gaol. Second, Thomas Ashe, president of the IRB supreme council, backed the political strategy. Third, Sinn Féin benefitted from the intervention of Archbishop William J. Walsh of Dublin, the preeminent Catholic prelate. He suggested in a letter to the press that those not alive to the dangers of partition were 'living in a fool's paradise' and added his belief that 'the country is practically sold'.[49] The timing of the letter had the effect of linking the partition issue to the Sinn Féin cause and contributed to McGuinness's narrow victory. There was also a handbill featuring a remark by Bishop O'Dwyer of Limerick, likening the dangling of home rule before Redmond to a carrot before the nose of a donkey with the punchline: 'No Donkey MP for Longford'.[50] Fourth, McGuinness's candidature was proposed by Collins and was an early indication of the influence that he would wield in this regard. Lastly, the by-election focused renewed public attention on the remaining penal servitude prisoners in Britain.

Less than two weeks after the Longford by-election, a meeting was organized in Dublin's Mansion House on 21 May 1917 to protest against the treatment of nationalist prisoners. Brugha was one of several speakers to address the crowd. That the meeting attracted the support of a range of organizations, including Catholic clergy and some members of the hierarchy, was a further indication of the growing loss of confidence in the IPP and steady drift towards Sinn Féin. Archbishop Walsh, who was cautiously supportive of Sinn Féin moderates, sent a message of support as did Bishop O'Dwyer of Limerick.[51]

Further protest meetings followed to demand the release of the prisoners. Following revelations of the harsh regime endured by Irish prisoners in Lewes in a letter written by Harry Boland and smuggled out to his family, the Irish National Aid and Volunteer Dependents' Fund organized a large-scale protest on 10 June 1917 at Beresford Place in Dublin.[52] The prominent and widespread display of posters and placards around Dublin advertising the meeting concerned the authorities. The DMP recommended to Henry Duke, the chief secretary, that the meeting be prohibited lest it endanger the peace; he agreed.[53] Nevertheless, the DMP prepared for trouble on a significant scale. On the evening of 10 June, a force of eighty constables, eight sergeants and two inspectors under a DMP superintendent was assembled at Store Street police station with a similarly sized contingent at Great Brunswick Street station. In addition, 400 soldiers were placed on standby at Dublin Castle. By 7.15 p.m. all of the assembled police were divided into parties of ten constables under a sergeant and placed at strategic locations close to Beresford Place.[54]

Despite the security arrangements, police reports described how a crowd of about three or four thousand had rushed into Beresford Place by 7.30 p.m., whereas press accounts suggest a more modest 1,000 people.[55] A moustachioed Brugha and Count Plunkett arrived by hackney car. As the crowd surrounded them near Liberty Hall, they stood up in the car with the intention of addressing the gathering. When Brugha ignored a warning from Inspector John Mills that the meeting was banned and persisted to speak he was seized from the car and taken into custody. The noise of the crowd, with tempers inflamed by the action of the police, rendered Plunkett's words inaudible. He was also arrested and taken with Brugha to Store Street (see plate 7). As the 51-year-old Mills escorted them, he was struck on the head with a hurley by Éamonn Murray, a member of the Fianna, and died of a fractured skull a few hours later.[56] When disturbances persisted in that general area, extra police

7 Cathal Brugha under arrest by the Dublin Metropolitan Police on 10 June 1917.
Behind him is Count Plunkett.

were drafted in to disperse the crowd and were eventually stood down at
midnight. A detachment of forty men from the Royal Irish Fusiliers was also
placed on standby at Store Street station.[57] Brugha and Plunkett were
subsequently removed to Arbour Hill military barracks to be tried by court
martial but were released on 18 June without charge.[58] Remarkably, this was
the first of just two occasions on which Brugha was arrested and it was the
only time that he was kept in detention. His second arrest occurred on 3
January 1919 in Thurles as he returned to Dublin, having been elected for
Waterford County. His offence was to refuse to give his name 'in plain English'
when asked to do so by a local constable. Brugha was taken to the local police
barracks but was released without charge later that night.[59]

Within a week of the Beresford Place protest, the penal servitude prisoners
had been granted a general amnesty and released. This, along with the
relaxation of the Defence of the Realm Act, was part of a government strategy
to remove the amnesty issue as a rallying point for extremists and to create a
better atmosphere for the Irish Convention – an Irish conference on home rule
which met under the chairmanship of Horace Plunkett between July 1917 and
April 1918.[60] It was both a final and ill-fated effort to throw Redmond a

lifebuoy, and a means of placing responsibility on the Irish themselves to settle the future administration of the country. Revealingly, Sinn Féin declined the five seats allocated to it on the grounds that the convention would not lead to complete Irish independence. Its non-participation was not seen as fatal because its political progress was still nascent. In the event, the convention broke down on the issues of an all-Ireland parliament and control of customs. It was also overtaken by the rapid pace of events, both in Ireland and in the Europe. Writing to Duke in December 1917, James O'Connor, the Irish attorney-general, named Brugha in a list also containing the names of Collins, Boland, Stack and Countess Markievicz as likely to cause trouble whatever the outcome of the convention.[61]

Before the advent of opinion polls, by-elections were the most reliable means of gauging the mood of the electorate. Sinn Féin's successes in Roscommon and Longford were augmented by two further victories in East Clare and Kilkenny city. No victory was more emphatic than East Clare and no winning candidate more central to the future history of Ireland. The victor was a political novice with little experience of public speaking outside the classroom. The senior surviving Volunteer from 1916, he was largely unknown before the by-election. But after it he was catapulted to national prominence, became president of Sinn Féin and represented East Clare for the next four decades. That soldier-turned-politician was Éamon de Valera. He had only been released from prison on 16 June, and while campaigning in his Volunteer uniform told the electors that 'every vote you give now is as good as the crack of a rifle in proclaiming your desire for freedom'. Everyone expected a Sinn Féin victory but few expected so large a winning margin of 5,010 votes to 2,035 for the IPP's Patrick Lynch. The East Clare by-election was a milestone for Sinn Féin because it secured a striking popular mandate that helped the organization to continue its rapid growth ahead of the 1918 general election. For de Valera, his victory was a pivotal episode in his progression from militant to political republican. Membership of Sinn Féin and the Volunteers overlapped and many of the party's leading activists were Volunteers who retained their military priorities.[62] The election of W.T. Cosgrave, Brugha's comrade in the South Dublin Union, in the Kilkenny by-election in August concluded a very successful period for Sinn Féin.

At a leadership level within Sinn Féin there were acute divisions, particularly between Griffith and Plunkett, that persisted until the October 1917 ard fheis. Brugha was instrumental in laying the foundation for the amalgamation of Sinn Féin and Plunkett's Liberty League, which had been established in April 1917 to challenge the IPP but instead threatened to duplicate and fragment Sinn Féin's efforts.[63] The unification was agreed at a lengthy meeting of the Mansion House Committee (established by Plunkett following the Roscommon by-election to co-ordinate the various separatist factions) in Brugha's home in June. Half the standing committee of Sinn Féin resigned to make way for six members of the Liberty League, Griffith remained president, and a convention in October would reassess the situation.[64] The intense process of developing the party machine proceeded during the summer of 1917 and, despite quarrels within the leadership cadre, de Valera, Brugha, Griffith and Plunkett generally worked in unison.

The most divisive issue was the demand by moderates such as Griffith, Seán Milroy and some of the pre-1916 Sinn Féin adherents that the dual monarchy idea in the 1907 party constitution be retained. Unsurprisingly, de Valera, Brugha, Plunkett and Collins insisted on a republic. William O'Brien recalled Brugha's somewhat forbidding remark that if Griffith did not accept the overarching goal of a republic and de Valera's leadership, he would have to 'walk the plank'.[65] Griffith's resistance to an outright declaration of republicanism was rooted in a belief that it was unattainable; it led to disagreement between the opposing sections.[66] Negotiations almost collapsed when Brugha and Collins threatened to walk away in protest. According to Robert Brennan, Brugha and Griffith were at 'daggers drawn ... so much so that Brugha had threatened that if Griffith stumped the country for Sinn Fein, he would get the Volunteers to stop him'.[67] A week before the October ard fheis, the matter was defused by de Valera's proposal that Sinn Féin would commit to securing international recognition of Ireland as an independent republic after which the people could freely choose their own form of government.[68] Such an ambiguous formula and the postponement of any consideration of what a republic actually meant beyond its emotive power created intense difficulties during the treaty debates. The acceptance of this policy was a personal achievement for Brugha and a reflection of the influence that he and the more radical republican wing exerted at this time on what remained a disparate political party.

The Sinn Féin ard fheis on 25 and 26 October 1917 confirmed the ascendancy of separatist republicanism. Held in the Mansion House, it was attended by about 1,700 delegates, representing 1,200 local branches, to decide the party's leadership, organizational structure and constitution. Griffith stood aside to allow de Valera's election unopposed as president of Sinn Féin. Griffith retained significant support and was elected a vice-president with 1,197 votes; Fr O'Flanagan was also elected a vice-president with 780 ballots. Brugha was elected to the party's national executive – in effect a shadow cabinet – having received 685 votes. This was the second-highest vote of the twenty-four members elected, eclipsed only by Eoin MacNeill's 888 votes, and was a measure of the esteem in which he was held. The last spot was filled by Michael Collins with 340 votes.[69] Laurence O'Neill, the Dublin lord mayor, recalled widespread canvassing for seats on the executive.[70] A further indicator of the respect enjoyed by Brugha came from Austin Stack, who had been elected secretary of Sinn Féin *in absentia* as he was a prisoner in Mountjoy. Writing to de Valera immediately after the ard fheis, Stack suggested that someone should deputize until he was released and that 'Brugha (if he could find time for the work) would be the best selection'.[71] In the event, Stack was freed in November.

In terms of structure, de Valera and Brugha put forward separate, but similar, proposals at the ard fheis. Interestingly, considering how their future relationship would deteriorate, Brugha's proposals were seconded by Collins. Ultimately, de Valera's scheme was overwhelmingly adopted.[72] Brugha also proposed the adoption of Sinn Féin's new constitution, impressing on delegates that an Irish republic could be attained by 'the weapon of the suggested constitution'. He reassured some concerned attendees that the proposed constitution did not entail connections with any secret societies and that a reference in the document to 'using any and every means' against a foreign government did not imply any intention 'to meet English rule by assassination'.[73] Within six months, however, Brugha himself would embark on an assassination mission to Westminster, the heart of the British political system. The constitution, which contained many aspects influenced by Brugha, was approved with ease.[74]

The language of Sinn Féin was suffused with three political demands. The first was the attainment of an Irish republic – the governing thesis of Brugha's life. Abstention from the House of Commons in favour of an Irish assembly was the second. This had been a stated aim of Griffith's original party. The third reflected the zeitgeist of Wilsonian self-determination. Sinn Féin intended to seek recognition for Ireland as an independent republic at the international peace conference that would follow the First World War. The national newspapers dismissed such goals as hopeless and absurd, with the *Irish Times* suggesting that such a political programme would lead to 'the infliction of untold calamity on Ireland'.[75] The same newspaper did, however, acknowledge that Sinn Féin had become 'a powerful and popular movement', that 'all classes of Nationalists, including large numbers of Roman Catholic clergy' had joined its ranks, and that it was well organized.[76] All proved key ingredients in Sinn Féin's success in the 1918 general election.

A national convention of the Irish Volunteers – the first to include the penal servitude prisoners released in June – took place at the same time as the Sinn Féin ard fheis. Holding the two meetings concurrently had been decided at a meeting of the Keating branch attended by de Valera, Ashe, Brugha, Collins, Diarmuid Lynch and Mulcahy. It would explain the presence of people from outside Dublin and thereby avert suspicion. Ashe did not live to witness either convention. He was arrested for making a seditious speech in July 1917 and died in Mountjoy Prison on 25 September from forcible feeding while on hunger strike. As Townshend put it, his death was 'a volcanic moment: Ashe was an iconic figure who combined revolutionary glamour with fervent religiosity. He had unique prestige as the most successful military figure of the rebellion'.[77] Ashe's death and funeral greatly boosted the Volunteers and Sinn Féin. Making his first public appearance, Collins, who succeeded Ashe as head of the IRB, delivered a pithy graveside oration: 'The volley which we have just heard is the only speech which is proper to make above the grave of a dead Fenian'.[78]

The Volunteer convention was a clandestine affair 'for the purpose of action rather than exchange of views or discussion'.[79] Elaborate security arrangements were made by the Dublin Brigade to ensure that the meeting on 27 October in a hall just inside Croke Park proceeded without interference. The precise location was communicated verbally two days before. The Volunteer convention was less than a quarter of the size of the Sinn Féin ard fheis. Between 250 and 300 delegates closely associated with the revitalization of the Volunteers from all parts of Ireland attended; several delegates were liable to arrest and some were in prison. Many delegates had also been in the Mansion House but, according to Mulcahy, the difference of purpose of the Sinn Féin and Volunteer conventions 'was completely appreciated and required no discussion by the Volunteers'.[80] Some prominent in the Volunteers before the Rising – Eoin MacNeill, Bulmer Hobson, J.J. O'Connell and Seán Fitzgibbon – were excluded given their opposition to the Rising. MacNeill had written to de Valera that the surviving members of the general council and executive should be given an opportunity to give an account of their stewardship.[81] While O'Connell resumed his association with the Volunteers, Hobson's active participation in Irish political movements ended for good.[82] Frank Henderson recalled that the position of MacNeill was discussed early in the proceedings. He had handed over all remaining funds to de Valera, who refused to allow any censure to be passed on MacNeill. Brugha's consideration was characteristically sincere and remorseless. Referring to the transfer of monies, he described MacNeill as 'an honourable man and a good Irishman' but one who should 'never be allowed to hold any position again in the Volunteers'.[83]

The significance of the convention was twofold. First, it marked the fusion of the military and political wings of the separatist movement. Having been

8 Richard Mulcahy, IRA chief of staff.

elected president of Sinn Féin two days earlier, de Valera was also unanimously acclaimed president of the Irish Volunteers. His dual mandate symbolized this fusion. The second importance lay in the other appointments that were made. Fresh elections were held for the national executive by province with Dublin regarded as a fifth province. Ulster, for example, was represented by Seán

MacEntee (Belfast), Joseph O'Doherty (Donegal), Paul Galligan (Cavan) and Eoin O'Duffy (Monaghan). The danger of arrest meant that holding monthly meetings of the national executive became increasingly difficult. Seán McGarry, a member and future president of the reconstituted IRB supreme council, was appointed honorary secretary to the Volunteer executive, a position he retained until the outbreak of the civil war. Notably, a quintet of directors was appointed to standardize aspects of the military work: Michael Collins became director for organization, Diarmuid Lynch director of communications, Richard Mulcahy director of training, Michael Staines director of supplies, and Rory O'Connor director of engineering. The resident executive was reconstituted to comprise the directors and McGarry. Brugha remained chairman and had the authority to co-opt six additional representatives in the Dublin area for specific duties. These were Éamonn Duggan, Gearóid O'Sullivan, Fintan Murphy, Diarmuid O'Hegarty, Dick McKee and Paddy Ryan.[84] Duggan became director of intelligence until the establishment of general headquarters in March 1918. Following the lead of Piaras Béaslaí, many writers have erroneously suggested that Brugha was chief of staff or mistakenly conflated the position of chief of staff and chair of the resident executive.[85] The role of chief of staff did not come into existence until the establishment of a general headquarters (GHQ) in March 1918 and was first held by Richard Mulcahy (see plate 8).

There was considerable overlap in the leadership of the political and military wings of the separatist movement. Six members of the national executive were also members of the Sinn Féin executive: de Valera, Brugha, MacEntee, Collins, Lynch and Stack. Eleven were elected to the first Dáil in December 1918, of whom five served as a minister (de Valera, Brugha, Mulcahy, Collins and Stack) and thirteen were elected to the second Dáil in May 1921. The influence of the IRB over the Volunteers had grown inexorably despite Brugha's forceful opposition. Of the six directors appointed by the convention, only Staines and O'Connor were not members of the IRB but were certainly trusted by it. Four of those co-opted to the resident executive were also in the IRB. Brugha was affected by ill health in the early months of 1918 and this militated against a greater involvement in the direction of Sinn Féin and the Volunteers. When the Sinn Féin national executive convened for the first time in December 1917, it elected an influential fifteen-member standing committee. This body met regularly and conducted its affairs with impressive efficiency.[86] Brugha was not a regular attendee and resigned in April, something that was accepted with 'regret'.[87] Within the Volunteers organization, training and the gathering of arms and ammunition were the main tasks prioritized by the various directors.

The establishment of a full-time general headquarters staff in March 1918, mandated by the Volunteer national executive, was testament both to the progress made since the Croke Park convention and to the growing fear that conscription would be imposed on Ireland. Mulcahy recalled that prior to the meeting of the national executive, the directors of the resident executive met at the Keating branch to consider nominations to the GHQ staff. Brugha does not appear to have been involved in these deliberations. The national executive approved the appointment of Mulcahy as chief of staff, Dick McKee as director of training and commandant of the Dublin Brigade, Collins as adjutant-general and director of intelligence, Rory O'Connor continuing in engineering, and Diarmuid O'Hegarty as director of organization. That appointment was brief as O'Hegarty became secretary to the cabinet with Éamon Price succeeding him as director of organization. On Mulcahy's nomination, Austin Stack was appointed deputy chief of staff but he was arrested soon after and played no role in the work of GHQ. Brugha continued as chairman of the increasingly redundant resident executive and was not on the formal military staff. In this capacity, he provided a link between the military and political leaderships and was the obvious choice for minister for defence in the first Dáil from April 1919.[88]

Compulsory military service was introduced in Britain in January 1916 for unmarried men between the ages of eighteen and forty-one, but Ireland was excluded from the measure. From the end of 1916, Lloyd George came under increasing pressure from within the war cabinet, his generals and British public opinion to conscript Irishmen for the remainder of the war. However, fears for the electoral future of the IPP and concerns about undermining the Irish contribution to the war effort through food production and work in British factories prevented the imposition of conscription.[89] The situation changed decisively in March 1918 when the German army began a great offensive on the western front and broke through British lines. The war appeared to have reached a turning point. In desperation and under severe public pressure, the cabinet considered imposing conscription on Ireland, where it was estimated there was an untapped reservoir of 150,000 men of recruitment age, and a further 50,000 if the age limit was increased to fifty.[90] Both Bryan Mahon, British army commander-in-chief, and Joseph Byrne, RIC inspector general, believed conscription could be enforced but expected a massive protest against it and recommended that known troublemakers first be removed.[91] Duke was not so sanguine. He warned Lloyd George that it would be impossible to enforce conscription in a way that would materially help the war effort and that the authorities might 'as well recruit Germans'.[92] The prime minister proposed combining the extension of the Military Service Act with an immediate grant of home rule.

When the scheme was introduced on 9 April Ireland was plunged into crisis and, in the words of the RIC inspector general, was 'ablaze with furious resentment'.[93] John Dillon led the IPP out of the House of Commons, which appeared to vindicate Sinn Féin's policy of abstention. An all-party conference at the Mansion House to coordinate resistance to conscription was organized by Laurence O'Neill, the lord mayor. De Valera informed him that he was 'quite ready to meet representatives of other Irish parties so as to give expression to the united determination of the Irish people to defeat conscription, and to devise the best means for effectively resisting this final invasion of our public and private liberties'. He finished his letter with the declaration that 'Sinn Féin will calmly, in the full consciousness of the justice of its cause resist conscription to the death'.[94] Other members of Sinn Féin – Brugha and Collins in particular – were averse to collaborating with the IPP. It may even have been a factor in Brugha's resignation from the Sinn Féin standing committee. Collins shared Brugha's suspicion, describing the leaders of the IPP as traitors to their country.[95] Both believed that only the Volunteers stood between Ireland and conscription. The national executive of the Volunteers decided unanimously to resist the imposition of conscription in Ireland with all military force. The menace of conscription caused a sudden influx of new Volunteers, whose enthusiasm in many cases proved short-lived.

A deputation from the Mansion House to Maynooth secured the support of the Roman Catholic hierarchy, which issued a statement declaring conscription 'against the will of the Irish nation' and calling on Catholics to resist 'by all means that are consonant with the law of God'. An anti-conscription pledge, modelled on the Ulster solemn league and covenant, was taken after masses on 21 April 1918 and clergy were actively involved in raising a national defence fund of which Archbishop Walsh was a trustee. The whole-hearted involvement of the church prevented widespread disorder but, as the authorities quickly realized, the clerical-nationalist collaboration ended any prospect of conscription being applied in Ireland. On 20 April the RIC inspector general reported that public feeling was 'in a state of extreme tension and it would be difficult to exaggerate the gravity of the situation', which 'has meant an enormous accession to the power of Sinn Féin'.[96] The mobilization against conscription 'crystallised the nationalist front which had been in gradual formation since 1916'.[97]

In the event, the government opted not to enforce conscription, but the threat remained until the sudden end of the war. The damage to public opinion was then compounded by the blundering German plot arrests of

17–18 May 1918. Seventy-three members of Sinn Féin, including de Valera and Griffith, were arrested under DORA on the allegation that Sinn Féin was colluding with Germany to stage another uprising. The 'German Plot' has generally been dismissed as a fabrication.[98] However, one prominent activist stated in his military service pension application that about this time Collins requested him to make arrangements for the landing of German arms on the west coast.[99] When Brugha, who had some intelligence sources in Dublin Castle, confronted Collins about this he emphatically denied any knowledge. Typically, Brugha remained sceptical.[100] Not alone were the arrests a propaganda gift to Sinn Féin but they also ensured that the immediate direction of the separatist movement came under the control of a radical hardcore who remained at liberty, including Collins, Boland, Mulcahy and Brugha. The latter's name featured on a list of prominent nationalists whose arrest and detention were recommended by the authorities.[101] It appears that Brugha and others had been tipped off by Ned Broy, a member of the DMP with republican sympathies who regularly passed on information between 1917 and his arrest in 1921. By contrast, de Valera dismissed a warning about his imminent arrest, claiming that he was sick and tired of such warnings.[102] Brugha may well have evaded capture in any case as he was by then on his way to London on an extraordinary mission to assassinate members of the British cabinet if and when conscription was implemented. As Macardle observed, Lloyd George 'spoke more literally than he was aware of when he expressed the opinion that to attempt to impose conscription would be "suicidal" at this time'.[103]

Brugha's assassination plan was an indication of how conscription had electrified the political atmosphere. J.J. O'Kelly recalled that the depth of opposition to conscription created a 'language' and a 'temper' among people 'in every parish' that were 'quite in line with Cathal Brugha's state of mind' which was willing to use both political and violent methods to advance Irish independence.[104] Brugha regarded the imposition of conscription on an unwilling people by an alien government without legitimacy and in the face of overwhelming majority resistance as a veritable act of war. The declaration of the Mansion House conference had also equated compulsory military service with 'a declaration of war on the Irish nation' and called on Irishmen to resist it 'by the most effective means at their disposal'. Brugha placed the locus of blame on the cabinet as the decision makers. As O'Farrell has argued, the assassination plan was 'not borne out of some psychotic Anglophobia or a sense of despair … Fundamentally, Brugha believed that politicians were responsible for the violence of their armies'. Seán Healy, a Cork Volunteer, recalled Brugha making this very point in his interactions with him.[105] The lack of any assessment of the profound personal and national and international political consequences seems astonishing. It was an example of the contradictions in Brugha's make-up, the oscillation between inherent caution and impulsive action. It has been argued that had the assassination been carried out, it would have proven counter-productive and led to the crushing of Irish republicanism to the benefit of Irish unionists.[106] Several colleagues called on Brugha to reconsider, believing his services more valuable in Ireland. But characteristically Brugha insisted on leading the expedition. The assassination proposals were presented to the Volunteers in a manner that, surprise aside, did not generate disapproval or excessive debate.[107] Although Richard Walsh claims that Brugha's plan was supported by de Valera at a meeting of the Volunteer executive, in 1964 de Valera was unable to recall such a meeting but maintained that Brugha 'would not act without an Executive decision in favour of his action'.[108] This is an important point. Brugha's mission may have been audacious or foolhardy, but it was not a maverick action without broader approval. Most accounts suggest that while Collins facilitated the mission, he may have derided the plan in private. Some such as Ernest Blythe described the mission as 'absolute lunacy'.[109]

Of over seventy candidates initially considered for the mission, just a few volunteered: Joseph Good, Bill Whelan, Matt Furlong, Thomas Craven, John Gaynor, Séamus McNamara and William Corcoran.[110] All were members of the Volunteers and travelled from Dublin. Good was born in London and from a young age was involved in the nascent Irish revolutionary movement there. He joined the Volunteers in London in 1914 and was in the same company as Michael Collins, who was then working as a clerk in the postal service.[111] Craven had joined the Volunteers in Liverpool. Both he and Good, along with many other English-based and English-born Irishmen, travelled to Dublin in April 1916 to take part in the Easter Rising.[112] In mid-April 1918, they had been interviewed by Brugha and Mulcahy and informed of the plan to assassinate members of the British cabinet if conscription was imposed on Ireland. The dangerous nature of the assignment was emphasized by Brugha who suggested that their chances of survival were slim but assured them that provision would be made for their dependants. The selected men were given a week to consider and to make any necessary arrangements with their families. Brugha also stressed that he would be in sole charge and would take no advice or instruction from anyone, prompting Whelan to reflect in hindsight that Brugha was 'the most cold-blooded man he had ever met'.[113]

In May the assassination team left for London in groups of two and three, and stayed in various safe houses around the city. Some travelled on fictitious passports and on the pretence of looking for work. They were ordered not to carry firearms or documents. Firearms were to be supplied in London by

Brugha. Each man was provided with an allowance of £5 per week. Following their arrival, arrangements were made for the group to convene at the Irish Club House near Smithfield Market.[114] Good and Whelan reached London on 18 May and stayed in the home of James Nunan, father of Seán, a veteran of the Rising and one of the four clerks of Dáil Éireann in 1919 before becoming de Valera's private secretary. They stayed there for three months. The Nunan home was used regularly by Irish republicans, including Brugha and Liam Mellows, and for that reason was often raided by Scotland Yard. The precise date on which Brugha left for London is unclear but it was certainly before the 'German Plot' arrests on 17 May. It may have been on 12 May because on the boat Brugha met Thomas Barry, a Corkman prominent in the GAA and the Volunteers. He was going to London in connection with the purchase of arms and later recalled departing Dublin about 12 May.[115] Brugha was accompanied by a young daughter, probably 5-year-old Nollaig, his eldest child who was born in 1912. On reaching Liverpool, Brugha met Neill Kerr who organized eight more British-based men for the mission. Originally from Armagh, the Kerr home in Liverpool was frequently used by Collins, de Valera and others and the family were heavily involved in acquiring and transporting arms to Ireland.[116] Although some urged Brugha to remain at home, his departure was not totally unwelcome in Dublin. Mulcahy and others in GHQ were 'glad that Cathal had something to concentrate on and occupy him, leaving us free to feel and act … as we wanted to do on our own'.[117] As Mulcahy's biographer puts it, Brugha's 'edgy watchfulness did not have to be endured', allowing the chief of staff, as he later humorously recalled, to 'look after the work of the staff … in complete harmony with the absent Cathal'.[118]

Seán McGrath, a native of Leitrim, who lived and worked in London was Brugha's main contact. Active in the Gaelic League, McGrath joined the Irish Volunteers in London and enjoyed a strong working relationship with Art O'Brien, the key figure in Irish nationalist circles in London.[119] He played a significant role in sourcing arms in Britain for supply to the Volunteers and IRA and operated under the direction of Collins, Brugha and Mulcahy. On his arrival in London, Brugha made contact with McGrath and outlined his plans to assassinate the British cabinet in the House of Commons from the public gallery. McGrath assisted with the plans by visiting parliament, marking out the government front bench places, and arranging passes for the visitors' gallery for Brugha and his henchmen. Art O'Brien attested to 'the most valuable assistance' provided by McGrath during the special mission in London for which Brugha 'expressed great appreciation'.[120] A few days after his arrival, Brugha again met Thomas Barry as McGrath was his principal contact for the purchase of arms. Brugha asked Barry to take his daughter back to Dublin and also gave him letters for Mulcahy and Collins. Barry recalled that on his return to Dublin, he 'found it very hard to find anybody' as many of the nationalist leaders had been arrested. He eventually found Mulcahy and Collins together in a house in the north of the city.[121]

Accommodation had been secured for Brugha in a large house near Tavistock Place and close to Regent's Park. It would appear that his entire family joined him there on at least one occasion, which suggests that Brugha expected to remain in London for a considerable time. Understandably, given the dangerous nature of the mission, Whelan found the presence of Brugha's young children unsettling. He assumed that they provided 'a kind of disguise or camouflage or as a cover for his [Brugha's] activities'. It seems likely that by travelling with his daughter Brugha, then a wanted man in Ireland, reduced the potential of being detected by the police as he boarded his boat. On reaching London Nollaig's function as a cover had been fulfilled. It is a measure of how desperately Brugha wanted to lead the London mission. By contrast, Mulcahy suggested less plausibly that Brugha brought over his children 'to soothe his loneliness'.[122] Brugha met the men in small groups at appointed times over the following months to detail the nature of their assignment and familiarize them, through photographs, with members of the British cabinet and prominent newspaper publishers and editors. Regent's Park, Hyde Park and Hampstead Heath were generally used as meeting venues because they provided a better opportunity for escape if required. As in Dublin, the bicycle was Brugha's preferred mode of transport in London. However, his tendency to take risks and his disregard for a prohibition on cycling in Regent's Park drew him into an unnecessary confrontation with a policeman to the consternation of his men. Fortunately, the incident ended with just a verbal reprimand.[123]

The assassination plan does not seem to have been clearly formulated. Some of the men appear to have had a vague understanding of where, how and when the attack would occur. Gaynor recalled that they 'had no definite idea of how we were going to do the job'.[124] Brugha decided that each man would target a specific cabinet minister. During a meeting in a London park, Brugha arranged for each man to draw the name of a cabinet minister from a hat. They were then required to acquaint themselves with the House of Commons, Downing Street and the photograph and place of residence of their assigned target. The men were issued with either a .38 revolver or an automatic pistol.[125]

Utilizing the ticket of maverick nationalist MP Laurence Ginnell, Brugha visited the public gallery of the House of Commons a few times with one or two of his men. On one occasion, Brugha's eagerness to examine the layout of the floor of the House from the gallery prompted the intervention of an usher who demanded that he not stand up or look over the gallery. During such visits he also took the ludicrous risk of bringing his 'Peter the Painter' semi-automatic weapon with him, telling Bill Whelan that he 'only wanted to get the feel of this thing here in the gallery'.[126] On another occasion in the gallery with Whelan, Brugha insisted that he alone would do all the shooting and that it would be the task of the other men to give him protection and then to shoot their own way out.[127] Gaynor was puzzled by this naïve plan and wondered how a party of fourteen Irishmen 'with their Irish brogues' could gain easy access to the public gallery.[128] Brugha expected to be informed in advance by contacts in London if and when the imposition of conscription on Ireland would be announced so that his team would be in position. Collins feared that 'Cathal might become over hasty, shoot first and do the thinking afterwards'.[129] Brugha became such a familiar visitor to the House of Commons that some policemen and officials assisted him as he entered and left the building. He later told J.J. O'Kelly that they seemed to think that 'he was a wounded soldier back from Flanders, and … they did everything they could to facilitate him'.[130] It is probable that Brugha emphasized his limp.

During his sojourn in Britain, Brugha also visited Liverpool with McGrath on a number of occasions, probably in connection with the latter's gun-running operations. On one occasion Brugha unexpectedly encountered Ernie O'Malley, who had been sent on a secret mission by Collins to purchase arms for the IRB. When asked by Brugha as to his business, O'Malley simply replied that he was on 'special work' and no more was said.[131] He vividly recalled Brugha's attire:

> He wore a double-reefer jacket; he looked at times like a seaman; of medium height with broad shoulders, steady grey-blue eyes and a determined chin. He wore a green tie. That to me typified the man. It seemed the symbol of his nationality in a hostile country. He might change his appearance, but the tie meant the cause to him. He was the most uncompromising of all the army officers.[132]

The men who formed part of Brugha's special team underwent a range of emotions during their stint in London. That they had little to do or occupy their minds compounded the tension they experienced in 'waiting for the affair'. Gaynor described his time in London as 'terrible, monotonous and trying'. The stress caused some of them 'to look old and haggard under the strain'. However, they also found time for 'dancing and walking and other exercises to keep themselves fit'.[133] On their return to Dublin, some of the men let it be known that they had 'the times of their lives' while in London and had 'plenty of enjoyment'.[134] Brugha only interacted with the men when discussing and planning tactics and strategy, and otherwise remained aloof. Good recalled one occasion when they enticed him to go rowing on the Thames near Kew and Whelan another when to his amazement Brugha, a teetotaller, brought him to a pub for a bottle of stout.[135] O'Malley contrasted Brugha who 'neither cursed, smoked or drank' with Collins who was 'adept at all three'.[136]

By August 1918 the British position in France had improved, any threat of conscription in Ireland subsided, and Brugha's mission in London became redundant. After approximately three months in London, most of Brugha's men returned to Dublin with a sense of 'great relief'. Caitlín joined her husband in London in early August and spent a few weeks with him before returning home alone. Brugha remained in London and also spent some time in Manchester and Liverpool before reaching Dublin in mid-October 1918.[137] Batt O'Connor's wife Bridget recalled

> One morning when I was finished doing my door-brasses ... I saw a small man coming up the path. He was slightly lame and had a green shade over one eye. He asked was Mr O'Connor in and I said: 'Yes, Cathal'. He laughed and took the shade off his eye and said – 'That is bad; I thought nobody could recognise me in this disguise'. He had just come off the boat from England where he had spent several months.[138]

While Brugha rested at the O'Connor home in Donnybrook, Batt O'Connor went to fetch Brugha's wife. In her BMH statement, Mrs O'Connor indicated that Collins was in the Brugha home where he occasionally spent a night. On hearing of Brugha's return, Collins wished to see him but was prevented by Mrs O'Connor who did not want Brugha disturbed until Caitlín first arrived. The Brughas then went into the city to buy a present for their son, Ruairí, as it was his first birthday on 15 October; the boy had been named Ruairí Mac Diarmada Brugha after Roger Casement and Seán Mac Diarmada.[139] That Collins occasionally overnighted in the Brugha home suggests that a friendship and respect existed between them at this time and that their enmity was a gradual and later development as the next chapter will discuss.

Brugha's absence for five months coincided with a period of feverish activity by both Sinn Féin and the Volunteers in anticipation of a long-expected general election. At the end of September 1918, the standing committee of Sinn Féin, which was dominated by Collins and, in particular, by Harry Boland as joint honorary secretary, approved Brugha as the party's candidate for the Waterford County constituency.[140] Ahead of the election, the number of Waterford constituencies had been reduced from three to two. Waterford city was now combined with its immediate hinterland while the rest of the county became the new Waterford County constituency, doubling in size. Sinn Féin selection rules required candidates nominated in a constituency with a Gaeltacht population to have a command of Irish; this proviso had been first proposed by Piaras Béaslaí.[141] For this reason, Boland, whose Irish was rudimentary despite membership of the Keating branch, was forced to decline the Waterford County nomination and instead contested Roscommon South. Brugha was no stranger to Waterford through his work as a commercial traveller with Lalors. He also had a strong attachment to the Ring Gaeltacht, which he visited often to camp, fish or cycle, and to perfect his spoken Irish, which bore a slight Déise intonation.[142] Brugha's election opponent was James John O'Shee, a solicitor, who had been an IPP MP in the old West Waterford constituency since 1895.[143] Seán Ó Murthuile, who had campaigned successfully on behalf of Joe McGuinness in South Longford, was assigned to assist with Brugha's campaign.[144] Brugha's presence on the election trail was severely curtailed by Caitlín contracting influenza in mid-November. Dangerously ill for fifteen days and also pregnant with Fidelma, who was born in May 1919, fears were expressed for her life. She was cared for by Dr Kathleen Lynn, Sinn Féin's director of public health and a proponent of vaccination, at 37 Charlemont Street, Dublin. This centre was created by Lynn and others to provide medical services for infants, but during the influenza pandemic was used to care for adult sufferers of the flu.[145] In her diary Lynn recorded how Caitlín appeared to be recovering before being gripped by pneumonia. One entry recorded starkly: 'terrible anxious day with Mrs C. Bruagha [sic], stayed in hosp. till 7am', but by 30 November she was 'much better' and returned home two weeks later.[146] Captain William Archer Redmond was the sitting IPP MP in Waterford city. He had first won the seat in March 1918 in a by-election occasioned by the demise of his father, John Redmond. Sinn Féin was confident that it would win both Waterford seats; Dr Vincent White contested Waterford city for Sinn Féin.

At the beginning of 1918, the IPP had been strong enough to win three by-elections on the trot and arrest Sinn Féin's seemingly inevitable progress. But thereafter it was fatally undermined by British policy in Ireland – conscription and the German plot arrests in particular – which rallied support for a revitalized Sinn Féin, and the disruptions and dislocations of the First World War. In his report for November 1918, the RIC inspector general suggested that the IPP had 'outlived their popularity' even with Catholic clergy and was abandoned by the electorate for failing to obtain a satisfactory guarantee with regard to home rule on the outbreak of the war.[147] In addition, the IPP's dilapidated electoral machinery was unfit for battle and bankrupt; its candidates were mercilessly depicted as conscriptionists and corruptionists by Sinn Féin. A majority of the Irish electorate was drawn to Sinn Féin's alluring electoral promises of abstaining from Westminster in favour of creating a constituent assembly in Dublin and presenting Ireland's claims of statehood at Versailles.

Campaigning in Waterford County was generally low key and newspaper interest focused on the Waterford city contest. On 18 November local Sinn Féin activists, including Dan Fraher and P.C. O'Mahony, addressed a large crowd in Dungarvan under a banner which read: 'For Cathal Brugha and Independence'. The dominant theme in the speeches was Brugha's cachet as a 1916 veteran.[148] Pax Whelan recalled that many locals had never heard of Brugha when he was nominated, 'but when they heard he was a 1916 man, that he carried a few British bullets in him … they were happy enough … all rallied around'.[149] Although there was a significant increase in the presence of Volunteers within the county immediately prior to the poll, no serious disturbances were reported. By contrast, the campaign in Waterford city was pockmarked by violence. Speaking at an election rally in Cappoquin in early December, Brugha told the assembled crowd: 'He only did in Easter Week what he was prepared to do again, and he would make any sacrifice to break the English government'.[150]

On 14 December 1918, just weeks after the end of the First World War, voters in Britain and Ireland went to the polls for the first time since 1910. Under the Representation of the People Act (1918) there was a near three-fold increase in the size of the Irish electorate, which expanded from 700,000 to just under two million. All men over the age of twenty-one were entitled to vote as were women over the age of thirty, subject to certain property qualifications. For the first time, over one-third of the Irish electorate was female and in total three-quarters of the adult population could now vote. There was 'a rush' on voting in Waterford County as soon as the polls opened. In Dungarvan great interest was reported, as was the 'most perfect discipline … on the side of Sinn Féin'.[151] The result was awaited with eager anticipation by large sections of the rural electorate, mainly Sinn Féin supporters who were confident that Brugha would prevail. After the polls closed, they lined the streets of Dungarvan to watch the ballot boxes arrive at the courthouse from the surrounding districts. That evening the streets 'resounded' with Sinn Féin songs, while a body of Volunteers paraded in front of Brugha's hotel waving flags and singing 'The Soldiers Song'.[152]

The election result was announced on 28 December. In Britain Lloyd George and the coalition government won a landslide victory. In Ireland the results were seismic. Under the 'first past the post' electoral system, Sinn Féin won 73 seats or three-quarters of the 105 Irish seats at Westminster; the once-untouchable IPP secured just six, of which four were in Ulster where Cardinal Michael Logue brokered an election pact between Sinn Féin and the IPP; and Ulster Unionists 26, consolidating its grip on power in what would become Northern Ireland. Notably, the Irish Labour Party opted not to contest the election and thereby complicate the national question. When it initially considered a pact with Sinn Féin, Brugha acerbically pronounced that it was 'a pity that Labour people have not the intelligence and patriotism to let their class claim wait until we have cleared out the enemy'. Labour's decision to stand aside may have pleased the likes of Brugha, who exuded 'could not be better', but it ensured that the party missed a vital opportunity to appeal to a newly and massively enfranchised electorate.[153] The scale of Sinn Féin's victory in what became the twenty-six counties was immense. In all of Leinster, Munster and Connacht only one IPP survivor remained standing: Captain Redmond in Waterford city who described his constituency as 'an oasis in the political desert of Ireland'.[154] By contrast, Sinn Féin won only three seats in the territory that subsequently became Northern Ireland. In the Waterford County constituency Brugha coasted to victory by 12,890 votes to 4,217, or 75.3 per cent of the vote. He was one of fifteen Sinn Féin victors in the forty-seven contested constituencies to achieve over three-quarters of the vote.[155] Brugha moved a vote of thanks to the returning officer and speaking 'with a nice gentlemanly feeling, devoid of all bitterness', wished his 'worthy opponent' well, and asked those who differed with him to now join with the majority. Revealingly, O'Shee congratulated 'his friends' on their tremendous majority.[156]

The 1918 general election was the most momentous Irish electoral contest of the twentieth century and the consequences for the future of Ireland and Brugha were profound. His contribution to this success was substantial if understated. Despite debilitating injuries after the Rising and the absence of interned and jailed colleagues, Brugha worked relentlessly to revive and consolidate the Volunteers. Essentially a shy man uncomfortable with public attention and not an innate politician, he nevertheless embraced the dual strategy of the post-Rising separatist movement and straddled its political and military wings. Throughout 1917 and 1918, Brugha was an organizer, a galvanizer, a fixer, a unifier, a facilitator and a zealot with an unwavering commitment to the attainment of an Irish republic. That Brugha regarded the election result as a retrospective democratic endorsement of the Rising was clear in a victory speech made in Cappoquin. He told the assembled crowd that

The people had now by their votes endorsed the Rising of Easter Week, that the work they had begun then would now continue, that the RIC had better understand that they were the armed persecutors of the Irish people and would henceforth be treated as enemy garrison troops. Sinn Féin had now the authority of the Irish people to govern them and that they would do so without delay.[157]

So it proved with the meeting of the first Dáil and the ambush at Soloheadbeg on 21 January 1919.

CHAPTER 5

Minister: from the first Dáil to the Anglo-Irish truce, 1919–21

IN JANUARY 1919 there was an unmistakeable sense of a new political era, both in Ireland and in Europe. The zenith of Sinn Féin's policy was reached on 21 January with a political revolution: the opening of the first Dáil. The *Freeman's Journal*, the newspaper of the IPP, was dignified in defeat: 'whatever democratic nationalists may think of the wisdom of the people's decision, whatever their doubts about the practicability of the republican policy ... as democrats, nationalists are bound now to give the republicans a fair field'.[1] The British government demurred, and much blood was spilled in consequence during the War of Independence between 1919 and 1921. An in-depth survey of that conflict is beyond the scope of this chapter which instead focuses on Brugha's contribution to the political and military struggle. He fulfilled the roles of speaker of the first Dáil and temporary president until April 1919 when he became minister for defence. Brugha's influence as minister was modest. His desire to ensure that ultimate authority over the IRA should lie with Dáil Éireann was not shared by IRA GHQ, the IRB, or the formidable Michael Collins. Brugha's antipathy towards Collins has attracted considerable attention but the underlying reasons are less well understood. An animosity towards Collins from 1920 onwards was nourished by Brugha's post-Rising wariness of the IRB and Collins's pronounced tendency to interfere in other Dáil government departments. Brugha's distrust of the IRB was not simply in terms of his own position as minister for defence, which was frequently undermined. He also viewed the IRB as a danger to the authority of the Dáil itself.

Sinn Féin sought to undermine the British administration in Ireland through the creation of a rival government and by appealing to world opinion. So confident was the party of success at the polls that its standing committee decided 'to convoke the Dáil Éireann' on 19 December 1918, nine days before the election result was officially announced. Prompt action was necessary because Woodrow Wilson, the president of the United States, had arrived in Europe in mid-December ahead of the Versailles peace conference. The Sinn

Féin executive instructed Robert Barton, Michael Collins, George Gavan
Duffy and Seán T. O'Kelly to proceed to London to get in touch with the
president. This fanciful scheme was in vain. By contrast, arrangements for a
national assembly were pragmatic and far more fruitful. The term Dáil
Éireann had been used by Sinn Féin at its 1918 ard fheis and was derived from
the name of a council of elders in Gaelic Ireland.

Arguably, the very first meeting of the Dáil took place in the Mansion
House on 7 January 1919.[2] Chaired by Count Plunkett, this was a private
session attended by twenty-nine of the thirty-five Sinn Féin TDs not in jail.
Thirteen of those present, including Brugha, became ministers and four of the
five future signatories of the Anglo-Irish treaty were present. Arthur Mitchell
has characterized the freshly elected TDs as young (Brugha was forty-four),
lower middle class and predominantly Dublin-based.[3] The deputies signed the
roll and a pledge in Irish (with an English translation) to abstain from
Westminster, 'to work for the establishment of an Independent Irish Republic'
and 'nothing less than complete separation from England'.[4] A motion declared
Dáil Éireann constituted and established. The meeting appointed select
committees. The first was charged with drawing up standing orders for the
house and a constitution; the second, of which Brugha was a member, was to
draft a declaration of independence and to produce a message to the free
nations of the world. The committees set to work immediately. It was decided
that all persons elected for Irish constituencies at the general election would
be invited to attend the public assembly of Dáil Éireann.

Strikingly, the parliamentary procedures adopted by the rebel parliament
in Dublin adhered closely to established practice at Westminster. The standing
orders largely followed the British pattern with, for example, written orders
governing parliamentary sessions, daily question time, and precedence of
ministerial business. An amendment in April in the name of Éamon de Valera
and Countess Markievicz ensured that deputies would be referred to by the
names of their constituencies, just like the House of Commons. In addition,
the constitution enshrined the Westminster model of cabinet government and
ministerial responsibility to parliament.[5] Some charged that the Dáil was
'simply Westminster put into Irish'.[6] Subsequent efforts by some disgruntled
TDs to introduce an American-style committee system were resisted. Even
after the Dáil was suppressed in September 1919 and went underground, the
doctrine of executive responsibility to parliament was maintained with
ministers making periodic reports as their circumstances permitted. The
constitution was largely drafted by George Gavan Duffy, who came to
prominence as solicitor for Roger Casement in 1916. In five short articles it
laid down a provisional scheme of government and not just a framework

for the Dáil.[7] There was one significant innovation. Unlike the British constitution, the Irish constitution was a written one.

Further preparatory meetings took place on 14 and 17 January at which final drafts of the standing orders, constitution, declaration of independence and message to the free nations of the world were adopted. Irish translations of the documents were also prepared. Much of that work was carried out by Piaras Béaslaí, TD for North Kerry, founding member of the Irish Volunteers and Gaelic Leaguer. The declaration echoed the 1916 proclamation in protesting the injustice of foreign rule 'maintained by military occupation against the declared will of the people'. It declared 'a new era in history' following the Irish electorate's endorsement of the Irish Republic at the general election and ordained that 'elected Representatives of the Irish people alone have power to make laws binding on the people of Ireland, and that the Irish Parliament is the only Parliament to which that people will give its allegiance'.[8] The document also called for international recognition of Irish independence. This was made more explicit in the message to the free nations to uphold Ireland's 'national claim to complete independence as an Irish Republic against the arrogant pretensions of England'.[9] The 'democratic programme', a statement of social and economic principles, has often been either misunderstood as suggesting the radical intentions of the first Dáil, or regarded as recompense for Labour for abstaining from the general election. Emmet O'Connor has deemed it neither democratic nor a programme and suggests that its true purpose was to have the Irish labour movement recognized at the International Socialist Conference in Berne in February 1919. In return, the democratic programme might elicit international support for Sinn Féin's claim to representation at Versailles.[10] The Irish Labour Party told the conference in Berne that it supported the self-determination of peoples in choosing the sovereignty and form of government under which they live without external military, economic or political pressure.[11]

Dawson Street was bustling on Tuesday 21 January 1919. The biggest event was not the meeting of the first Dáil. Some 400 members of the Royal Dublin Fusiliers, who had been prisoners of war in Germany, were treated to a celebratory dinner in the Mansion House followed by a concert in the Theatre Royal. The press reported good-humoured banter as they trooped out and Sinn Féin supporters and over sixty journalists filed into the Round Room, unsure of what to expect. The timing was significant, coming three days after the beginning of the Versailles peace conference and two weeks before the new parliament at Westminster was due to assemble on 4 February. The authorities watched on but did not intervene. They were fully aware of what was planned because a police raid on Sinn Féin headquarters on

9 The meeting of the first Dáil Éireann, 21 January 1919. Brugha is seated in the front row centre between Count Plunkett (*left*) and Seán T. Kelly (*right*). Piaras Béaslaí is standing directly behind Brugha.

11 January yielded drafts of the constitution and the declaration of independence. The heads of the DMP and RIC observed the Mansion House from an adjoining building and regarded the assembly as a charade.[12]

The first public meeting of the Dáil – the apogee of Sinn Féin's policy – was carefully stage-managed. Decades later, Béaslaí recalled how he put his knowledge of the theatre to work. The *Cork Examiner* reported that 'the proceedings were conducted with a decorum and sense of responsibility that even the Mother of Parliaments could not hope to excel'.[13] At 3.30 p.m. twenty-four deputies of the new assembly entered the round room (see plate 9). Count Plunkett proposed and Pádraig Ó Máille, TD for Connemara, seconded the appointment of Brugha as speaker or ceann comhairle. In this capacity, Brugha reminded those present that this was the most important work in Irish history since Ireland had been invaded.[14] Fr Michael O'Flanagan, vice-president of Sinn Féin, then read a prayer to open the session. The roll of all elected representatives was called in alphabetical order by constituency. The usher replied: 'Níl sé i láthair' for those of other parties (the Ulster Unionists and IPP naturally declined their invitations), 'níl

sé i láthair – fé glas ag gallaib' (for those in jail) and 'ar díbirt ag gallaib' (for
those exiled from Ireland). Those in prison included Countess Markievicz, the
first woman elected to Westminster, Griffith and de Valera. Collins and Harry
Boland were also absent and were in England to organize de Valera's escape
from Lincoln Jail.[15] The proceedings, conducted in Irish, were solemn and
formal. The constitution was the first document presented. It was read in Irish
alone. By contrast, the declaration of independence and the message to the free
nations were read in Irish, French and English, and the democratic
programme in Irish and English. Each document was proposed and seconded.
Fittingly, Brugha read the declaration of independence in Irish and after its
adoption told those present: 'you understand from this we are now done with
England'.[16] Darrell Figgis remarked at the time that Brugha had 'a Republic
as clear before his eyes as the sun in heaven', the public declaration of which
'was all that to him was required to complete the reality that existed indivisibly
in his mind'.[17] The declaration may have reflected Brugha's dominance but
Figgis thought it a strategic error in international terms.[18] Lord Decies, the
press censor, allowed the press to publish a full account of the proceedings but
not the declaration of independence, the democratic programme, or the
speeches of Brugha and Béaslaí.[19] A delegation to the Versailles peace
conference was appointed, comprising de Valera, Plunkett and Griffith. At
5.20 p.m. the house adjourned.

That evening a reception, hosted by Brugha as ceann comhairle, was held
in the Oak Room in honour of the visiting journalists who were treated to
clear soup, roast beef, and apple tart and custard.[20] And so began the careful
cultivation of the press at which Sinn Féin excelled during the War of
Independence. At the reception a vote of appreciation was made to Brugha by
William O'Brien, the labour and trade union leader. He knew Brugha well and
attended as Brugha's personal guest.[21] Other leaders of the labour movement
were also at the reception and in fact Cathal O'Shannon of the ITGWU
assisted Sinn Féin's J.J. Walsh with the arrangements. The labour movement's
close involvement with Sinn Féin in the struggle for independence from 1916
to 1921 is often overshadowed by James Connolly's role in 1916. Brugha took
a keen interest in labour affairs. He initially approached O'Brien on the street
in Dublin in either late 1916 or early 1917 and, having introduced himself,
stated that he 'wanted to keep in touch with the labour movement'. Thereafter,
Brugha contacted O'Brien regularly to elicit the labour perspective on a range
of issues.[22]

The following day the Dáil assembled in private session. The standing
orders were approved, a secretariat was appointed, and Seán T. O'Kelly was
elected ceann comhairle. He retained this position until August 1921, even

though for much of the period he was in Paris, first in an unsuccessful attempt to represent the Dáil at the peace conference, and then as Dáil envoy to France. During his absences J.J. O'Kelly (Sceilg) deputized as ceann comhairle. But the most important business was the election of a cabinet. In the absence of the imprisoned de Valera and Griffith, Brugha was elected acting president (príomh-aire). Four ministers were nominated by Brugha and appointed by the Dáil: Eoin MacNeill to finance, Michael Collins to home affairs, Count Plunkett to foreign affairs and Richard Mulcahy to national defence. The assembly then adjourned and did not reconvene until April when de Valera and Griffith were in attendance and the cabinet was reconstituted and enlarged.

The first public meeting of the Dáil was significant for four reasons. First, it demonstrated an acceptance of the ballot box as a source of representative authority. Second, the founders of the national parliament were constitutionalists and the model adopted by them remained the basis of Irish parliamentary government.[23] Third, the meeting was in itself revolutionary because Irish resistance would take the form of a rival democratically elected government. Despite enormous difficulties during the War of Independence, the Dáil established a functioning counter-state to its British rival and gained a wide measure of effective authority. Lastly, the Dáil would provide the authority and the personnel to negotiate the Anglo-Irish treaty in 1921. Brugha attached paramount importance to the authority of the Dáil, emphasizing in a speech in Waterford city on 25 April 1919 that

> The sole authority in this country is the authority of her own government – the authority of the elected representatives of the Irish nation. This authority alone has the right to our support. The Acts of the usurper have no authority ... our attitude towards this Power shall be such that we can show the world we don't recognize it.[24]

In his report for January 1919, Lord Decies claimed with some accuracy that there was 'an undercurrent of disappointment that neutral countries have not taken more notice of the proceedings' of the first Dáil.[25] At a Sinn Féin concert in the Mansion House at the end of January, Brugha criticized the press for not doing enough to promote Ireland's claim for representation at the peace conference. The Irish people wanted a republic, he stated, and 'they were going to let the world know it'.[26] Brugha's ominous warning that 'the time might come when Sinn Féiners would be given an order, the carrying out of which would entail sacrifices' was censored from the press report.[27]

The Dáil's mission to Paris was an inevitable failure. The appointed delegation could not travel because de Valera and Griffith were in prison and Plunkett was refused a passport. To surmount this difficulty, Dublin Corporation appointed another delegation headed by Seán T. O'Kelly who set up his office in the luxurious Grand Hotel in February 1919.[28] He was joined two months later by George Gavan Duffy. Their efforts to petition delegations and gain admission proved futile for predictable reasons. First, as Ireland sought independence from one of the victorious powers her claims were never going to be entertained. Second, the republican association with Germany in 1916 and its stance on conscription damaged Irish standing in Europe. Lastly, O'Kelly's tactics and lavish accommodation were ill-judged.[29] As a result, the delegation operated on the margins of the great debates with 'other outcasts' of the British Empire.[30] There was some success, however, in promoting the Irish case among the many foreign journalists in Paris and subsequently at the Vatican, where O'Kelly had an audience with Pope Benedict XV.[31]

On the same day as the historic events in the Mansion House, Constables Patrick O'Connell from County Cork and James McDonnell from County Mayo were killed at Soloheadbeg in County Tipperary during an ambush by Irish Volunteers. This is commonly regarded as the beginning of the War of Independence. Sinn Féin was not formally in favour of violent revolution and the Dáil did not take responsibility for the military campaign until 1921. Within Sinn Féin there was a variety of positions on the use of political violence. Moderates such as Griffith were deeply critical as Soloheadbeg had no democratic mandate and shocked public opinion.[32] Though often cast simplistically as an extremist, Brugha's stance was more complex. He dismissed Griffith's criticism by claiming if popular consultation was required 'we would never have fired a shot'.[33] However, he often objected to independent action by the IRA (as the Volunteers gradually became known from 1919) and was determined to ensure that the IRA was accountable to the Dáil.[34] The sense of horror occasioned by the Tipperary killings forced IRA GHQ and Brugha as acting president and chairman of the resident executive to issue a clarifying statement in *An tÓglach* on 31 January. This affirmed the Volunteers as the legitimate army of the republic. It declared that a state of war existed between Ireland and England for which reason

> Every Volunteer is entitled, morally and legally, when in the execution of his military duties, to use all legitimate methods of warfare against the soldiers and policemen of the English usurper and to slay them if it is necessary to do so in order to overcome their resistance. He is not only entitled but bound to resist all attempts to disarm him. In this position he has the authority of the nation behind him, now constituted in concrete form.[35]

Despite such vehemence, Brugha worried that further unauthorized military action would jeopardize the strategy of seeking international recognition. As he put it to a Waterford audience, 'the more the world has known about England the less the world likes her'.[36]

If Irish efforts in Paris made few headlines, de Valera's spectacular escape from Lincoln Jail on 3 February 1919 certainly did. De Valera went into hiding in Manchester and to the dismay of his colleagues in Dublin seemed reluctant to return home. He believed that he could best advance Irish self-determination by going to the United States to rally Irish-American opinion and to fundraise.[37] Brugha travelled to Manchester on 12 February to impress on de Valera the need for his presence in Ireland.[38] Collins was keen to propagandize de Valera's triumphant return to Dublin as head of state. However, these plans were intercepted by the police and opposed by the Sinn Féin executive, and by de Valera and Brugha.[39] Instead de Valera was quietly smuggled back to Dublin on 20 February and the American plans were set aside until June. On arrival, de Valera contacted Brugha and shared a bed with Collins in Brugha's house that night.[40] De Valera remained in hiding in various locations until the release of the 'German Plot' prisoners in early March on humanitarian grounds due to the influenza pandemic.[41] The release was due in part to the death Pierce McCan. As a 'German Plot' prisoner in Gloucester Jail, he had been elected Sinn Féin TD for East Tipperary before contracting influenza. At his funeral in Dualla near Thurles on 9 March, Brugha delivered a provocative graveside oration. He suggested that 'had an Englishman been treated thus in Germany, a war would have resulted between the two nations'.[42] What did the men of Tipperary and Ireland intend to do to avenge McCan's illegal detention and death he asked, before suggesting they

> put an end to the system by which that young man was kidnapped. They had amongst them creatures going around their country spying upon their people and sending their stories to Dublin Castle. They should remember that it was by their goodwill that such creatures existed amongst them. If the people withdrew that their existence would be impossible.[43]

Brugha's direct attack on the police anticipated by a few weeks the Dáil-sanctioned boycott of members of the RIC and DMP. This is not to suggest that Brugha encouraged or approved the killing of police without justification. Rather, it signalled the Dáil's tactic of undermining the British system of law and order in Ireland.

The Dáil did not convene between 23 January and 31 March as most TDs were in prison or on the run. At its second sitting on 1 April, Brugha resigned as president in favour of de Valera who reconstituted the cabinet the following day. Brugha became minister for defence in place of Richard Mulcahy. He declined a ministerial salary of £300 on the basis that his business interests were sufficient to support his family and that the money should instead support a newly created position of assistant minister for defence which was occupied by Mulcahy, who was also IRA chief of staff.[44] It seems that Brugha and Mulcahy had agreed on this. In theory at least, Mulcahy kept Brugha appraised of policy developments at IRA GHQ as the minister did not attend those meetings. This may have been subsequently regretted by Brugha as it allowed Collins's ascendency and the influence of the IRB to flourish.[45] Brugha made it clear that his decision to refuse a ministerial salary was not a reflection on his colleagues, many of whom had no other income. But it meant that Brugha would in effect be a part-time minister, something he acknowledged when pledging to be as committed to his responsibilities as any other minister.[46] As we shall see later, this also facilitated Collins's growing control over the army. Brugha's ministerial colleagues included Countess Markievicz as minister for labour, W.T. Cosgrave as minister for local government, Griffith as minister for home affairs, Collins as minister for finance, Plunkett as minister for foreign affairs, MacNeill as minister for industry, and Robert Barton as director for agriculture, which did not carry cabinet rank. In straitened circumstances, the Dáil met just thirteen times between its first assembly in January 1919 and its suppression the following September; there were a further eight meetings before the truce in July 1921. Arthur Mitchell has described the Dáil government as 'government by bicycle', given how ministers and officials circulated freely around Dublin presenting themselves as 'ordinary citizens going about their business'.[47] Máire Comerford, a courier, knew the ministers by their bicycles: Collins had a high framed black Lucania and Brugha an Irish-made green Pierce.[48]

    Two significant decisions were approved by the Dáil in early April that heralded the beginning of a functioning counter-state. The first was the launch of the Dáil loan campaign, spearheaded by Collins, to finance the new government through the sale of bonds. Brugha impressed on a Waterford audience the need to 'buy up these bonds' and expected the entire 'Irish race' at home and abroad to 'invest their money' in the republic's future.[49] The campaign raised an impressive £371,000 in Ireland.[50] The second decision was the social ostracization of the police. In introducing a motion on this policy, which was passed unanimously, de Valera accused the police of brutal treason against the Irish people.[51] De Valera was not present to witness the results of either decision. On 1 June 1919 he departed for the United States to promote the cause of the republic and did not return until December 1920. At a private session of the Dáil on 17 June, Griffith became president substitute on a motion proposed by Brugha.[52]

From April 1919 there was a flurry of Dáil 'decrees' on issues ranging from land purchase to afforestation. Given the Gaelic League background of many TDs, there was strong support for the Irish language. In August Brugha advocated the establishment of a special committee to foster the use of Irish where it was still spoken. Two months later at the October meeting of the Dáil, Terence MacSwiney proposed that a minister for Irish be appointed, a suggestion originally mooted by the Gaelic League. Brugha proposed and MacSwiney seconded the appointment of J.J. O'Kelly.[53] He was an appropriate choice, having succeeded Eoin MacNeill as president of the Gaelic League in 1919. He had also read the Irish version of the address to the free nations of the world at the first sitting of the Dáil.[54] Like Brugha, O'Kelly declined a ministerial salary and saw his work for the language and the republic as 'a labour of love'.[55] In 1920 Brugha wrote a foreword for *Irish without a teacher*, a series of booklets for those unable to attend Irish classes, in which he maintained that if Irish was allowed to die there would be no Irish nation.[56]

A cornerstone of the Dáil's efforts to undermine the British administration was the creation of a rival legal structure in the shape of the Dáil or republican courts. By August 1920 they operated throughout Ireland, with the exception of Antrim, and further undermined the morale of the boycotted police and Crown court system. One telling measure of the widespread acceptance of the Dáil courts was that they were welcomed by the resident gentry, despite their aversion to republicanism, as a remedy for the collapse of the British civil administration.[57] The Dáil courts became a means of demonstrating the Irish capacity for self-government. Brugha's initially favourable disposition toward the Dáil courts was short-lived. According to Kevin O'Shiel, one of the architects of the system, Brugha soon had no use for courts.[58] His stance was less a criticism of the court system itself than a concern that land disputes, which occupied much of the courts' time, would fragment Sinn Féin's base and divert attention away from the pursuit of the republic. He told O'Shiel that both the country and the republican movement should have only one objective: 'to get the English out of Ireland. Nothing should deflect or distract us from that purpose'.[59] Brugha also opposed the creation of a separate republican police force, fearing that it would deplete the ranks of the IRA and weaken the military campaign. O'Shiel recalled approaching the minister for defence for assistance in dealing with 'delinquents' who defied court orders in the west of Ireland. Brugha listened 'in complete silence, his utterly immobile and expressionless countenance confronting me with steely impenetrability', before dismissing the value of courts or police.[60] In the event, after a week and without informing O'Shiel, Brugha sent an IRA unit to enforce the will of the court by arresting the offenders and imprisoning them on a Lough Corrib island.[61] This episode suggests that the contemporaneous criticism of Brugha as inflexible and un-cooperative was not always justified.

The IRA campaign was highly de-centralized and varied markedly in intensity both within and between counties. GHQ attempted to maintain control by requiring brigade commandants to seek sanction for any planned actions and to submit monthly reports. In his classic analysis of the War of Independence, Charles Townshend identified three broad phases of the guerrilla offensive.[62] The first phase was a long period of low-level operations against the RIC from 1917 until the winter of 1919–20. It was characterized by raids for arms, even though forbidden by GHQ, of which Soloheadbeg represented an intensification. During this period GHQ was reactive rather than proactive as local units took the initiative, many of which did not readily accept central control. Townshend suggests that as late as September 1919, local Volunteer units had little idea what, if any, overall plan of action was favoured by GHQ. Accordingly, the bolder and more adventurous were 'testing the limits, experimenting with possibilities'.[63]

The second phase saw a contraction of the police presence due to a combination of boycott and increasing levels of violence. The social ostracization deployed against the police, their immediate families, and those who associated with them was so systematic in some areas that the police had to commandeer food supplies. Steadily, the scale of violence increased: eighteen policemen were killed in 1919 but twenty-two were killed in the first four months of 1920 alone and almost 200 by the end of that year. The combination of boycott, violent attacks and mounting casualties demoralized the RIC. By the end of 1919, smaller outlying police huts, staffed by three or four policemen, had become untenable and were evacuated. By the summer of 1920, one third of the police barracks in the country had been closed, ceding large swathes of territory to the IRA. The beleaguered RIC was then concentrated in larger more fortified barracks and issued with better weaponry. Policemen resigned or retired in droves. The number leaving the force was twice as high in 1919–21 as it had been between 1910 and 1919. Potential recruits were intimidated and so vacancies went unfilled. The British government was slow to grasp the scale of the dislocation of law and order in Ireland, having been preoccupied by the Versailles peace conference and distracted by labour unrest at home. The IRA was deemed a 'murder gang', and the Irish problem was viewed as a policing job. When sufficient police recruits could not be found in Ireland, the British government tapped the large pool of unemployed British veterans of the First World War, who had the hardened military experience to implement counter-insurgency measures. The first recruits arrived in Ireland in February 1920. Their mixed kit of khaki trousers and dark green tunics gave rise to the sobriquet, the Black and Tans. In July 1920 a second force – the RIC Auxiliary Division – was recruited from ex-army officers. They were deployed in companies of 100 to the most disturbed areas of the country and with their own transport were highly mobile.

The third phase from August 1920 witnessed an intensification of British control under the Restoration of Order in Ireland Act, a 'halfway house towards martial law', which granted the Crown forces a high degree of immunity from the civil law.[64] This forced unprecedented numbers of IRA men to go on the run as full-time revolutionaries in groups known as 'flying columns' or active service units. The War of Independence then entered a more brutal phase. An unofficial system of reprisals by the Crown forces was tolerated in response to IRA attacks. Homes and businesses were burned or looted, beatings and mock executions became commonplace as did extra-judicial killings. Both civilian and combatant deaths increased significantly during 1920. So did arrests and internment, which depleted the ranks of the IRA. By the summer of 1921 the military balance had tilted towards the British side.

Several historians have drawn attention to the ambiguous relationship between the Dáil and the IRA.[65] There was a tendency, as Laffan has observed, for the Volunteers 'to regard the Dáil with a vague, benevolent deference, provided that it made no serious attempts to limit their freedom of action'.[66] That several figures held dual roles made this situation more complex: Collins was director of intelligence and minister for finance, Mulcahy was IRA chief of staff and assistant minister for defence, and Brugha was chairman of the largely defunct resident executive and minister for defence. This raised intractable questions around accountability and where ultimate authority resided. For instance, although Mulcahy acknowledged the authority of the cabinet over the army, he criticized Brugha's desire for parliamentary control over the IRA.[67] The traditional Fenian position that politicians could not be trusted was also alive and well. Brugha and de Valera adhered to the concept of the supremacy of the Dáil. Collins saw the IRB as the guarantor of republican principles, whereas Brugha and de Valera saw a shadowy 'government within a government'.[68]

Before his departure to the United States, de Valera put down a marker regarding the civil-military relationship: 'There is in Ireland at this moment only one lawful authority, and that authority is the elected Government of the Irish Republic'. He added that 'The Minister of Defence is, of course, in close association with the Volunteer military forces which are the foundation of the National Army'.[69] Nevertheless, many Volunteers believed that their only allegiance was to their own executive. Brugha and de Valera wanted to curtail the fervour of the more hot-headed IRA units. For this reason, on 20 August 1919 a Dáil motion proposed by Brugha as minister for defence required Dáil deputies, IRA men, and officers and clerks of the Dáil to swear allegiance to the Irish Republic and the Dáil 'against all enemies, foreign and domestic'.[70] Brugha had spent the previous three months trying to reach agreement with the army executive on the matter. Dick Walsh recalled a series of 'heated' meetings that gave rise to 'an acute difference of opinion' on the proposed oath.[71] It was opposed, among others, by Diarmuid O'Hegarty, secretary to the Dáil and a senior IRB figure, and Mulcahy. The latter was irked that the issue was distracting GHQ from its primary purpose of keeping the fight at a controlled high intensity.[72] In the end Brugha's tenacity and the respect in which he was held won out.[73] Brugha's motion occasioned some debate in the Dáil with Tom Kelly deeming the oath 'a species of coercion' against the Volunteers. In defending the motion, which was passed by thirty votes to five, Brugha maintained that if the IRA was considered a standing army, then they should be subject to the government. The minister for defence opted against holding a Volunteer convention on the matter given the security risks this entailed.[74]

A desire to consolidate civilian control was not Brugha's only motivation. The oath was clearly a means of limiting the influence of the IRB within the army and by implication Collins. The oath was not in itself the cause of the breakdown in relations between Brugha and Collins but it was, as Townshend points out, partly 'a symptom of the growing personal antagonism' between them, as well as of the awkward relationship between the Dáil and the IRB.[75] Mulcahy believed that Brugha's primary motivation in proposing the oath was 'to outflank the IRB' and to curb its influence.[76] In September 1919 the IRB acknowledged the Dáil as the legitimate government of the country.[77] The oath of allegiance to the Irish republic and its government altered little. It did not prevent the IRA evolving its strategy and tactics independently of the Dáil government and its own GHQ. Brugha's ability to direct defence policy was curtailed by the GHQ executive. As Michael Staines put it, the minister had no more power than any ordinary member of the executive.[78] Nor did the oath ensure that the minister for defence was in control of his military subordinates. It did not disrupt the bonds of loyalty within the IRB. A further consideration for Brugha was a desire to prevent a wholescale militant onslaught against the police lest it alienate American public opinion and undermine de Valera's mission. When Michael Lynch raised the issue of shooting 'enemy forces',

Brugha asked him to instruct his men to 'keep their powder dry', pending a response from de Valera, and 'if it's fighting they want, I will give them their bellyful but, in the meantime, no shooting'.[79] Mulcahy also followed this moderate course until the suppression of the Volunteers, Sinn Féin, Cumann na mBan, the Gaelic League and the Dáil itself on 10 September 1919. Thereafter, he no longer restricted Volunteer activities. The restrained attitude of the minister for defence also changed. Lynch recalled that within weeks of their earlier conversation Brugha 'gave the word "go" … [and] we went'.[80] Nevertheless, Brugha remained cautious. For instance, an unsuccessful attempt by the Squad (Collins's elite group of assassins established in September 1919) to assassinate Lord French in December 1919 came after months of prevarication due to Brugha's concerns that 'the people would not stand for it' and that it would create a negative impact abroad.[81] No such concerns were evident a year earlier when Brugha planned to assassinate the British cabinet.

As David Fitzpatrick has observed, personal and factional divisions were 'an unavoidable by-product of the revolutionary struggle'.[82] By September 1919 several individual relations had deteriorated within the cabinet and within GHQ. However, as Christopher ('Todd') Andrews remarked, these strained relations were contained during the War of Independence and did not impede the regular business of the Dáil or the army. The ordinary IRA man was unaware that 'Griffith loathed Childers or that Brugha loathed Collins. Nor that Collins despised [Austin] Stack. Nor that De Valera regarded Cosgrave as a "ninny"'.[83] As the next chapter will discuss, these personality clashes were revealed in all their viciousness when the Anglo-Irish treaty was debated. The animosity between Brugha and Collins, so evident during those debates, has attracted more attention than other instances of personality clashes because it was so bitter. But it was not always thus. Joe Good, who knew Collins well in London and was a member of Brugha's assassination team in 1918, described them as the 'closest of friends' and Robert Barton recalled 'a close harmony'.[84] Collins was a regular visitor to the Brugha home until the end of 1918 and, as indicated in chapter 4, stayed there on occasion.

Contemporaries such as Barton and Mulcahy suggest that the tensions surfaced towards the end of 1920 and increased thereafter. The causes were varied but three factors stand out: Brugha's hostility towards the IRB, their ill-matched personalities and Collins's undermining of Brugha's ministerial authority. Brugha's opposition to the IRB did not affect his relations with Collins until after the latter became president of the supreme council in 1919. Collins's stature increased while de Valera was in the United States. The IRB became a means of aggrandizing his influence within the Dáil and within the IRA. His increasing control over the IRA led to an encroachment on Brugha's responsibilities as minister for defence. According to Robert Barton, by expanding his duties as director of intelligence to the limit, Collins undermined Brugha's authority.[85] Peter Hart claims that Collins was driven into many conflicts by 'his desire to acquire or exercise power'.[86] Membership of the IRB and control over the army were at the base of a broader division within the cabinet between Brugha, de Valera and Stack on one side, and Collins and Mulcahy on the other. As John Regan has put it, 'the long-festering disagreement which spread between these two factions was multifaceted and bitter, but the common denominator was control of the army'.[87] Each camp also attracted their respective supporters. Ernest Blythe, for example, 'sympathised entirely with Collins in the sarcastic exchanges which took place between himself and Brugha' and was especially disparaging of Brugha, whom he described as 'of limited intelligence'.[88] By 1921 the power struggle had an unsettling effect on some IRA officers. Frank Henderson recalled travelling to Wexford to visit IRB circles and of being warned beforehand to avoid Brugha who was on the same train. He was 'deeply troubled' by this 'serious estrangement between the chiefs, whom I regarded up to that moment as peerless in their unity and their leadership'.[89]

The respective personalities of Brugha and Collins were almost antithetical. The brash and abrasive Collins had a fondness for whiskey, cigarettes and swearing, was anti-clerical and displayed an interest in atheism.[90] Such traits were far removed from Brugha's sense of propriety and religious devotion. In retrospect, Mulcahy reflected on the destructive consequences of Collins's behaviour. He suggested that 'weaknesses' in Collins's character and personality created antagonism and 'spoiled his approach to persons' while he lacked the self-awareness to notice.[91] Brugha had ample character flaws of his own, in particular a rigid single-mindedness and at times an explosive temper. Mulcahy put it delicately when describing Brugha as 'not naturally a committee man or one for council. He liked the feeling of being a ball on the run with decision and direction'.[92] Collins did, however, respect the sincerity with which Brugha doggedly defended his principles. Despite their sharp differences, Mulcahy claimed that Collins retained a certain affection and admiration for Brugha 'as one would have for a difficult but natural child'.[93]

Collins's propensity to interfere in various ministries has been noted by many historians. For Anne Dolan and William Murphy 'he meddled too much' and 'overstepped too many marks'.[94] This was particularly true in relation to the minister for defence. Some IRA officers grumbled about Brugha's distance and inaccessibility. Similar criticisms were made about IRA GHQ, that no member of its staff 'ever came down the country to see things for himself' as one put it, or 'knew the tides of our military effort' in Ernie O'Malley's phrase.[95] O'Malley criticized Brugha for not knowing his army officers well and suggested that this was because he could not devote all his energies to his ministerial portfolio.[96] While there is no evidence to suggest that Brugha's responsibilities in Lalor Ltd led to a neglect of his ministerial duties, his capacity to develop personal relationships within the army was certainly impeded. This afforded Collins the space to cultivate IRA officers, many of whom were IRB members, who were drawn to his big personality and sense of camaraderie. They often chose to report to him rather than to Brugha and increasingly Collins was seen as the man in control, 'the type of man the IRA wanted, and so the Minister of Defence was forgotten'.[97] This was naturally resented by Brugha.[98] Pakenham and O'Neill suggest that Brugha 'could be forgiven for wanting complete control of his own department, unimpeded by a secret society'.[99] The localized nature of the IRA campaign and the independence of local units who carried on 'as though there was neither an executive nor a minister' were further constraints on Brugha's authority.[100]

Overlapping spheres of authority did much to poison relations between Brugha and Collins. As cabinet ministers they were equals. On the army side, Brugha was Collins's superior but as president of the supreme council of the IRB Collins would have regarded himself as the senior figure. Brugha's authority was necessarily limited by the political standing of several members of the headquarters staff. His efforts as minister for defence to oversee Collins's actions as unofficial director of purchases and director of intelligence – as 'a subordinate in a subordinate office to my office' – heightened tensions between them.[101] In October 1920 Brugha engaged in a powerplay by having Liam Mellows appointed director of purchases at GHQ.[102] Collins saw this as a move against his IRB network, which controlled gun-running activities at home and abroad and whose first loyalty was to him. As early as 1917, Brugha became aware that his efforts to source arms in Liverpool were stymied because he was not a member of the IRB.[103] Collins simply dismissed Brugha who suffered 'the daily humiliation of holding an emasculated portfolio as a sinecure while real power remained outside his influence in GHQ and by inference with the IRB and Collins'.[104] As the War of Independence entered its third and more brutal phase, Brugha was left in the invidious position of having to justify particular killings committed by the IRA that as minister he had objected to. A prime example was the unauthorized abduction and killing of Mary Lindsay, a unionist, and her butler by Cork No. 1 Brigade in March 1921. Collins was aware of this but did not bring the matter to the attention of GHQ or Brugha.[105] In July 1921 Brugha was delegated to issue a response to Ethel Benson, Mrs Lindsay's sister, who, unaware of her death, sought her release from captivity:

> Madam, in accordance with instructions from the President, I have made enquiries from our local commanders into the case of Mrs Lindsay. The information sent us is that she was executed as a spy some months ago. The charge against her was that she was directly responsible for conveying to the enemy information which led to the execution of five of our men by the British authorities, to the death of a sixth, from wounds received in action, and to a sentence of twenty-five years penal servitude passed upon a seventh … We regret the circumstances and the stern necessity to protect our forces which necessitated this drastic action by our local commanders.[106]

The Lindsay affair clearly demonstrated that there was a lack of control in the army, that GHQ directives had been broken, and that a code of honour had been transgressed by killing a woman.[107] It reflected badly on the secretive modus operandi of Collins and on Mulcahy as chief of staff.

Brugha's relationship with Mulcahy also merits comment. Although they had known one another through the Keating branch of the Gaelic League, a close association only began during the post-Rising reorganization of the Volunteers. Temperamentally, Mulcahy, noted for his self-control, forethought and calm nature, was almost the opposite of Brugha.[108] They maintained close contact on policy and operational matters with Mulcahy reporting to Brugha at Lalor's or in Rathmines. However, he recalled that speaking with Brugha was 'never a great pleasure' due to the intense nature of Brugha's character and his 'staccato way of thinking'. To Mulcahy this suggested a mind that was limited in its expression, prone to act on impulse, devoid of any vision and lacking organization. Despite this criticism, Mulcahy held that the GHQ staff worked in unison with the minister for defence, whose agreement 'flowed naturally and readily with us'.[109] The relationship between Mulcahy and Brugha was generally harmonious until a controversy about gun-running in Scotland in March 1921 (discussed below) shattered this accord. Risteárd Mulcahy found it difficult to determine whether his father spoke about Brugha with resentment or compassion, but he did speak of Brugha 'with sympathy and respect'.[110]

Remarkably, throughout the War of Independence the department of defence essentially operated from Lalor Ltd. Dáil and GHQ correspondence was collected and delivered from 14 Ormond Quay, some of which was addressed to 'Mr Murphy'.[111] A steady stream of callers sought 'Mr Vincent' (Brugha's alias). They were generally met and screened by Vincent Lalor. From

Brugha's office on the second floor a mirror allowed him to see anyone coming up the stairs. Mitchell suggests that Dublin Castle failed to act due to ineffective police intelligence but Liam Kavanagh, who worked in Lalor's, recalled that the premises was raided on several occasions. William ('Bill') Reid, then a 10-year-old boy and later a floor manager in Lalor's, was asked by Brugha to burn documents in the furnace for security reasons.[112] As a minister constantly in danger of arrest, Brugha rarely presented written reports lest critical information fall into the hands of the Crown forces. J.J. O'Kelly, who was present at cabinet meetings, claimed that no reports were as enthusiastically received as those presented by Brugha, whom Béaslaí described as 'a model of brevity'.[113] Brugha addressed the Dáil on military matters only seven times, and in just two instances was any information included in the record.[114] Máire Comerford, who worked as a courier, described Brugha as 'very kind, humble and gentle, but … a disaster as an administrator'.[115] This may refer to his practice of not using a typewriter, which led Collins to suggest a lack of efficiency in administrative matters.[116] This depiction of Brugha is open to question as his successful business career suggests he had good organizational and managerial skills. Furthermore, Collins was acerbically critical of the performance of several of his ministerial colleagues, not just Brugha.

Incontrovertibly, Brugha's role as minister was hampered by the fact that he was always in danger of arrest and frequently on the run.[117] His capacity to evade arrest might simply have been because the British 'took no interest in him' as Townshend asserts.[118] However, there is evidence to contradict this. Robert Brennan, who produced the *Irish Bulletin* during the War of Independence and was appointed under-secretary for foreign affairs by de Valera, claimed that by the end of 1920 Dublin Castle had offered an award of £5,000 for information leading to Brugha's arrest.[119] When Andy Cope, assistant under-secretary at Dublin Castle, was exploring options for a negotiated peace, with Lloyd George's covert approval, he had a specific interest in meeting Brugha, 'the man with the quare name'.[120] In the event, this did not transpire and it is questionable whether Brugha would have engaged with Cope.[121] Brugha was especially security conscious. He generally carried a gun, avoided being photographed, and rarely slept at home. He regularly stayed in Lalor's, where a bed, furniture and a gas stove were installed on the first floor. For emergencies, the roof could be accessed by a narrow ladder and Brugha often worked there with a gun at his feet. Liam Kavanagh recalled that Brugha was 'very cool, calm and courageous'.[122] According to Ó Dochartaigh, to conceal his identity when attending Mass or meetings outside the office Brugha grew a long red moustache to hide his distinctive mouth.[123] Lalor's became the source of minor controversy in 1919 when the *Voice of Labour* suggested that an employee had been dismissed for seeking a wage increase. Brugha complained that this had no foundation and after an investigation by the newspaper the statement was retracted in October 1919.[124]

Safe houses were widely used by republicans at this time. Batt O'Connor's home in Donnybrook was often frequented by Brugha, Collins and Austin Stack.[125] Both Robert Brennan and Frank Gallagher claim to have first introduced Brugha to John Burke, a boilerman at Temple Street Children's Hospital, and Brugha regularly stayed in the Burke home at the rear of the hospital between October 1920 and May 1922.[126] Bridie O'Reilly, a typist in IRA GHQ, often brought communications to the minister for defence at Lalor's and Burke's.[127] On 23 October 1920 Brugha had a narrow escape when twelve houses in Fitzwilliam Terrace, Rathmines, were raided in an effort to apprehend him. The searches lasted several hours and involved five lorry loads of troops supported by armoured cars. Caitlín was seized by armed soldiers and detained in a Crossley tender in her nightdress for over an hour. Her pleas to tend to her frightened children were ignored. Bloodhounds were brought into the house to sniff Brugha's clothes. The officer in charge maintained the dogs had detected that Brugha had recently been in the house and had left through a window. Caitlín insisted that she had no information regarding his whereabouts.[128] Having been tipped off about the presence of detectives by Frank Gallagher, Brugha did indeed escape through the window and sought refuge with the Burkes.[129] Caitlín's rough treatment by the military was not unusual. As Hanna Sheehy-Skeffington remarked:

> When a man is on the run, is not his wife … frequently threatened, separated for hours from her terrified children, and sometimes compelled to stand in the street under the rain barefooted in her nightdress when her house is sacked and even burned.[130]

Brugha also hid regularly in the home of Áine O'Rahilly and her sister Nell Humphreys at 54 Northumberland Road where a secret room had been installed, 'principally to harbour' Brugha, who often offered it to younger Volunteers if they could not find sanctuary elsewhere.[131] There was also a 'safe house' in Sutton where it was possible for Brugha's family to join him. J.J. O'Kelly recalled that Brugha sometimes dressed up as a 'parson' and told his wife that she could tell strangers that she was a 'minister's wife'.[132] The British intelligence file on Brugha recorded that he dressed in clerical garb.[133]

To strike back at an increasingly effective British intelligence effort in the latter part of 1920, Collins, who displayed a 'rudely functional approach to killing', planned the assassination of twenty intelligence agents in what became known as Bloody Sunday on 21 November 1920.[134] The action was sanctioned by the cabinet, following a scrupulous examination of the evidence against each man by Brugha. This trimmed the number on the initial target list which some accounts suggest was more than fifty.[135] It was a notable instance where Brugha had asserted some authority over Collins. Determining evidence of guilt was a policy on which the minister for defence insisted, often to the irritation of impatient colleagues.[136] It subsequently became clear that some of the fourteen suspects killed were not involved in intelligence work, something admitted by Collins.[137] The night before Bloody Sunday, Collins, Brugha, Mulcahy, McKee, Peadar Clancy and Seán Russell met the assassination teams on Lower Gardiner Street to finalize arrangements.

Given the dangers of crossing the city, Brugha and Mulcahy stayed with John Burke in Temple Street. Their departure the following day was prevented by the increase in military activity following the IRA killings and the shooting in nearby Croke Park during a botched search operation by Crown forces. Mulcahy provided an evocative portrayal of Brugha's response to the danger they were in:

> Cathal went upstairs ... opened up the window, pulled over a chair alongside it, pulled out two revolvers and put them on the bed beside him, and took off his boots, and sat down on a chair alongside the window to meet like a man, anything that came his way. Now my tactics would have been entirely different. I would have my bicycle out and been out the gate at the back, and I would have been off up Drumcondra; but noblesse obliged, I had to sit alongside my minister on the side of the bed there, praying at whatever was going to pass.[138]

Alfred Burgess claimed that on returning home Burke found Brugha sitting in the garden with two revolvers. When he urged him indoors as the Crown forces were flooding into the neighbourhood, Brugha remained as he was with the reply: 'If those people come in, you will find my dead body ... and don't be surprised to find six or seven of the bodies of our visitors'.[139] Such defiance was a testament to Brugha's zeal and reckless courage.

Bloody Sunday was not a knockout blow and the British intelligence system quickly recovered. The assassinations and the Kilmichael ambush a week later (the most celebrated IRA ambush of the War of Independence where seventeen Crown forces and three IRA men were killed or later died) led to a more militarized response to the Irish situation, hitherto viewed as a policing issue. Martial law was introduced in Munster, Kilkenny and Wexford; the use of detention without trial (in one week alone, there were 500 arrests), courts martial for capital offences and official reprisals all increased. On 25 November Griffith and MacNeill were jailed. According to J.J. O'Kelly, Brugha was Griffith's first preference to replace him as acting president of Dáil Éireann with Stack and Collins as his second and third choices. Both Brugha and Stack refused to act in place of Griffith. Brugha claimed that the importance of his army work prevented him from accepting the temporary post. The nomination then devolved on Collins, who declared: 'As no one else will, I suppose I must'.[140] This may have come as a surprise to de Valera who had expected Brugha to replace Griffith.

De Valera returned to Ireland on 23 December, the day the Government of Ireland Act (1920) that partitioned Ireland came into force. The British cabinet did not impede his return to the dismay of Sir Nevil Macready, general officer commanding in Ireland.[141] At this time, the British government pursued a dual policy of war and exploring the possibility of peace, of which the failed effort of Archbishop Patrick Clune of Perth in December 1920 was one of several examples.[142] Brugha's response to earlier feelers for peace was that they should be ignored and that any serious proposals should be made directly to the Irish government.[143] Collins and Brugha were among de Valera's first visitors at the home of Dr Robert Farnan. Indicating his lack of appreciation of the volatile situation that then existed, de Valera rebuked Brugha for arriving with a gun in his pocket. The minister for defence insisted that he would use it if necessary.[144] Drained by the feud with Collins, Brugha welcomed de Valera's return with relief and suggested had he not returned, 'there would be a split from top to bottom'.[145] De Valera dismissed the differences between Brugha and Collins as trivial. Following de Valera's return, the frequency of cabinet meetings increased and there was growing pressure on GHQ to give more direction to IRA units. There was also a concerted effort by de Valera to link the military campaign to the mandate of the Dáil which, he stated in March 1921, should take 'full responsibility' for the actions of the IRA.[146] This was followed by the publication of *The Irish Republican Army*, a pamphlet, in which he formally declared that the government was responsible for the actions of the army. This change of stance also appears to have prompted Brugha to become more involved in military strategy, particularly in terms of operations in Britain and gun-running, an intrusion regarded as 'inappropriate' by Mulcahy as chief of staff. It soured relations between them.[147]

Brugha proposed to cabinet that industrial installations in Liverpool should be bombed in reprisal for atrocities by the Crown forces in Ireland. Although curtailed by the capture of Mulcahy's papers, under the direction of Rory O'Connor, director of engineering at GHQ, nineteen warehouses in

Liverpool and Bootle were set ablaze on 28 November 1920 causing £250,000 damage. This action proved counterproductive as IRA activists in Liverpool and elsewhere were arrested, leading one Liverpool Volunteer to recall: 'There was no one left to direct operations.'[148] There is no evidence to support the assertion by Frank Owen, a journalist and biographer of Lloyd George, and later repeated by Tim Pat Coogan, that Brugha contemplated machine-gunning civilian crowds in British cinemas and theatres.[149] One withering review of Owen's work suggested he had 'been more than negligent in the almost total lack of documentation', which was both poor history and poor journalism.[150] The November attacks were part of a larger and debatable strategy to influence British left-wing organizations. In mid-1920 Brugha and Collins asked Seán McLoughlin, a revolutionary socialist and republican, to undertake agitational work with the British left to generate favourable support for the Irish cause and to identify individuals who could facilitate gun-running or sabotage. A few days after 'Bloody Sunday', McLoughlin departed on this mission. He later claimed to have visited every big town in England and Scotland and to have been 'in touch with every revolutionary element in Britain'.[151] He remained in Britain until the truce and kept in regular contact with Brugha as he was 'anxious to join any activities [Brugha] would conduct in London'.[152] This was a reference to mooted plans for various assassination campaigns which are discussed below.

We have already seen how Brugha's attempts to monitor gun-running created tensions in 1920. This simmering issue reared its head explosively in March 1921 when Brugha discovered that £2,700 assigned for the purchase of arms in Scotland was unaccounted for and he informed de Valera that a 'very serious situation' had arisen.[153] A cloud of suspicion hung over Collins. An audit revealed sloppy procedures and a lack of financial accountability. In a personal letter to de Valera, Collins complained that Brugha's behaviour was 'not gentlemanly' and that he was 'raking up petty technicalities'.[154] An embarrassed Collins was being held to the standards he himself imposed as minister for finance.[155] He later wrote: 'The whole thing is a heart scald to me and I am awfully anxious to get it cleared up'.[156] While he assumed the right to stick his fingers into other departmental pies, Collins fended off any scrutiny of financial affairs or the procurement of arms. When asked by Robert Briscoe about altering an arms requisition list submitted by Brugha, Collins remarked: 'I'm giving the money and I run this stuff [gun-running]'.[157] To defuse the row, Mulcahy approached Brugha, who made it clear that his main concern related to financial control and accountability. In the meantime, arms purchases were suspended to the alarm of the IRA. In this context Béaslaí's criticism of Brugha's 'eminently unreasonable' timing seems entirely valid.[158]

De Valera tried but failed to bring the parties together.[159] Brugha displayed a marked lack of judgement in subsequently relating his version of events to GHQ staff. Understandably, Mulcahy was incensed and complained to de Valera that Brugha was trying to stir up dissent. De Valera suggested Brugha was jealous and to let matters blow over.[160] Brugha was too obsessive a patriot for personal vanity but too rigid and inflexible a patriot to grasp the full implications of his dogged stance. The episode was one of the lowest points before the Anglo-Irish truce in the fractious relationship between Brugha and Collins; it also harmed relations with Mulcahy.

Some accounts of this incident accuse Brugha of 'Javert-like' tendencies in his pursuit of Collins.[161] Their difficult relationship aside, Brugha's well-known fixation with financial accountability was not exclusively reserved for the minister for finance. Later in 1921, Brugha's gimlet financial eye focused on gun-running in the United States. Harry Boland had been dispatched there in February 1919, ostensibly as Dáil envoy but also to coordinate an ambitious covert programme for procuring arms through the IRB and its American affiliates. Brugha did not oppose this scheme and even placed an order for some sub-machine guns, revolvers, ammunition and silencers in March 1921.[162] The following month, relations with Boland became difficult when Brugha relentlessly queried accounting discrepancies for 650 Thompson sub-machine guns which cost \$133,034.40.[163] The situation soured further when the authorities captured 495 Thompson guns in Hoboken, New Jersey in June. This greatly damaged Boland's reputation. He provided the minister for defence with documentation on monies spent and goods purchased and in an agitated letter on 19 July asked:

> Am I to understand … that you did not authorise me to purchase 650 Thompson sub-machine guns? Where do you think I could get cash to pay on the nail for these? … You are making it very hard for me if you deny me an ok on the purchase … I have had no help from your Department … although I have asked time and again for help to land the tremendous amounts of goods we have here … I have already written you saying that I cannot account for discrepancies in the amounts received by you and amounts invoiced; you must settle that up at home … I close with deep regret of the gun-running.[164]

Two days later, Boland was more contrite. He apologized for any embarrassment to Brugha and undertook to repay 'money borrowed from the Trustee Reserve' through voluntary subscriptions. The minister's response was light-hearted:

I take it that your liver was out of order, or that you had eaten something that disagreed with you when you wrote to me of 19th consequently, I shall not reply to it in kind. I don't rail at people and if I ever do, you will not be the man I'll start upon.[165]

Brugha made it clear to Boland that his main concern was to ensure that any money spent out of the defence fund was properly authorized. The episode was a reminder of the importance Brugha attached to financial accountability, even during the surreal world of arms smuggling by an underground government in a foreign country. Boland's purchasing efforts were beset with difficulties, financial and otherwise. Eventually, Brugha cancelled the importation of a major consignment of arms as the transportation costs were unsatisfactory.[166] Reports by Seán Nunan, who assisted Boland in the United States, were later furnished directly to Brugha, who, in addition to financial statements, also demanded to know what arms had been sent to Ireland and to whom.[167] Brugha's insistence on full disclosure was driven partly by suspicion of Collins and the IRB, and partly by his obsessive desire to economize. Liam Mellows complained that Brugha 'would sit all night with his mouth like a rat trap over half a crown'.[168]

A persistent trope in historical writing on the War of Independence is the portrayal of Brugha as a bloodthirsty advocate of political violence and of assassination plots in Britain.[169] His position was more nuanced. As discussed above, Brugha insisted on a sufficiency of evidence before targeted killings or the execution of alleged spies. For Brugha deaths had to have an obvious political or military purpose. He was particularly concerned about safeguarding civilians from the use of mines and grenades in urban ambushes. After an IRA ambush on Camden Street, which resulted in civilian casualties, the commandant was upbraided by Brugha for conducting an attack on a busy Saturday. The minister for defence also forbade shooting from inside houses as it would implicate the inhabitants.[170] Many assassination plots in Britain were planned but they did not materialize. The list of potential targets was long and included, among others, the British cabinet, the Prince of Wales, Lord Fitzalan (the last viceroy of Ireland), Sir Basil Thomson (head of the Special Branch at Scotland Yard) and several Unionist MPs, including Field-Marshal Sir Henry Wilson, former chief of the Imperial General Staff. Of these only Wilson was killed but this did not occur until 1922. Many of these schemes were plotted by Collins and were not the sole preserve of Brugha. In 1919 the possibility of 'wiping out the British Cabinet, and several other prominent people' was assessed by Liam Tobin and others. They advised Collins, Brugha and Mulcahy against it due to insufficient support from the

London Volunteers. Brugha demanded that the mission should proceed but the matter was dropped.[171]

When Terence MacSwiney, the lord mayor of Cork and Sinn Féin TD, began a hunger strike in Brixton prison in August 1920 Collins made plans to assassinate the British cabinet in the event of MacSwiney's death.[172] Three Volunteers from Cork, led by Patrick ('Pa') Murray, went to London at the end of August where their preparations were assisted by Sam Maguire, Art O'Brien and London Volunteers. The context of the mission changed dramatically as MacSwiney's ordeal lasted two months and captured the attention of the world in an unparalleled propaganda coup for Irish republicans. Before MacSwiney's death on 25 October, which occasioned an outpouring of sympathy in Ireland, Britain and further afield, Collins shrewdly cancelled the assassination mission. On returning to Dublin, Murray met Collins first and then Brugha, who believed the mission should never have been considered in the first place.[173] MacSwiney and Brugha had a strong rapport through involvement in the Gaelic League and attendance at the Ballingeary summer school. A letter from Brugha on 30 September went to MacSwiney's 'heart, consoled and comforted me ... I wish I could say all that's in my heart for your beautiful letter'. He expressed the hope that Brugha would be 'among the survivors to lead Freedom'.[174] Brugha's condolences to Muriel, MacSwiney's widow, mixed the heartfelt loss of an admired friend with a glorification of the cause:

> All of us who knew Traolach intimately were pained beyond measure when we heard what he had embarked upon; but we recognised that his clear vision foresaw that such a sacrifice from one in his position was necessary in order to draw world attention to our country. This has been done, and I believe that Traolach's death has achieved more for Ireland internationally than anything that has happened since Easter Week.[175]

Brugha also lauded Muriel's fortitude: 'After what you have done no Irish wife can hesitate to tread the same path. And it may well be that before we drive out the foreigner, many will be given a choice such as you were given'.[176] This was a grim reminder of Brugha's readiness to put the republic before all else, including his own life and the welfare of his family. Twenty months later, Caitlín Brugha joined Muriel as a republican widow.

The sense of disquiet at the proposed assassination to avenge MacSwiney was short-lived. In October 1920 members of Cork No. 1 Brigade met Collins and Brugha in Vaughan's Hotel in Dublin where the assassination of Lloyd

George and his cabinet was yet again on the table. The operation, which had been strenuously opposed by Griffith, was cancelled possibly due to the contact between Archbishop Clune of Perth and Lloyd George about a possible truce in Ireland.[177] A further assassination plot against the cabinet was floated in early 1921. The details were revealed by Seán Mac Eoin, the Longford IRA leader, in his statement to the BMH. He recalled meeting Brugha in March 1921 and accepting an assignment to lead an assassination party to London in retaliation for the outrages perpetrated by members of the Black and Tans and Auxiliary Division.[178] In the event, Brugha's instruction was countermanded by either Collins or Mulcahy or both, and significantly this was accepted by Brugha. If Collins halted Brugha's 1921 plot to assassinate members of the British cabinet, in the manner outlined by Mac Eoin, it was not, as Dolan and Murphy suggest, 'because it had crossed some ethical line for him'.[179] Collins had planned too many assassination missions for that. No record survives of the precise reasons for the cancellation. Damaging tentative efforts at peace negotiations or the prospect of overwhelming British retaliation and international opprobrium are obvious, but animosity towards Brugha in the wake of the gun-running imbroglio should not be dismissed. The choice of the inexperienced and untravelled Mac Eoin, who was known to Collins but only slightly acquainted with Brugha, seems odd.[180] Earlier plots generally involved Volunteers with knowledge of British locations. When Mac Eoin published his account in the *Sunday Independent* on 7 December 1958 its intent was questioned. One critic deemed it an attempt 'to represent Brugha as a ruthless assassin'.[181] Another saw it as an effort to demonstrate Collins's 'unique position' within government and his ability to overrule decisions by superior officers, including the minister for defence.[182]

Despite the failure of earlier peace initiatives, there were renewed attempts in 1921 so much so that in March de Valera remarked to Collins: 'Feelers are being thrown out in all directions just now'.[183] De Valera's insistence on direct negotiations impeded progress. Short of surrendering arms, Collins was flexible about conditions for a truce. Brugha, however, was increasingly concerned that some of his colleagues were 'probing away' from 'the declared status of the nation' – the Republic – in pursuit of a deal with the British. In April 1921 Lloyd George told the House of Commons that he was willing to meet any representative Irishman 'not under suspicion of murder' to discuss any subject of public importance without laying down conditions.[184] Privately, he was not prepared to receive a delegation that included Collins, Mulcahy or Brugha.[185]

The general election of May 1921 was intended to select representatives for the northern and southern parliaments established by the Government of Ireland Act (1920). In the south all 124 seats were won unopposed by Sinn Féin candidates. The election was the first held under proportional representation and Brugha was returned as one of five TDs for the new Waterford-East Tipperary constituency. He continued as minister for defence in the second Dáil. Despite some regional successes, such as the Crossbarry ambush in March 1921, and some spectacular failures, such as the botched operation to burn the Customs House on 25 May, it was increasingly clear to IRA GHQ that the military balance was moving inexorably toward the Crown forces. However, the British public and international opinion were ever more opposed to the methods deployed in Ireland. Furthermore, the British government was distracted not just by Ireland but by its unprecedented military commitments from Siberia to the Middle East to India. At the opening of the Northern Ireland parliament on 22 June 1921, King George V made a plea for reconciliation and events moved swiftly thereafter. On 7 July, de Valera met with Brugha, Collins, Stack, Griffith, Plunkett and MacNeill to consider 'a very important decision to be made'.[186] Brugha expressed some reservations that 'if the fighting were stopped it might not be easy to get things going again' but did not insist on this point.[187] Terms for a truce, which provided for a ceasefire and no provocative actions by either side, were agreed on 9 July and came into effect on 11 July. For very different reasons, the British and Dáil cabinets agreed to negotiate a peace. The scale of the republican success in securing a truce, which bestowed legitimacy on both the Dáil and the IRA, has been underappreciated. The political and military effort to attain that achievement, however, created a superficial sense of unity that belied deep fissures within the Dáil cabinet and between prominent personalities. What should have been a moment of triumph instead gave oxygen and space for festering resentments to flourish.

CHAPTER 6

Custodian: truce, treaty and split

THINGS FALL APART. On his return from the United States in August 1921, Harry Boland observed 'a feeling of distrust where formerly there was comradeship'.[1] The truce did not neutralize the personal animosities that had emerged since 1920. If anything, it heightened them. Diarmaid Ferriter's observation that personality clashes in 1922 proved a more decisive factor than politics or ideology in determining sides in the Irish civil war is equally applicable to the treaty.[2] During the truce period, Brugha cast off the caution he had exhibited as minister for defence during the War of Independence to reassert his authority and that of the Dáil over the IRA. During the Anglo-Irish negotiations he was continually perturbed by fears that others, including even de Valera, wavered in their commitment to the republic. This outweighed any consideration of the magnitude of the Irish achievement in negotiating the treaty. Arthur Griffith claimed that de Valera had sought his assistance to escape from 'the strait-jacket of the republic', the straps of which had been securely fastened by Brugha, its tenacious custodian.[3] For Brugha approval of the treaty meant the disestablishment of his cherished republic. It occasioned an extraordinarily vicious contribution to the treaty debates that cast him in an unforgiving light of his own making.

The Irish public greeted the cessation of hostilities with relief and optimism that it would be a 'precursor of a genuine and lasting peace'.[4] The terms of the truce were intended to create an atmosphere conducive to peaceful discussions between Dublin and London. The IRA agreed to cease all attacks on Crown forces and civilians, to discontinue military manoeuvres and prohibit the use of arms, to abstain from interference with public or private property, and to 'prevent any action likely to cause disturbance of the peace which might necessitate military interference'.[5] In return, all raids by the Crown forces were stopped, curfew restrictions were lifted, the dispatch of reinforcements from Britain was suspended, and military activity was restricted to supporting the police in their normal civil duties.[6] The truce allowed normal life to resume. For the Brugha family it meant reunion in Rathmines for the first time in several months. After his narrow escape from arrest in October 1920, Brugha feared that the family home would be burned and sent his family first to Ring in Waterford, and then to Ballybunion in north Kerry

10 Éamon de Valera about to depart for London for preliminary discussions in July 1921. *Left to right*: Arthur Griffith, Robert Barton, de Valera, Count Plunkett and Laurence O'Neill.

where they remained until the truce.[7] Brugha enjoyed the simple pleasures of getting to know his children, having breakfast with the family and listening to Caitlín play the piano.[8] Shortly after the truce, he joined his wife and children for a short break in Ballymoney on the north Wexford coast. Máire Comerford recalled meeting Brugha, Liam Mellows and Seán Etchingham, the Wexford TD and minister for fisheries (non-cabinet), at Harcourt Street Station before they boarded the evening train to Wexford: 'they were like schoolboys going home, with laughter and larks and handwaving'. Mellows and Etchingham were visiting their mothers in Courtown and Castletown respectively. Arrangements had been made in Gorey to collect the three at short notice, should it be required, to bring them back to Dublin.[9] The seaside at Ballymoney was a rare occasion for relaxation and an opportunity for Brugha to engage in one of his favourite pastimes – swimming. He was particularly pleased to see the advancing swimming skills of his eldest daughter. The family also enjoyed picnics together in Howth. But, as ever, political matters soon called Brugha away.[10]

On 12 July, the day after the truce came into effect, de Valera went to London for exploratory talks with Lloyd George (see plate 10). The British prime minister insisted that dominion status was the maximum offer on the table. Furthermore, there was no promise to end partition, and additional restrictions were likely on issues such as defence and the British war debt, among others. De Valera ceded nothing and pushed for full Irish sovereignty. On his return to Dublin, he hosted a meeting of his 'inner cabinet' at his home in Blackrock. Collins, Griffith, Brugha, Stack, MacNeill, Mulcahy and Childers were present. Collins, Griffith and Mulcahy appeared favourably disposed to negotiations and may have resigned themselves 'to an acceptance of dominion status from the moment it was first offered'.[11] Brugha insisted that it was unacceptable to consider an offer that effectively dismissed any consideration of a republic. Griffith contended that the offer should be referred to the people, while a pragmatic Collins suggested it was a 'step on the road'. Given the enduring singularity of his commitment to an Irish republic, Brugha 'was having none of it'.[12] In a letter to William O'Brien, de Valera set forth the delicate balancing act required to ensure cabinet accord:

> I made it my own peculiar function to forestall crisis where sharp differences might arise by steering along a line of policy which would be in accord with the aspirations of both [Brugha and Griffith] ... My sentiments and associations were mainly with Cathal Brugha and the group he represented, whilst in the majority of cases my reason inclined to the other side.[13]

To conciliate Brugha and others who shared his views, de Valera proposed the concept of 'external association'. In internal matters Ireland's sovereignty would be recognized but in matters of external affairs Ireland would voluntarily associate with the British Commonwealth and as such would recognize the authority of the Crown as head of that association. Designed to maintain the unity of Sinn Féin, it was a construct that anticipated aspects of the future development of the Commonwealth. Patiently and skilfully, de Valera won Brugha over to his compromise.[14] Ultimately, external association was not sufficient to address the fundamental fault-line between purists and pragmatists that fractured the Dáil cabinet, or to dispel the vagueness of the Irish demands.

Following de Valera's meeting with Lloyd George a significant alteration was made to the constitution of Dáil Éireann. As approved in 1919, Article 2(b) described the president as 'President of the Ministry elected by Dáil Éireann', not as a head of state. In July 1921 this matter was raised by Brugha in correspondence with Diarmuid O'Hegarty, secretary to the government. At a private meeting of the Dáil on 23 August, Brugha proposed amending Article 2(b) to read: 'The Ministry shall consist of the President of the Republic who shall also be Prime Minister and be elected by Dáil Éireann'.[15]

This move to regularize de Valera's legal standing can be interpreted as a continuation of the debate of the previous month on the terms of engagement for negotiations. In this regard, as Laffan suggests, it certainly 'raised the stakes and created a new obstacle to any settlement with Britain'.[16] But it can also be viewed as an attempt to protect the Dáil from the IRB because the president of the supreme council also bore the title president of the republic.

On 12 September de Valera wrote to Lloyd George to accept his invitation to enter a conference. Two days later, the Dáil selected a negotiating team of five: Arthur Griffith (minister for foreign affairs and chairman of the delegation), a reluctant Michael Collins (minister for finance), Robert Barton (minister for economic affairs), Éamonn Duggan (solicitor, director of IRA intelligence and chief liaison officer during the truce) and George Gavan Duffy (TD, solicitor and former Dáil envoy to Paris).[17] De Valera's astonishing decision not to lead the delegation took many by surprise. Notwithstanding his justifications for remaining in Ireland, it has never been satisfactorily explained. As W.T. Cosgrave commented at the time, 'they were leaving their ablest player in reserve. The reserve would have to be used some time ... and now was the time'.[18] This position did not change once the negotiations got underway. However, de Valera's stance was supported by Collins and other Sinn Féin TDs such as Kevin O'Higgins. The British too had a notable absentee in the person of Andrew Bonar Law, who, due to ill health, stood down temporarily as Conservative Party leader and in effect deputy prime minister. The British side was dominated by the 'Big Four' – Lloyd George, Austen Chamberlain (lord privy seal and Conservative leader), Lord Birkenhead (Conservative lord chancellor) and Winston Churchill (Liberal colonial secretary). They were joined by Laming Worthington Evans, Gordon Hewart (solicitor-general) and Hamar Greenwood (Irish chief secretary). Both delegations had secretaries of ability: Erskine Childers on the Irish side and on the British Tom Jones and Lionel Curtis. Further assistance to the Irish delegation was provided by Fionán Lynch, Diarmuid O'Hegarty and John Chartres. The Dáil cabinet ratified the Irish negotiating team on 7 October. By a unanimous vote, the Dáil granted plenipotentiary powers to the Irish delegates, who, in theory, had full authority to negotiate and sign an agreement. But privately de Valera issued additional contradictory instructions: any draft settlement had to be referred to the cabinet in Dublin before being finalized.[19] This incongruous position would prove a bitter point of contention when the treaty was later debated in the Dáil. Notably, an Irish republic as an objective was not specified in the instructions. It was expected that in addition to providing regular progress reports, the Irish delegates would take the boat back and forth to Dublin to report on progress in person.

In December 1921 de Valera revealed to Joseph McGarrity, the leader of Clan na Gael to whom he was close, that he would have liked Brugha to go to London but deemed him too argumentative: 'Cathal is the honestest and finest soul in the world, but he is a bit slow at seeing fine differences and rather stubborn'.[20] In any case, Brugha insisted that 'he could not leave the army'. But by that very logic he should have been a member of the delegation given the centrality of defence to any settlement between Ireland and Britain.[21] In 1937 Caitlín Brugha refuted a bogus claim in a review of Dorothy Macardle's *The Irish Republic* that a lack of confidence was the main reason for Brugha's non-involvement: 'With Cathal Brugha there was no question of any "want of confidence in himself" where the rights and the liberty of the people of Ireland were concerned.'[22] She maintained that his objection centred on the location of the negotiations in London and that her husband was willing to participate had the negotiations been in Ireland or in a neutral country. Brugha had stated this in a public address on 12 February 1922.[23]

It certainly suited Brugha to remain at home while Collins was busily engaged in London. During the truce he attempted to reassert his ministerial authority, reform aspects of the IRA, and explore a few of his own military strategies in the event of negotiations breaking down. As a result, relations with Mulcahy reached a bitter dénouement. Mulcahy later suggested that Brugha took advantage of the truce to augment his status by meeting people and listening to their complaints, and by interfering in army matters.[24] This upsurge of activity by Brugha may have been an effort to counter the dominance exerted by Collins and Mulcahy over the IRA both in fact and in the public mind. As chief of staff, Mulcahy was in an invidious position. He refused to facilitate any attempt by Brugha to 'get at Collins' or weaken his position: 'I was just a stubborn kind of understanding rock because I couldn't see the organisation of the GHQ Staff at that stage changing in such a way that Collins would move off it.'[25] But Brugha's greater involvement also reflected a new reality during the truce, where political considerations outweighed military concerns and presented the minister for defence with an opportunity to put the Dáil more firmly in charge. The British military noted how the IRA had been transformed during the truce from being in 'a precarious condition' and 'functioning under the greatest difficulty' to a situation where it could freely recruit, organize, drill, equip and restore morale. The acquisition of Thompson sub-machine guns made the IRA 'a more formidable organisation from a military point of view' and the enforced inactivity on the intelligence front was a significant handicap for the Crown forces.[26] This resurgence of the IRA was accompanied by an increasing number of complaints directed to the minister for defence. Ill-discipline was a particular concern. For example, when complaints about the imposition of unauthorized local IRA levies reached Brugha, he issued a strong condemnation against such extortion: '[n]o pressure of any kind is to be used to make unwilling persons subscribe to our funds ... Our national reputation for honour and discipline is involved in this matter'.[27] One grieving mother wrote to him to have the name of her son Michael J. O'Dempsey cleared; he had been killed by the IRA as an alleged spy in March 1921. An empathetic Brugha went to considerable lengths to investigate the circumstances of the shooting. In October he informed Mrs O'Dempsey that the charges against her son were 'without any foundation in fact' and tendered the condolence and 'sincere regret' of the government before adding: 'We feel that the tense conditions of the time alone could make such a tragedy possible in our country.'[28] The voluminous correspondence associated with the truce period made clear Brugha's greater engagement in GHQ affairs.[29]

In July 1921 the smouldering tensions between Brugha, Mulcahy and Collins reignited when, based on flawed IRA intelligence, W.G. Robbie, an ex-British army officer who managed the Dublin office of the Yost typewriter company, was ordered to leave Ireland. Brugha was incensed at how the matter was handled because it displayed 'an amateurishness that I had thought we had long ago outgrown'.[30] As director of intelligence, Collins was the focus of Brugha's ire, and he expected Mulcahy to sanction him. Furthermore, Brugha threatened to put the 'Department of Information on such a footing that things of this kind cannot occur in future'.[31] Unwisely, Mulcahy waited a month before replying to Brugha's demand for an explanation, which only deepened the sense of crisis. While on one level understandable, his belated response was inflammatory. Mulcahy was sharply critical of the 'very unfortunate' tone of Brugha's communication that had 'a very destructive influence on the harmony and discipline of the staff'. His patience clearly wearing thin, Mulcahy made it clear that 'unless something can be done to eliminate the tendency to revert to this tone when differences arise, I cannot be responsible for retaining harmony and discipline among the staff'.[32] Unsurprisingly, Brugha viewed this as insubordination. His response to Mulcahy was sarcastic and ruthless in equal measure and laid bare Brugha's grievance at the undermining of his ministry:

> The concluding paragraph of your note is scarcely worthy of notice, and I would not refer to it at all, except that if I passed it without comment, you might be tempted to write in the same strain a second time, and it is only fair to warn you that should such occur, I shall very seriously consider the advisability of suspending you, if not terminating, your connection with this Department. What good purpose was served by

your writing thus 5 weeks after the event is probably known to yourself. To me it seems a further development of that presumption on your part that prompted you to ignore for some months past the duly appointed Deputy Chief of Staff [Austin Stack]. However, before you are very much older, my friend, I shall show you that I have as little intention of taking direction from you as to how I should reprove inefficiency or negligence on the part of yourself or the D/I [Collins], as I have of allowing you to appoint a Deputy Chief of Staff of your own choosing. In regard to your inability to maintain harmony and discipline among the staff: it was scarcely necessary to remind me of the fact, as your shortcomings in that respect – so far at least as controlling the particular member already mentioned is concerned – have been quite apparent for a considerable time.[33]

A week later, Brugha sacked Mulcahy and ordered him to hand over his books and accounts to Austin Stack as deputy chief of staff.[34] One must question both the proportionality of Brugha's response and his judgement. As we have seen in chapter 5, Brugha attached great importance to establishing the guilt of IRA targets and was within his rights as minister to highlight shoddy practice by GHQ. The expulsion of Robbie clearly lacked sufficient evidence. But Brugha could scarcely have been less tactful in how he approached the matter, preferring a sledgehammer to common sense. It is difficult to avoid the conclusion that the Robbie case was seized on by Brugha as an opportunity to admonish and humiliate Mulcahy. On the cusp of the London negotiations, the timing of this unedifying display of ego and petulance by both the minister for defence and the IRA chief of staff was astonishing, if not reckless.

No longer willing to contain his anger, Mulcahy appealed to de Valera for immediate support lest the 'toxic atmosphere' destroy 'the vigour and discipline of the Staff'. Mulcahy made it clear that he could no longer discuss the matter directly with Brugha and could not allow him to chair or be present at staff meetings.[35] With the possibility of a resumption of hostilities with Britain never far away, de Valera could not risk the loss of either the IRA chief of staff or the minister for defence. Mulcahy's resignation could cause turmoil within the IRA, while Brugha's removal might occasion political divisions within the country.[36] A meeting was held in Sighle Humphreys' house at 36 Ailesbury Road attended by Mulcahy, Brugha, Stack and de Valera. Mulcahy later claimed that when de Valera demanded an explanation, Brugha broke down crying and insisted that 'he could do no wrong'. It is unclear what precisely he meant but it seems to imply that as minister for defence Brugha had acted with the best of intentions. This was as close to an apology as Mulcahy could expect.[37] The fundamental breach in the relationship between Brugha and Mulcahy was not adequately addressed, let alone repaired. De Valera brushed over it as he attempted to mollify both men. He also attempted to nullify Mulcahy's sacking by suggesting that as assistant minister for defence Mulcahy should attend cabinet meetings before dismissing the idea: 'No, you would probably be as bad as the rest of them after a fortnight.'[38] Although a throwaway remark, it indicated the tensions that beset the cabinet.

Hostilities resurfaced the following month when Brugha complained that Stack was not being summoned to GHQ staff meetings. In 1918 Mulcahy wished to have Stack on his staff and suggested the position of deputy chief of staff. Following his escape from Strangeways prison in Manchester in October 1919, Stack did attend GHQ meetings but resigned in August 1920 to concentrate on his responsibilities as minister for home affairs. For reasons that are unclear but probably at Brugha's instigation to strengthen the control of the Dáil, Stack resumed his role as deputy chief of staff.[39] Mulcahy, however, had other ideas. Without informing Brugha, he offered the post to Eoin O'Duffy, who had been director of organization since June 1921. A protégé of Collins, O'Duffy was a member of the IRB supreme council and his appointment as deputy chief of staff consolidated the IRB's influence within GHQ. As Fearghal McGarry notes, the 'lines of demarcation between the functions and powers of the GHQ triumvirate of Mulcahy, Collins and O'Duffy were by now remarkably vague', although Mulcahy was technically in command, Collins 'effectively called the shots'.[40] By not advising Brugha of such a significant appointment, Mulcahy knowingly created a fresh source of discord with his minister.

In mid-September the cabinet introduced measures to remove ambiguity in the relationship between the army and the government. In essence, the army was to be reconstituted and officers would have to apply for new commissions. Furthermore, while the chief of staff was to chair staff meetings, the minister for defence could preside if he wished to meet staff on a particular matter. The deputy chief of staff (Stack) was also to attend staff meetings.[41] This new arrangement provided Brugha with more control over the army at the expense of Collins, Mulcahy and the IRB. On 17 November Brugha offered fresh commissions 'to put the army in an unequivocal position as the legal defence force of the nation, under the control of the civil government'.[42] The reconstituted army came into being on 25 November, the anniversary of the founding of the Irish Volunteers in 1913. O'Duffy treated the new commission as a demotion and 'a personal slight and a grave dishonour which … I do not deserve'.[43] This prompted an immediate response from Brugha, who maintained he had no prior knowledge that O'Duffy had been acting as deputy chief of staff. The minister had no intention of reducing O'Duffy's rank or causing offence, and claimed 'no one in the army or outside it has more confidence in you than I have'.[44] Brugha's words may have been carefully chosen, as his 'confidence' in O'Duffy was linked to the position of director of organization. Brugha's anger was reserved for Mulcahy for elevating O'Duffy without ministerial approval.[45] In a rather curt note, O'Duffy expressed surprise that Brugha had not been aware of his 'active' role as deputy chief of staff.[46] Whether O'Duffy believed Brugha's claim of ignorance is questionable, but what is not in doubt is that he harboured a sense of grievance and ill-feeling towards Brugha thereafter.

Mulcahy made it clear that he would continue as chief of staff only if he rather than Brugha had responsibility for appointing GHQ staff. When Brugha insisted that Stack be offered a new appointment as deputy chief of staff and O'Duffy offered the post of director of organization, Mulcahy threatened to resign.[47] At a cabinet meeting in the Mansion House on 25 November, to which the GHQ staff were invited, new arrangements to strengthen the constitutional position were approved. Henceforth, the cabinet was 'the supreme body' directing the army. While the chief of staff was to be 'the professional or technical head' and 'supreme on the field of battle', the minister for defence was 'the administrative head of the Army'. All commissions derived their authority from the cabinet and, pointedly, all appointments had to be sanctioned by the minister for defence. The cabinet meeting ended Mulcahy's efforts to secure the right to sanction appointments.[48] It seems that de Valera was also anxious to restrain the independent nature of GHQ and curb the growing influence of Collins, his most powerful cabinet rival.[49] For Tom Garvin, this 'crucial decision, by which the Public Band was to be replaced by a force controlled by civilians responsible to the Dáil, marks the beginning of the transition to genuine statehood from the semi-imaginary underground republic of 1919'.[50] The oddity of Stack and O'Duffy both occupying the position of deputy chief of staff required a creative but not very workable solution. They became joint deputy chiefs of staff but in Mulcahy's absence O'Duffy was to be his 'full representative'.[51] This was an obvious effort to appease Mulcahy. At the end of November GHQ sent a note that officers should accept the new commissions.[52]

The tension at the cabinet meeting was palpable. When de Valera explained that Stack, as deputy chief of staff, would hold a 'watching brief' for Brugha, each member of the GHQ staff objected, thereby emphasizing their support for both Mulcahy and Collins. O'Duffy, who viewed Stack's joint appointment as a diminution of his role, became agitated and proceeded to regurgitate his personal grievances. Mulcahy later recalled that O'Duffy's 'slight touch of hysteria' provoked an alarming scene. Losing his temper, de Valera 'rose excitedly in his chair … and declared in a half-scream, half-shout "ye may mutiny if ye like, but Ireland will give me another army," and dismissed the whole lot of us out of sight'.[53] Both Collins and Griffith hurriedly left the meeting to catch the mail boat for the long journey back to the negotiations in London. For all the controversy generated, it appears that Stack did not attend any GHQ meetings.[54] Mulcahy later claimed that the hostilities directed at him by Brugha were a form of collateral damage emanating from Brugha's desire to keep Collins in check: 'I was a bad contact for the transmission of these attacks, and in that way Cathal became somewhat antagonistic to myself'.[55] The spat over the deputy chief of staff revealed the marked tensions that divided the republican leadership eleven days before the Anglo-Irish treaty was signed. While de Valera's exasperation may have been understandable, he failed to provide the necessary leadership to address the personal animosities within his cabinet. It was an ominous omen of things to come, 'a pre-echo of the eventual split'.[56]

A belief that the truce might be short-lived led to Brugha's active involvement in procuring arms. According to Robert Barton, this 'was a rather sub rosa business' as the cabinet had 'no fixed plan' to take advantage of the truce to stockpile weapons.[57] In December 1921 the quartermaster-general reported to Brugha that procuring arms had become much less difficult but transportation still presented challenges. He also emphasized 'the freedom of movement and the advantage of being able to work at night as well as day' conferred by the truce conditions.[58] According to this report, between July and December 1921, 51 machine guns, 313 rifles and 637 revolvers and automatics were imported and distributed compared to respective figures of 6 machine guns, 96 rifles and 522 revolvers and automatics between August 1920 and 11 July 1921.[59]

Brugha spent significant time exploring various strategies to implement attacks in Britain. In August 1921 he summoned Gilbert Barrington and Richard Purcell, members of the Tyneside IRA and the British-based Irish Self-Determination League, to a meeting in Dublin with a view to developing plans to attack infrastructure in Britain in the event of the truce collapsing.[60] In June 1922 Brugha would again encounter Barrington as a comrade in the Hammam Hotel during the fateful opening week of the civil war. Brugha's most absurd scheme was an unrealistic attempt to harness the ranks of the unemployed in Britain. William O'Brien recalled Brugha indicating that the cabinet had approved £5,000 to support a 'special campaign' in Britain, if required. When discussing the campaign, Brugha mentioned his *idée fixe* of 'attacking British Ministers in the House of Commons'.[61] O'Brien poured cold

water on the idea of enlisting the unemployed who 'would not do any of the
things he had in mind … [as] … they were not that kind'.[62] This led Brugha
to enquire about assistance from 'communists'. He was subsequently
introduced to Arthur McManus and William Gallacher, two leading figures
in the British Communist Party, who dispelled much of Brugha's naivety.[63]
One wonders if Brugha's unrealistic schemes reflected a growing sense of
desperation or a dawning realization that compromise in London was
probable.

The London negotiations can be divided into three phases. The opening
period from 11 October to 3 November consisted of seven plenary sessions
and three 'sub-conferences'. The Irish team was willing to consider an element
of compromise on a range of issues, such as defence and trade, if the 'essential
unity' of Ireland was maintained. The second segment from 5 to 16 November
largely concerned efforts by Lloyd George to persuade Sir James Craig,
Northern Ireland premier, to join the conference. The final phase saw Lloyd
George press a settlement on the Irish delegation. Although the conference
met for the first time at 11 a.m. on 11 October, an Irish memorandum of
proposals was not submitted until 24 October, 'too late', Lloyd George stated
for effective examination.[64] This ceded the advantage to the British for
whom three cardinal points remained constant throughout the negotiations:
dominion status with allegiance to the Crown, Irish entry into the
Commonwealth, and defence and security considerations. So adamant was
Lloyd George on the first point that he contemplated resigning in November.
This opened the highly unpalatable prospect of a diehard Conservative
government under Bonar Law taking office. Intriguingly, the word 'elucidation'
appeared on a number of documents underlining the sense that the conference
was breaking new constitutional ground regarding dominion status. The
Crown remained the crux. The Irish alternative was de Valera's external
association concept. The second major issue was 'essential unity' and partition.
Craig believed that the future of Northern Ireland had been settled in 1920
and that the London conference was solely a matter for Dublin and London.
His refusal to countenance any arrangement for an all-Ireland parliament led
to the proposal of a boundary commission as compensation.

Although Brugha was kept abreast of the negotiations by Erskine Childers,
particularly on matters pertaining to defence and the retention by the British
of port facilities, he was increasingly suspicious that decisions were being taken
without adequate consultation with the cabinet in Dublin.[65] For instance, he
was aggrieved that the Irish delegation agreed to halt the importations of arms
to Ireland without referring to him. Stack suggested that Brugha was 'at first
inclined to ignore the arrangements altogether' but reluctantly accepted

11 Michael Collins and Arthur Griffith.

them.[66] Such a benign recollection is open to doubt. During the negotiations Brugha provided Michael Brennan, commandant of the East Clare Brigade IRA, with £1,000 to acquire arms. Brennan dispatched Michael Hogan and Edward ('Ned') Lynch to London to this end in November with, according to Lynch, an instruction to avoid Michael Collins 'at all costs'.[67] When Collins became aware of their presence, he made clear the paramount need to avoid any action that might jeopardize the negotiations. Assurances were given and promptly ignored. Military barracks in Chelsea and Windsor were raided on 18 and 22 November with the assistance of sympathetic Irish Guards. The British police recovered machine guns but not rifles, which made their way to Ireland; Hogan and four others were later jailed.[68] When news of this incident broke, the embarrassed Irish delegates were confronted by their British counterparts. Collins convinced the British that the raids were conducted without proper authorization.[69] In their statements to the BMH, both Brennan and Lynch suggested that Brugha had no knowledge of what was an opportunistic operation; no arms had been purchased as originally intended. On returning to Dublin, Lynch visited Brugha at Lalor's, suggesting that at the very least Brugha was aware that Hogan and Lynch were in London and that their presence had the potential to derail the negotiations by contravening the understanding on the importation of arms. Not for the first time, it called into question Brugha's judgement.

A potential breakdown of discussions came not on Ulster, as de Valera had sought, or due to arms raids but on the intractable issue of status. The Irish delegation returned to Dublin for a final cabinet meeting on 3 December. It was a stormy affair. The most contentious issue in the draft treaty provisions was the requirement that Irish TDs and public servants swear an oath of allegiance to the British Crown. Brugha flatly refused to contemplate this and insisted 'if the British wanted an oath from us ... we might give it, provided they swore to us in return'.[70] Both Brugha and de Valera rejected the provisions for a boundary commission contained in Article 12. Brugha also attacked the use of sub-conferences, whereby Griffith and Collins (see plate 11) did most of the negotiating, leaving the other delegates 'not in possession of full information'. When advised that the British suggested the arrangement and the Irish delegation approved it, he poisonously responded: 'the British Government selected its men'.[71] This insinuation drew an angry response from Griffith who demanded that Brugha withdraw his remark. He did but only after Griffith insisted it be recorded in the minutes.[72] Brugha's warning that Griffith risked splitting Ireland 'from top to bottom' if he signed the treaty proposals caused Griffith to reflect. He indicated that he would not do so before submitting the terms to the Dáil and 'if necessary the people'.[73] This bitter exchange was a microcosm of greater eruptions to follow. The delegation returned to London with no clear idea of the cabinet position beyond an instruction to extract better terms. Critically, de Valera once again refused to join the negotiations. Collins appears to have made a genuine effort to push de Valera's concept of 'external association', but Lloyd George refused to budge from a traditional imperialistic position and Irish hopes regarding status were hobbled. Using a mixture of persuasion and intimidation, the British prime minister demanded that the agreement be completed. And so, in the early hours of 6 December 1921 articles of agreement between Great Britain and Ireland were duly signed.

Given the background historical context, the Irish achievement was substantial: formal recognition of Irish statehood in the territory of the proposed Irish Free State (due to come into being after twelve months) had been granted. The first article of the treaty set out Ireland's status as a dominion on the same footing as Canada, Australia, New Zealand and the Union of South Africa. The second and third articles defined the Irish relationship to the imperial parliament. The fourth article set out the terms of the oath. It displayed considerable creativity as the oath to the Crown was by means of the constitution. Yet, as would become apparent, the existence of *any* oath was offensive to those committed to an abstract republic. Articles 5 and 10 dealt with financial liabilities; 6, 7 and 8 concerned defence and security, while article 9 covered free trade. Articles 11 and 12 related to Northern Ireland, which had the right to opt out of the agreement within one month of the Free State coming into existence on 6 December 1922. Should that come

12 *Front row left to right*: Mary Rynne, Éamon de Valera, Stephen O'Mara (bacon manufacturer, former IPP MP and supporter of the treaty), Cathal Brugha. *Second row left to right*: Michael Rynne (grandson of O'Mara and a future diplomat) and Richard Mulcahy. The photograph was taken at O'Mara's residence Strand House, Limerick on 6 December 1921.

to pass (which it did) a boundary commission would be established. Articles 13–18 concerned the means for putting the treaty into effect and various issues arising from the transfer of authority from London to Dublin. The *Irish Independent* suggested this historic document, if ratified by both parliaments, would leave the Irish Free State 'mistress in her own house, and in a position to work out her own salvation in peace and without hindrance'. It expressed confidence that 'after the years of agony we have endured, after the many fluctuations at the Conference itself, with its moments of tension and anxiety, Ireland will today joyfully receive the news that the long and arduous deliberations have culminated in a Treaty which assures her the best possible terms that in existing conditions could be secured'.[74]

Historians have often pondered why the Irish delegation did not contact Dublin by telephone. That instrument had hitherto not been used for security reasons. Astonishingly, even if a call had been made, de Valera was not at his desk. After the cabinet meeting he and Brugha travelled to Loughrea, County Galway, where they spent a night in the residence of Bishop Thomas O'Doherty of Clonfert, who was a strong supporter of Sinn Féin but privately critical of IRA violence.[75] They were later joined by Mulcahy who retired to bed early. The bishop, Brugha and de Valera sat by the fire and discussed the possible outcome of the treaty negotiations. It seems that de Valera wished to establish the prelate's views on what would constitute a satisfactory settlement and to expose Brugha to significant opinions other than those of members of the Dáil and cabinet. It was unlikely that Brugha was swayed in any way by O'Doherty, whose only priority was fiscal autonomy from Britain.[76] News of the settlement reached de Valera, Brugha and Mulcahy on 6 December when they were in Limerick (see plate 12).[77] The British communist William Gallacher had been tipped off about the settlement before leaving London for Dublin, where he sought a meeting with Brugha. He urged the arrest of the returning plenipotentiaries and the encouragement of Irish workers and peasants to fight for a republic. Brugha dismissed any suggestion of arrests and on saying goodbye to Gallacher stated: 'you are always welcome in Ireland, but we do not want any of your communism'.[78]

The settlement was considered at a cabinet meeting in the Mansion House on 8 December which lasted from 12 noon until 9.30 p.m. with two adjournments. The minutes of the meeting starkly revealed the depth of division over the treaty with Griffith, Collins, Barton and Cosgrave in favour and de Valera, Brugha and Stack against.[79] Laurence O'Neill, the lord mayor, noted that the 'fierceness of the language could be heard outside. The pent up animosity of Brugha towards Collins was let loose. De Valera was pleading … [and] … Cosgrave was battling with his conscience'.[80] Brugha, de Valera and Stack were enraged that the plenipotentiaries had signed without referring the settlement to the cabinet. When de Valera would not recommend acceptance of the agreement to the public, Collins proposed that the treaty be permitted to go through and that the republican question could be fought with the provisional government.[81] De Valera made a counter-proposal known as 'Document No. 2' which elaborated his 'external association' concept. No compromise was reached.[82] Brugha later professed that the events leading up to the treaty taught him more 'of the rottenness of human nature … than I ever learned during the forty-six years of my life'.[83] When his brother Alfred asked his views on the settlement, Brugha declared: 'If I were to be party to that, I would be ashamed to show my face to my youngest child'.[84]

The Dáil debated the settlement between 14 December and 7 January 1922 at University Buildings, Earlsfort Terrace. That the Dáil opted for a private session led the press to fixate on the arrival and demeanours of various figures. De Valera 'drove up in a somewhat old-fashioned car, Mr Michael Collins lolled back in a Rolls-Royce, Mr Arthur Griffith balanced himself on the side of a jaunting car, while Mr Cathal Brugha laboriously pedalled along on a bicycle'.[85] The *Freeman's Journal* reported that Brugha 'literally dashed up the steps to avoid the battery of camera men'.[86] In their analysis of the treaty, Mícheál Ó Fathartaigh and Liam Weeks observe that during the debates 'the Treaty seems a mere side issue with TDs using it as a means of settling old scores and grudges ... the preoccupation was less on the agreement delivered by the London delegation, and more on their instructions'.[87] In addition to the actions of the plenipotentiaries, the other dominant issue was the position of the king and the oath. Little was said about Ulster, partition or the boundary commission. Supporters defended the agreement as the best deal that could have been reached under the circumstances; critics accused the delegates of betraying the republic. Outside the Dáil, public reaction to the signing of the treaty was overwhelmingly positive. The *Freeman's Journal* believed the settlement to be 'a fair one, and full of blessings for the Irish people' and praised the 'patriotism, intelligence and prudence' of the delegation.[88] The *Irish Times* considered the treaty the best deal available to Ireland and that a return to war would be ruinous for the country.[89]

Apart from enduring some sneering from pro-treaty deputies, including an accusation by W.T. Cosgrave that 'except for war he was not worth a damn', Brugha remained largely silent throughout the increasingly raucous debates.[90] On Saturday, 7 January he spoke in both Irish and English for an hour and a quarter. The speech was that of an uncompromising republican. It was also venomous and 'pulsating with icy fury' in the words of Townshend.[91] Brugha unleashed the personal animosities that had developed over the preceding two years in all their viciousness. Incensed by Griffith's depiction of Collins as 'the man who won the war', Brugha claimed Collins's military reputation was no more than a figment of journalistic imagination. He described Collins as 'merely a subordinate in the Department of Defence ... [who] was made a romantic figure, a mystical character such as this person certainly is not'.[92] He dismissed Griffith with equal contempt, accusing him of winning the war for England.[93] Pro-treaty TDs called for no interruptions because Brugha was 'making [such] a good speech for the Treaty'.[94] He supported de Valera's 'external association' concept and rejected Griffith's claim that 'only a quibble' differentiated the treaty from de Valera's proposal: 'the difference for me, is the difference between a draught of water or a draught of poison'.[95] Brugha informed the house that if he accepted the treaty and did not do his best to defeat it, it would amount to 'national suicide'.[96] Máire Comerford recalled that when Brugha emerged from the chamber 'his lips were blue' from the strain and tension.[97] The reaction to Brugha's speech was one of shock, 'in every sense of the word shattering', as the *Freeman's Journal* put it.[98] Todd Andrews recounted the sense of disbelief and embarrassment created by Brugha's condemnation of Collins, which merely 'diminished Brugha's stature while evoking sympathy for Collins'.[99] Jennie Wyse Power described the contribution as the

> most dreadful public utterance I have ever listened to, apparently made to prejudice Collins, even Brugha's followers interposed to ask him to restrain himself … It was vicious and malignant and his face reminded me of a hound striking its fangs in an inferior animal and then licking its lips to satisfy itself that it had drawn blood … Oh the horror of it all … de Valera broke down, and there was dead silence in the chamber.[100]

Brugha's premeditated and *ad hominem* tirade gravely damaged his reputation and legacy. Counterproductively, it did nothing to secure a vote against the treaty which was approved by sixty-four votes to fifty-seven. In the aftermath of that vote, Brugha undertook to ensure that discipline – adherence to the decision of the Dáil – would be maintained in the army.[101] This has been widely ignored or misunderstood. Indeed, a RTÉ documentary to mark the centenary of the vote on the treaty suggested the opposite, whereas in fact Brugha adhered, as he had always done, to the authority of the Dáil, even if personally he opposed that decision.[102] The narrowness of the Dáil vote did not reflect the popular position because the TDs were unrepresentative of the country at large. At the general election of June 1922, effectively a referendum on the treaty, the electorate decisively backed pro-treaty TDs. On 9 January de Valera failed to be re-elected president by two votes and was replaced by Griffith. With the appointment of a new cabinet, Brugha's tenure as minister for defence was terminated and he was succeeded by Mulcahy. During the debate on de Valera's resignation, Brugha wanted to 'avoid saying anything of a contentious nature' and attempted to clarify some of the remarks he made two days earlier. He did not believe that 'any one man won the war' and that the position prior to the treaty was obtained by 'men whose names, if I mentioned them here would not be known'.[103] In a significant softening of his position, Brugha was 'perfectly satisfied that the five men who signed this document [treaty] thought that they did the best thing for Ireland' but 'if they

13 Cathal Brugha and Éamon de Valera after the Dáil vote on the treaty on
7 January 1922.

think they can absolutely rely on the word of Mr. Lloyd George and his
friends they are not as sensible men as I took them to be'.[104] In appealing for
unity, Brugha believed that de Valera should continue as president because he
was the only 'man who can lead us properly and keep us all together'. His
remark – 'If Eamon de Valera did not happen to be President who would have
kept Arthur Griffith, Michael Collins and myself together?' – generated
laughter.[105] It was a rare moment of levity (see plate 13).

Brugha's calmer and somewhat contrite contribution in the Dáil on 9
January did not undo the damage caused by his vitriolic speech two days
before but it does shed light on his thinking. Three reasons can be advanced
for the tone and fury of Brugha's remarks on 7 December. The first was his
self-anointed role as custodian of the republic declared in 1916. The body of
no other member of the Dáil bore as many wounds from the Rising. His
inflexibility, determination and tenacity in the pursuit of the republic were his
greatest strengths between 1916 and the truce, but during the treaty debates
and thereafter, when constructive political skills and greater compromise were
required, they became his greatest weaknesses. As one of the men 'of taut and
rigid principles' in Frank Pakenham's phrase, he could not countenance the

disestablishment of the republic that acceptance of the treaty entailed.[106] The second reason was his animosity towards Collins, which has generally been depicted as jealousy. For Piaras Béaslaí, for example, there was 'a general feeling of pain and shame at such a crude exhibition of personal jealousy on the part of one of our leaders at this great national crisis'.[107] While not denying that jealousy may have existed, Brugha's insistence on proper accountability and opposition to Collins's modus operandi, in particular his utilization of the IRB within the IRA and within the Dáil, better explains his enmity. As minister for defence, Brugha had an appreciation of the sacrifices made by a whole host of unheralded members of the IRA and Cumann na mBan. Lastly, Brugha and others, such as Mary MacSwiney (sister of Terence MacSwiney), were outraged at the way in which the IRB was used to sway the Dáil vote on the treaty. On 12 December Seán Ó Murthuile issued a directive that the IRB supreme council supported the settlement.[108] It is difficult to determine precisely how influential this was and suggestions by Brugha that forty votes may have been secured certainly seem too high. Nonetheless, it was a factor. The depth of Brugha's scorn for the IRB and his willingness to die for the cause to which he devoted his life are made clear in a stingingly bitter letter to Eoin O'Duffy, who had surreptitiously denigrated Brugha in the Dáil:

> that one whom I believed to be a brave man and a real fighter should have stooped so low as to stab in the back one who has made, and is willing to make, as least as great sacrifice as any others for our common country, is certainly the worst disillusion I have yet experienced. When I heard of the notice that was sent out to members of the IRB by the body which calls itself the Supreme Council I made up my mind that when fighting started again I would challenge those vile creatures, who thus prostituted the body that brought the Republic into existence, to follow a lead that I would give. Fighting has now been temporarily stayed, but only temporarily. I believe, that in our time, sooner or later, it will begin again. When it does you may expect to hear from me. I will give you and the creatures referred to above an opportunity of showing your willingness to face certain death for Ireland, and you may be sure that I will not ask you to do anything that I am not prepared to do myself.[109]

This was an ominous prediction of the inevitability of civil war. On the night of the Dáil vote, an anguished Brugha claimed 'it can't mean the undoing of our lifework'.[110] Things fall apart.

CHAPTER 7

Martyr: civil war, death and funeral

C ATHAL BRUGHA FOUGHT and died in a civil war that he opposed. For
Piaras Béaslaí, his death was 'one of the few heroic episodes in a generally
sorry and squalid story'.[1] After the Dáil vote on the treaty on 7 January, the
position of that assembly was complicated. A provisional government with
Michael Collins as chairman governed the twenty-six counties until the Irish
Free State was given effect after a general election. In tandem, Arthur Griffith
remained president of the second Dáil and his government continued to exist,
albeit gradually subsumed by the provisional government.[2] Brugha made clear
in the Dáil on 9 January that he had to fulfil his mandate to preserve the
commitment of Dáil Éireann to the republic until the electorate decided
otherwise.[3] As he put it to a meeting in Navan in April 1922, 'the Republic
should continue to function until the Treaty was brought before the
electorate'.[4] Brugha left undated notes on the treaty that elucidate his political
stance in the six months before the civil war. He maintained that peace was
'not likely to eventuate from the articles of agreement' for three reasons. First,
the IRA was 'solidly behind the Republic', and it was by no means certain that
an election on its own would settle the question of the treaty. Second, Brugha
believed that 'the intense yearning for national freedom that every Irishman
worth his salt feels in his heart is too strong to allow Ireland to be turned into
a British dominion'. This encapsulated his own position and was a theme that
he frequently aired in public meetings and on election hustings. Lastly, Brugha
doubted that a constitution could be drawn up to satisfy Irish aspirations
and at the same time pass through Westminster without amendment.
Consequently, 'the fight will be on again'.[5] Several efforts were made to prevent
the treaty split culminating in civil war such as postponing the general election,
preparing a draft constitution and allowing the occupation of the Four Courts
by anti-treaty forces for over two months from April 1922. Brugha strove to
win public opinion over to the anti-treaty side while maintaining a sense of
realism about the probability of armed conflict over the settlement. This was
expressed forcefully by him in March 1922 at the unveiling of a memorial at
Pickardstown in County Waterford to two IRA men killed during the War of
Independence. Brugha warned those in attendance that

The time would come soon when the Irish people would be called upon
to make a very serious decision. They should not allow any person or
any body of people to make up their minds for them. Every effort
should be made to achieve unity and maintain it, and almost any
concession short of a sacrifice of principle should be made in that
direction.[6]

The division over the treaty sundered not only the Dáil but Sinn Féin, the
IRA and the IRB, while pro-treaty members of Cumann na mBan were asked
to resign. The anti-treaty lobby was quickly labelled republican, irrespective of
the position that some members took during the treaty negotiations (for
example, de Valera never expected to obtain a republic). The initial prospects
for the republican side did not look promising as large sections of the press
rallied behind the treaty as did the Catholic Church and local representative
bodies. On 12 January the Sinn Féin executive called a special ard fheis to
consider the party's constitution in light of the treaty.[7] That it could only be
changed by a two-thirds majority gave some hope to the anti-treaty wing of
the party, which was determined to uphold the Irish republic and return to the
ideals on which the first Dáil was founded (see plate 14).

The republican campaign to win over public and party opinion was
launched with a monster meeting in O'Connell Street on 12 February with
speeches from three platforms that lasted for an hour and a half.[8] De Valera
was the principal speaker. His address rehearsed arguments against the 'so-
called Treaty', as he put it, namely that it was signed under duress, required an
oath to the king, and ceded Irish ports to the British. Although partition had
been largely ignored during the treaty debates, de Valera now emphasized it
'above all' and suggested this 'ancient nation that had been one from the dawn
of history is now to suit the exigencies of British politicians … to be broken
up into two warring States'.[9] Brugha's speech focused on the Irish language
and on the army. He claimed that efforts were being made to subvert the
discipline and morale of the IRA and if this continued before a general
election it would lead to trouble. Brugha stressed that he 'wanted the people
to have a fair chance of saying whether they wanted to become British subjects
or to remain citizens of the Irish Republic'.[10] The issue of citizenship, which
he had raised during the treaty debates, also featured in an article in *Poblacht
na hÉireann* – an anti-treaty bulletin managed by Joseph MacDonagh, brother
of the 1916 martyr Thomas, and edited by Liam Mellows and Frank
Gallagher.[11] Under the title 'Was it for this?', Brugha made clear his conviction
that the Sinn Féin constitution of 1917 'was broken when the Treaty was
signed' and 'Easter Week, and the work and sacrifices since, all went – for

14 Anti-treaty TDs in January 1922. Brugha is in the first row centre, holding his hat and coat.

what? To make us British subjects? To turn our country into a British Dominion, or two British Dominions?'[12] On 19 February de Valera, Brugha and other anti-treaty TDs spoke in Cork city. De Valera largely repeated his Dublin address with one notable exception. He invited the pro-treaty side to produce their constitution and hinted that the difficulties dividing Sinn Féin and the country might be surmounted if the constitution did not embody the king.[13] As chair of the drafting committee, Collins strove to make the constitution as republican and conciliatory as possible. As in Dublin, Brugha's opening remarks concerned the need to 'save the Irish language'. He criticized J.J. Walsh, the local Cork city TD and newly appointed postmaster general, for displaying a policy of surrender in the use of Irish within the postal service. Walsh subsequently refuted this by listing twelve actions he had taken to support the language – from encouraging post office staff to learn it, to repainting and re-lettering post boxes, to having instructions in Irish only on telegraph forms.[14] Brugha also promoted de Valera's 'Document No. 2' to his Cork listeners. He described it as 'a supreme effort by President de Valera, the captain of the ship, to pull the ship off the rocks upon which it had been driven by incompetent amateurs who had seized the helm'.[15]

The extraordinary Sinn Féin ard fheis held in the Mansion House on 21 and 22 February was attended by 3,000 delegates. An agreement was ratified to adjourn the ard fheis for three months to avoid the prospect of an immediate general election, to avert a formal split in Sinn Féin, and to allow the ratification of the constitution by the electorate.[16] This suited both sides. De Valera and his adherents needed time to build up a new political organization. Brugha strongly endorsed the adjournment and suggested that 'even yet they could achieve unity' by allowing the Dáil to function regularly, by ensuring no interference with the operation of government departments, by allowing the provisional government function in its own way, and by providing equal representation on the standing committee of Sinn Féin. His intervention was applauded.[17] For Collins the agreement removed the inherent danger of Sinn Féin repudiating the provisional government, the majority in the Dáil and popular opinion.[18] Both wings of Sinn Féin hoped that the postponement of an election would reduce tensions.

In the event, the election took place on 16 June 1922. It was required under the terms of the Irish Free State Agreement Act passed in Westminster at the end of March. The prospect of an election raised the related question of who should vote and whether the electoral register should be updated. At the beginning of March, Kate O'Callaghan, an anti-treaty TD and widow of the former mayor of Limerick, introduced a bill in the Dáil to have women between the ages of twenty-one and thirty added to the register before the treaty was put to the country.[19] Supporting the measure, Brugha called for recognition of the equal rights of women as enshrined in the 1916 proclamation because 'they have as true an insight in national matters as men'.[20] He also acknowledged the role played by Cumann na mBan during Easter Week and in the period since then. The bill was denounced by Griffith as 'an attempt to torpedo the Treaty' and as a 'dishonest trick'.[21] The measure was defeated. Brugha's support seemed to be motivated less by a commitment to equal rights than hopes that female voters would oppose the treaty.

Republicans launched a new political organization on 17 March 1922 called Cumann na Poblachta with offices at 23 Suffolk Street in Dublin. De Valera was president; Brugha, Stack and J.J. O'Kelly were trustees. Its chief aims were to uphold, strengthen and secure international recognition for the republic; to preserve the unity of the nation and the integrity of its territory; to restore the Irish language as the spoken language; to make Ireland economically self-sufficient; to maintain diplomatic representation abroad; to maintain a high standard of 'probity and honour in Irish public life'; and to repudiate the treaty 'as humiliating to the nation, and destructive of its status and rightful claims'.[22] One of its first actions was to dispatch J.J. O'Kelly, Austin Stack and Countess Markievicz to the United States to secure Irish-American financial and moral support for the anti-treaty policy of de Valera. The trio did not return to Ireland until May. In an address in Rhode Island,

Stack claimed 'for us there was only one possible government: The Republic, the whole Republic, and nothing but the Republic'.[23] Accompanied by de Valera, Brugha put this argument to his constituents at a large meeting in Waterford on St Patrick's Day. He recalled the Parnell split and appealed for unity: 'If they could not agree they should not fall out with one another. There should be no rows. Let them tolerate everyone's honest opinion.'[24] Brugha's moderate stance was almost immediately undone by his criticism of Collins for removing the Belfast boycott to the detriment of northern nationalists – a claim with little foundation because the boycott had never been effective. Brugha also warned ominously, as he had also done a week before in New Ross, that civil war was probable if the treaty was not defeated: 'unless the men who had borne the brunt of the fighting for the past few years were given votes, they would make themselves heard in a very strenuous way'.[25] As events transpired, Brugha did not have long to wait before the IRA made its opposition to the treaty crystal clear. On the same day in Thurles, de Valera infamously predicted that if the treaty was accepted the IRA would have to 'wade through Irish blood'.[26] Whereas opponents accused him of inciting civil war, he maintained he issued a warning as he had done on the same tour in Waterford and Killarney.

As Michael Hopkinson notes, the treaty came as a shock to an army that was under the impression that it had fought for an Irish republic.[27] Although a majority of the IRB and the leadership of the IRA supported the settlement, most of the rank and file – some estimates suggest three-quarters – did not.[28] Personal loyalties and factional animosities were often more significant factors than ideology in determining whether an IRA unit was pro- or anti-treaty. Michael Brennan in Clare and Seán Mac Eoin in Longford, both of whom were close to Collins, were pro-treaty. By contrast, in Kerry the leaders of the three IRA brigades took the anti-treaty side, even though public opinion was divided. In Brugha's constituency, the Waterford Brigade, led by Pax Whelan, was anti-treaty. P.S. O'Hegarty recorded that in the immediate aftermath of the signing of the treaty both Brugha and Mellows had travelled throughout the south and the west encouraging army units to oppose the settlement.[29] In the early weeks of 1922, the position of the army was complicated not only by the treaty but also by the rapid evacuation of the British army. Large areas of the country were dominated by anti-treaty IRA units and the provisional government had little choice but to allow evacuated barracks to be taken over by them. There was also a steady increase in lawlessness as armed groups conducted raids and settled private scores. When senior IRA officers met on 10 January, they condemned the Dáil vote in favour of the treaty as a subversion of the republic and maintained that the IRA no longer owed allegiance to the Dáil. Richard Mulcahy, the new minister for defence, parried a demand for an army convention to reaffirm allegiance to the republic by postponing the request for two months.[30] He used this interval to establish a pro-treaty National army, an effort assisted by British funding and equipment.[31] When the two-month moratorium expired, Mulcahy was secure enough to prohibit the convention.

Flouting the government ban, the now illegal army convention met in the Mansion House on 26 March and 9 April. At a press conference on 22 March, Rory O'Connor made the menacing comment that armies had overthrown governments in many countries. When asked if he proposed a military dictatorship, he replied infamously: 'you can take it that way if you like'.[32] The convention was attended by 220 delegates who represented 52 of the IRA's 73 brigades. On 9 April the authority of the Dáil was revoked in favour of an elected sixteen-member executive which oversaw the IRA, or at least those units prepared to submit to its authority.[33] Liam Lynch was elected chief of staff. Ironically, Brugha, who had written to the press that the convention was justified in meeting, was not allowed to address the gathering. The military men wanted no truck with politicians.[34] This prompted Seán T. O'Kelly to remark to a friend in Rome: 'They did not think even Brugha or Boland good enough fighting men to join them'.[35] Brugha did, however, oppose a resolution that aimed to prevent an election on the treaty which was defeated. The convention exposed the limits of Brugha's influence, or that of other political figures, on the IRA executive. Civilian control of the army, on which Brugha and de Valera had insisted during the War of Independence, had been decisively cast aside.

Less than a week after the convention, on the night of 13 April, anti-treaty members of Dublin No. 1 Brigade IRA occupied the Four Courts, the centre of the Irish judiciary, which was designated as the headquarters of the IRA executive. The seizure of the Four Courts was a clear retracing of the actions of the rebels of 1916. It was also a blatant challenge to the authority of the provisional government. As a statement by the Catholic hierarchy on 26 April expressed it, the treaty was a national question that could only be settled by the national will. In that context, the occupation of the Four Courts amounted to 'military despotism' and 'an immoral usurpation and confiscation of the people's rights'.[36] The occupation greatly alarmed the British government but a hard-line response, demanded by Churchill, was resisted in favour of efforts to find common ground. The capture of the Four Courts did not precipitate the start of the civil war and two months elapsed before hostilities began.

Under the shadow of looming civil war, Laurence O'Neill, the lord mayor of Dublin, and Archbishop Edward Byrne of Dublin attempted to broker an

15 Brugha outside the Mansion House in April 1922 during failed negotiations between pro- and anti-treaty TDs organized by Archbishop Edward Byrne of Dublin and Lord Mayor Laurence O'Neill.

agreement between pro- and anti-treaty sides. Between 19 and 29 April negotiations took place in the Mansion House that involved Collins, Griffith, de Valera and Brugha (see plate 15). William O'Brien, Thomas Johnson and Cathal O'Shannon also attended for the Labour Party which, despite its official neutrality, was in practice pro-treaty.[37] From the outset, the atmosphere was unfavourable. Brugha provided an egregious example of the absence of trust when on 26 April he accused Griffith and Collins of being British agents. He withdrew the remark at the behest of the archbishop but claimed that those who did the work of the British government were British agents.[38] When Collins then asked if he and Griffith were ministers whose blood was to be waded through in defence of the republic, Brugha calmly replied that they were. The bitterness was such that the two sides had to occupy separate rooms.[39] De Valera adopted a more balanced tone but his room for manoeuvre was circumscribed by the intransigence of Brugha. Unsurprisingly, the Mansion House conference ended in failure.[40]

Efforts to find common ground and avoid armed conflict continued. In early May a peace committee, comprising pro- and anti-treaty TDs was established in the Dáil, and this committee held sixteen meetings. The idea of presenting a joint 'national panel' to the electorate was floated but agreement could not be reached. On 17 May a dejected Brugha complained bitterly that he 'was absolutely sick of politics … It was completely against my will that I ever entered into public life'.[41] On the same day he proposed a free vote, based on an updated electoral register, on the issue of the treaty. When this was predictably rejected, he focused on partition and the plight of northern nationalists as 'a basis of unity between the two sides here in the Dáil'.[42] The birth of Northern Ireland was accompanied by intense communal violence and widespread civic disorder, the worst of the twentieth century until the modern Troubles. Beginning in July 1920 and persisting until June 1922, it claimed hundreds of lives.[43] Belfast was the epicentre of the sectarian violence, where the nationalist community comprised a tiny minority. Brugha wanted both sides in the Dáil to unite 'in defence of our people in the north' and revealed that during the Mansion House conference the previous month he had suggested to Collins that they 'should retire from public life and go to the north of Ireland on a defence crusade in favour of our people there'. Collins did not accept the offer which Brugha renewed in the Dáil.[44] J.J. O'Kelly recalled 'a very animated scene', but no one was willing to stand with Brugha.[45] This sincere but unrealistic suggestion was motivated by Brugha's intense desire to avoid the abhorrent prospect of civil war. He told the Dáil that he would

> prefer to die by an English bullet or an Orange bullet rather than by a bullet fired by one of the men with whom we have been fighting together during the last six years … I am never going to fire a bullet at any of those men and I hope that I am not going to die by a bullet from any of them.[46]

A final effort to prevent an open political division came on 20 May when Collins and de Valera agreed a controversial and undemocratic election pact that was approved by the Dáil and a reconvened Sinn Féin ard fheis. Essentially, the election would be uncontested. A national coalition panel comprising pro- and anti-treaty TDs, on the basis of their existing strength in the Dáil, would be rubberstamped by the electorate and after the election an executive would comprise the president, the minister for defence, and five pro- and four anti-treaty members.[47] Brugha let his name go forward on the national coalition panel for the five-seat Waterford-Tipperary East constituency.[48] Notably, the pact also allowed third-party candidates – the Labour Party, farmers' representatives and independents – to run against the

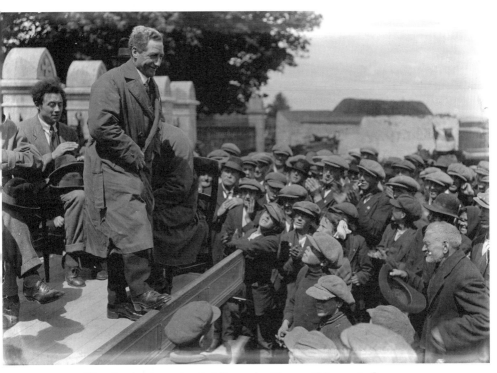

16 Brugha electioneering in Mooncoin, County Kilkenny in June 1922.

Sinn Féin panel. By and large, they were pro-treaty and came under pressure
to withdraw from the election in some constituencies. In Waterford-Tipperary
East the abduction of Godfrey Greene, a farmers' candidate, convinced him
not to contest the election.[49] Crucially, the feasibility of the pact depended on
British acceptance of the draft constitution. As Brugha had predicted, this was
not forthcoming. Regarding the draft as a radical revision of the treaty, the
British compelled Collins to retain the oath of allegiance and the office of
governor-general; both were unacceptable to de Valera. The constitution was
published on 16 June, the day of the election, by which time Collins had all
but repudiated the pact, telling voters in Cork two days before polling to vote
for whom they thought the best candidate.

In the days before the election, Brugha campaigned extensively, alongside
de Valera, Boland and others, throughout Waterford, south Kilkenny and
south Tipperary. They spoke to large crowds in Lismore, Cappoquin and
Dungarvan. In Waterford city, the Mall was so thronged that the speakers
addressed the meeting from the windows of the town hall. Brugha once again
repeated his claim that he was an unwilling participant in public life and had
contemplated not participating in the election. His main focus was on

partition and the fate of Catholics in Northern Ireland. In temperate language, Brugha explained that although he continued to disagree with 'friends on the opposite side [who] said that this Treaty was a step towards a Republic', he did not 'say that they were absolutely wrong'.[50] On 13 June Brugha addressed supporters in the south Kilkenny village of Mooncoin (see plate 16) after which further meetings were held in Carrick-on-Suir and in Clonmel, where Brugha spoke entirely in Irish.

The result of the election was a shattering blow to republicans, none of whom headed the poll. Over half of their candidates were defeated and well-known figures such as Childers in Kildare-Wicklow and Liam Mellows in Galway lost their seats. In Clare, where only the agreed national coalition panel candidates were nominated, de Valera came second. Brugha retained his seat in Waterford-Tipperary East, elected on the fourth count with 5,310 votes (15.5 per cent). He came third behind Vincent White, who topped the poll for pro-treaty Sinn Féin with 6,778 (19.89 per cent), and the Labour Party's John Butler who came second with 6,288 (18.45 per cent). Dan Breen, the celebrated IRA figure who unusually featured on both panel lists, was not returned.[51] J.J. O'Kelly recounted how he, Brugha and de Valera had an informal meeting after the election to reflect on the outcome. Although Brugha complained of pain in his foot, he was in a very 'buoyant' and 'hopeful' mood because there was 'no visible evidence of the imminent civil war'.[52]

Political affairs were quickly overtaken by military developments. On 18 June, before the results of the election were announced, a further army convention was held. A motion by Tom Barry to resume the war against Britain if all British forces were not withdrawn within seventy-two hours was opposed by Brugha and Liam Lynch and was only narrowly defeated. The convention broke up in confusion and division. One faction favoured an immediate attack on the residual British forces in Ireland. Another, led by Brugha and Lynch, favoured further discussion with the government. In London, Sir Henry Wilson, a retired British field marshal, former chief of the imperial general staff, adviser to the Northern Ireland government and Ulster Unionist MP for North Down, was assassinated on 22 June by two members of the IRA, both First World War veterans.[53] Placing the blame on those in occupation of the Four Courts, the British government demanded that the provisional government take action or threatened to do so itself. This forced a reluctant Collins to act. The kidnapping of J.J. 'Ginger' O'Connell, the National army assistant chief of staff, provided a pretext. At 4 a.m. on 28 June 1922 the Four Courts was shelled with two eighteen pounder guns borrowed from the British army. The long-anticipated Irish civil war had begun and Brugha's worst fears had come to pass.

Later that morning Brugha met Stack, de Valera and others in the Cumann na Poblachta office on Suffolk Street. De Valera suggested a last-ditch peace initiative by Archbishop Byrne, Lawrence O'Neill and Cathal O'Shannon, the labour leader, but this was rebuffed by the government.[54] Robert Brennan, who had served as first secretary of the Dáil department of foreign affairs until January 1922 and was anti-treaty, was present and recalled Brugha's belief that the situation had changed decisively. 'It's no use', he said to de Valera, 'these fellows have gone over to the British. We're going to fight back'. As Brugha started for the door, de Valera called out: 'Don't go Cathal'. Brugha returned within minutes to announce that 'he was joining up'.[55] De Valera issued a short statement that placed the blame on the British for scuppering the pact: 'at the bidding of the English, Irishmen are today shooting down on the streets of our capital brother Irishmen'.[56] On this basis, Brugha, de Valera, Stack, Barton and Markievicz gave their public support to the IRA executive. Early on 29 June Brugha sought spiritual guidance from a trusted priest and observed the Holy Hour adoration of the Eucharist, a devotional practice he frequently undertook, especially at times of anxiety. He bid farewell to his wife and six children. Nessa, the youngest, was just three months old and Nollaig the eldest was nine. According to O'Kelly, his departing words in Irish bleakly reflected how: 'I turned out in 1916, my heart throbbing with delight at the prospect of striking at the enemy we all knew; I go forth now scarcely knowing whereto I go'.[57] That night Brugha attended a meeting in the home of Dr Conn Murphy in Rathgar where arrangements were made for the mobilization of anti-treaty forces the following day.[58] Brugha favoured guerrilla warfare.

The headquarters of Dublin No. 1 Brigade IRA in Barry's Hotel on Gardiner Row was not well located to relieve the besieged garrison in the Four Courts. It also had insufficient accommodation, which reveals how unprepared the brigade was for civil war. This issue was solved when Oscar Traynor, the brigade commandant, commandeered the Hammam, Gresham and Granville Hotels along with adjoining buildings on the east side of O'Connell Street, such as the Dublin United Tramway Company offices, on 29 June – effectively the entire block between Earl Street and Parnell Street. Two buildings on the west side of O'Connell Street were also occupied. Liaison between the Four Courts and O'Connell Street was provided by Máire Comerford of Cumann na mBan.[59] Brugha, de Valera, Barton and Stack re-joined the IRA as privates and reported to Traynor. Seán T. O'Kelly was there before them armed with an umbrella.[60] Ten members of the Dáil (many future members of the Fianna Fáil front bench) were present along with doctors, nurses and four priests, who appeared to be inspired by patriotic motives as much as those of a religious nature. The garrison comprised seventy men and thirty women. Traynor promoted Brugha to staff commandant in charge of the O'Connell Street block. The interconnecting walls of the four adjacent hotels were breached to allow movement between the buildings. The billiard room in the Hammam Hotel was designated as the garrison's hospital and the hotels were well stocked with food.[61] In her memoir, Máire Comerford recalled there were too many National army prisoners from captured posts near O'Connell Street in the Hammam. Brugha was 'worried about the safety of these harmless and puzzled men' and asked Comerford and Muriel MacSwiney to lead the prisoners from the rear of the hotel to re-join their own forces on 1 July.[62]

After two days the Four Courts garrison surrendered. The subsequent fire and explosion in the Public Records Office, part of the Four Courts complex, caused the irreparable loss of centuries of Irish historical archives.[63] The National army then focused its attention on O'Connell Street which had little prospect of being relieved by anti-treaty forces. Before the bombardment began, a remarkable but unsuccessful effort to broker peace was made by John F. Homan, a primary school teacher and volunteer ambulance driver with St John Ambulance Brigade, who engaged with Collins and de Valera.[64] A sustained attack by the National army on 3 July forced most of the garrison to evacuate. De Valera, Stack, Traynor and others were smuggled out and taken across the city to Mount Street. This reduced the number under Brugha's command to seventeen men and three members of Cumann na mBan: Linda Kearns, Muriel MacSwiney and Kathleen Barry, older sister of Kevin Barry.[65] Their plan was to hold the position for as long as possible and then surrender without loss of life.[66] Barry recalled that the women were almost driven to mutiny in their determination to stay. 'I had to dodge Cathal all the time', she wrote, 'he approved of me making tea and Bovril, but not of me filling sandbags in my leisure moments'.[67] Brugha subsequently admitted to her that he would not have managed without the assistance of Cumann na mBan. Other women undertook dangerous dispatch duties. Comerford was sent to Suffolk Street where she met Caitlín Brugha and told her what she knew of the situation.[68]

Several members of the garrison commented on Brugha's demeanour. Writing on 7 July 1922, Robert Barton recounted how Brugha

> wandered all over the place, mostly on the roofs from Hammam to Gresham, armed with a Mauser automatic, with rifle-stock fitted. He seemed ubiquitous. I met him on the roof … and a few minutes later in the rear of the Granville, always cool and collected, with a rare occasional smile, all the more valued for its rarity.[69]

Barton also noted Brugha's concern for others and how he took practically no rest, something also remarked on by Comerford. John O'Sheehan, who remained in the Hammam until 4 July, recalled there 'was nothing frantic, frenzied or worried about Cathal Brugha … He was by no means an emotional type, but very, very determined'.[70] These accounts depict a man who, despite his abhorrence of civil war, had in the defence of the republic found an inner peace, was certain of purpose and reconciled to accept whatever outcome might unfold.

At approximately 10 p.m. on 3 July, Emmet Dalton, who commanded the National army forces, reported that 'the enemy is hemmed into the Gresham and Hammond [sic] Hotels on the east side of O'Connell Street' and that a message had been sent to Brugha that an attack would be launched if he did not surrender. Brugha's reply in Irish was received two hours later and read: 'Not dammed likely'.[71] Throughout Wednesday 4 July, artillery was used to dislodge the anti-treaty forces in O'Connell Street. A journalist who witnessed the assault recounted how

> the Hammam Hotel was shelled by an 18-pounder gun … The force of the explosion seemed to smash every window in Henry St[reet], and for one terrible moment, I thought that the street had crashed down about my ears. When the first shell cut its way through the walls, two armoured cars darted across the thoroughfare and, pulling up on the kerb outside the Hamman, proceeded to pound away with four Lewis machine-guns through the breech. There was no reply from the garrison, which seemed incapable of doing anything in face of this deadly bombardment. Time and time again the 18 pounder threw its shells into the building, and after each one the process was repeated of pouring machine-gun fire into the breaches from the armoured cars. Up to midnight this deadly attack was continued, and all over the city the chorus of death was taken up by hundreds of riflemen.[72]

According to Calton Younger, twenty-five shells were fired and caused enormous damage (see plate 17). Brugha was concerned for the safety of the Dublin Fire Brigade who were endangered by mines. He placed a white flag on the roof to allow an emissary to deliver a message to the National army. This caused confusion as the messenger should have carried the flag but, nonetheless, it was 'an action of extraordinary thoughtfulness in a moment of awe-inspiring crisis'.[73]

By the morning of 5 July much of the O'Connell Street block was engulfed in flames, forcing the small garrison from the Gresham and Hammam Hotels

17 Assault on the republican position in the Hammam Hotel, Upper O'Connell Street, July 1922.

into the Granville Hotel. Brugha received an order from Traynor to quit the building but had no intention of complying.[74] As defeat and surrender became increasingly likely, Kathleen Barry observed how Brugha, in a pensive mood during a quiet interlude in the fighting, walked up and down in touch with his own inner thoughts. 'On his face', she later wrote, 'a look that made me wonder … only afterwards I realised that we had been privileged to watch a man making up his mind to immolate himself'.[75] John Homan vividly described how Brugha's 'resolve was clearly imprinted on his face – a resolve not to leave that house alive if he could find death without committing suicide. It was not merely that he was *willing* to give up his life, he was *determined* to give it up – *to get away from it*'.[76] Likewise, Linda Kearns was certain that Brugha did not intend to surrender. Before the end, surrounded by fire and in the midst of collapsing masonry, she asked him if he was 'acting wisely in going to his death' as there had already been too many unnecessary deaths. Having considered the question, Brugha replied: 'Civil War is so serious that my death may bring its seriousness home to the Irish people. I feel that if it put a stop to the Civil War, it would be a death worthwhile'.[77] So profound a discussion in such surreal circumstances was for Kearns 'the most poignant moment of my life'.[78] Strikingly, in an opinion piece immediately after Brugha's death Stephen

18 The remnants of the Granville Hotel, Upper O'Connell Street, July 1922.

Gwynn, the writer, soldier and former IPP MP, suggested 'the war may die with him, and it is scarcely likely that he would have desired it to outlast his life'.[79]

As flames encircled them on three sides, Brugha and his small contingent were forced to retreat to a yard at the rear of the Granville (see plate 18). Their position no longer tenable, he ordered them to surrender and they entered Thomas's Lane with a white flag.[80] With Brugha's permission, Kearns and Dr J.P. Brennan remained behind with him. Moments later, Brugha, 'the embodiment of the assailed Republic', stepped out into the laneway which was crowded with National army soldiers and members of the fire brigade.[81] There are varying accounts of what happened. Kearns described how he had 'a revolver in each hand and he kept on shouting "no surrender"'.[82] Brugha was struck by a single bullet in the left thigh which ruptured his femoral artery. A Red Cross volunteer stated that when he did not obey a command to halt a 'volley of shots rang out, and Mr Brugha fell, blood spurting from his wound, and his weapons fell from his grasp. He made a desperate effort to rise but fell back again.'[83] Most witness accounts clearly state that Brugha did not fire a shot. By choosing death over surrender he fulfilled the advice of his friend

Éamonn Ceannt after the 1916 Rising to fight to a finish.[84] Brugha fell just as
he had predicted in his speech on the treaty, an extract from which Caitlín
later found in his pocket:

> if our last man was lying wounded on the ground, and his English
> enemies howling round him with their bayonets raised ready to plunge
> them into his body, and if they asked him, 'Now will you come into our
> Empire?' – true to the tradition that has been handed down to him, his
> answer would be – 'No I will not'.[85]

It was a final gesture of an unwavering fidelity to the Irish republic.

A gravely wounded Brugha was tended to by Linda Kearns and Seán
Brady until medical assistance arrived. Brady recalled that he briefly opened
his eyes to enquire if the others were safe. Assured that they were, he smiled
and closed his eyes again.[86] Brugha was taken by ambulance to the nearby
Mater Hospital with Kearns, a nurse, keeping her fingers on his severed artery
to stem the loss of blood.[87] She later criticized the lack of prompt attention
provided as an hour elapsed before Brugha was taken into theatre.[88] At the
inquest into Brugha's death, Dr Cotter, house surgeon at the Mater, deposed
that Brugha had been admitted at 8.30 p.m. with an entrance wound in the
upper thigh, a large gaping exit wound and a compound fracture of the left
femur. He was 'severely shocked, blanched and his pulse was barely
perceptible'. At 9.30 p.m. an operation was performed by Mr Smith to stop
the bleeding, suture the severed sciatic nerve and set the fracture. Cotter stated
that Brugha's condition was relatively good after the operation until noon on
6 July after which he gradually sank.[89] Unaware of the seriousness of Brugha's
wounds, de Valera wrote to him with a mild rebuke:

> had you gone down and been lost to us the cause would have suffered a
> blow from which it would have hardly recovered. You were scarcely
> justified therefore in taking the risk you ran – and we were all more
> than vexed with you – but all's well that ends well.[90]

Caitlín arrived at the hospital at 6 a.m. on 6 July and remained with her
husband, occasionally conversing with him in Irish, until his death. His
brother and sister, a priest, one of the nursing sisters, and Mrs Lalor, the wife
of his business partner, were also present.[91] Brugha received the last rites from
Father Ryan, a Dominican priest attached to St Saviour's parish in Dorset
Street, that night. Before his death, he was reportedly 'perfectly conscious,
happy and determined, but entertained no bitterness'.[92] Cathal Brugha died at

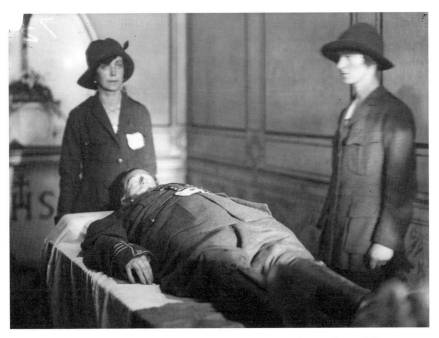

19 Cathal Brugha lying in state in the Mater Hospital with members of Cumann na mBan providing a guard of honour, July 1922.

10.45 a.m. on 7 July, eleven days before his forty-eighth birthday. At an inquest later that day, Dr Louis Byrne, city coroner, recorded that he died from shock and haemorrhage caused by a bullet fired by a person unknown.[93]

Brugha was the first high profile fatality of the civil war. His death did not shorten the conflict as he had wished. After the anti-treaty IRA was defeated in Dublin, the National army drove them from towns and cities. The conventional phase lasted about two months after which there was a reversion to guerrilla warfare until a ceasefire was called on 24 April 1923. The republican cause lacked public support and was further demoralized by the government's ruthless prosecution of the war, including the use of executions and reprisals. The division over the treaty subsequently dominated Irish politics for almost a century.

As preparations were being made for Brugha's funeral, Caitlín issued a statement to the press requesting that apart from family relations the chief mourners and the guard of honour 'should only include the women of the republican movement'. She made the request to protest against 'the immediate and terrible civil war made by the so-called Provisional Government on the Irish Republican Forces'.[94] Furthermore, she did not wish to see the presence

20 The family at Brugha's graveside in Glasnevin cemetery, 10 July 1922.

of any representatives or officials of the Free State at the funeral. Brugha's remains reposed in the mortuary chapel of the Mater Hospital on Saturday and Sunday, 9 and 10 July. The body was covered by a tricolour and members of Cumann na mBan stood guard as large numbers of people paid their respects (see plate 19). On Sunday afternoon, the remains were removed to the nearby St Joseph's Church, Berkeley Road, where Canon Daniel Downing, the parish priest, had a reputation for never refusing the services of his church on political grounds. After the funeral, Downing wrote to Seán T. O'Kelly that it 'will always be a comforting memory that it was given to me to honour so noble a character, so devout a Catholic and so superlatively brave a man as Cathal Brugha'.[95] The funeral took place the following morning followed by interment in the republican plot in Glasnevin cemetery (see plate 20). A large crowd and between ninety and one hundred priests from city parishes attended.[96] The cortège, which took fifteen minutes to pass a given point, diverted to O'Connell Street and stopped beside the ruins of the Granville Hotel, where the rosary, which Brugha had prayed daily, was recited.[97] As requested by Mrs Brugha, no government representative was in attendance and the police kept a low profile. Members of Cumann na mBan, such as Grace Gifford-Plunkett, distributed leaflets requesting anyone who repudiated Brugha's anti-treaty republicanism to leave the obsequies.[98] It appears that many treaty supporters, who had attended out of a sense of respect, honoured that wish. De Valera did not attend as he had sought safety in Munster but Boland, Stack and Traynor were present. Liam Mellows, who had been imprisoned in Mountjoy Prison following the surrender of the Four Courts garrison, applied to the provisional government for permission to attend the funeral along with six of his imprisoned comrades. This request was denied with 'regret'.[99] One newspaper reported that the 'silence which prevailed during the procession through the city and the service at the graveside was broken intermittently by the crack of an irregular sniper's rifle in the distance'.[100]

Tributes were paid to Brugha by friends, former friends and foes alike. Almost all of them admired his sincerity of purpose and courage. De Valera, the political figure who was closest to Brugha, noted in his diary: 'Our lion heart is gone' and later wrote that 'we are all robbed of the one man who could have made victory possible ... Oh cruel, cruel that it is by Irish men he should be killed'.[101] Stack, who knew Brugha for more than twenty years, wrote to Caitlín of his anguish and sense of disbelief.[102] Boland reverently described Brugha as 'easily the greatest man of his day; what a wonderful fight he made, with his 15 men against an army. May God rest his soul and give his comrades the courage of Cathal to fight till the fight is won'.[103] Collins praised his patriotism:

> Because of his sincerity I would forgive him anything. At worst he was a fanatic – though in what had been a noble cause. At best I remember him amongst the very few who gave their all that this country should have its freedom. When many of us are forgotten Cathal Brugha will be remembered.[104]

Within weeks of Brugha's funeral, both Boland and Collins were killed in the civil war and Griffith died of natural causes. Boland's dying words to his mother and sister were: 'I am going to Cathal Brugha ... I want to be buried in the grave with Cathal Brugha'.[105] Even the unionist *Irish Times* noted Brugha's final 'magnificent gesture of tragic defiance'.[106] A month after her husband's death, Caitlín Brugha wrote to Edmund Downey, the strongly republican editor of the *Waterford News*. Thanking him for his sympathy, she described Cathal's death as 'the deepest sorrow God could have given me' but she was consoled that 'he died for Ireland' and prayed that God would send 'that freedom for which he died and may his example keep our people from selling our beloved country into slavery'.[107] The result of the June 1922 general election suggested otherwise. It made clear that the Irish public was not going to stand by the republic. But for Brugha that cause was sacrosanct, a holy mission for which he was willing to make the ultimate sacrifice.

CHAPTER 8

After Cathal

THE DRAMATIC NATURE OF Brugha's last stand and death should not obscure the personal tragedy visited on his wife and six children who also made great sacrifices for an Irish republic. They endured his frequent absences from home, they experienced terrifying raids by the Crown forces, and they lived with the constant fear of his arrest or death until that became a bleak reality in July 1922. Caitlín Brugha (see plate 21) was as committed to the Irish republic as her late husband but after his death she moved from background to foreground for a period. During the civil war, she assisted the anti-treaty cause in whatever manner she could. For instance, her house in Rathmines was used for receiving arms and ammunition. As Mary McAuliffe points out, republican widows had power and a symbolic status that some chose to use in the political arena.[1] Caitlín did so in two ways. First, as a republican speaker and fundraiser and, second, by succeeding her late husband as a TD (see plate 22).

In September 1922 Caitlín travelled to Glasgow with two of her children on her first fundraising tour. The partisan Scottish edition of *Poblacht na hÉireann* gave extensive coverage of how the railway station in Glasgow was 'thronged' in anticipation of the arrival of 'the widow of Ireland's greatest Republican'.[2] The visit was not reported in other newspapers, however. Caitlín addressed a number of meetings. She told one gathering in the newly named Cathal Brugha Hall in Govan that her 'one consolation' was that her husband had 'died for the Irish Republic as a soldier, the death he wished for above all others', before appealing for funds to assist 'the battle for the Irish Republic'.[3] Even before Brugha died, the parallels between his defiance in 1916 and in 1922 provided an inexhaustible source for republican propaganda purposes. On 6 July *Poblacht na hÉireann* wrote:

> Just as he fell in Easter Week, riddled with wounds but unsubdued, fighting for a Republic born in blood and fire, so six years later he falls again unsubdued, in defence of the Republic he helped to erect on foundations as strong as his own dauntless spirit.[4]

Caitlín consciously cultivated this depiction of Brugha. On 6 December 1922 she joined Art O'Brien, the anti-treaty former London envoy of Dáil Éireann,

21 Caitlín Brugha, c.1923.

at an Irish Self-Determination League meeting in London to denounce the treaty.[5] It was her first visit to that city since 1918 when she had joined Cathal there. In January 1923 she returned to Glasgow with Dr Kathleen Lynn to address republican meetings. Cumann na mBan members in Glasgow were

22 Cathal Brugha, *c.* 1922.

involved in smuggling munitions directly to Ireland and Caitlín was believed
to have covered some of their travel expenses.[6] Writing from Glasgow, she
reported that 'the movement is on a turning point here' and added that 'things
are going splendidly in Ireland'.[7] Although the republican military campaign
was disintegrating from early in 1923, the result of the general election in
August, in which Sinn Féin performed much better than had been expected,
subsequently justified Caitlín's optimism.[8] On 21 January 1923 she was invited
to attend a demonstration to commemorate the independence of Dáil Éireann
in Beswick, Manchester with Kate O'Callaghan, widow of the mayor of

Limerick, Mary MacSwiney, Maude Gonne MacBride, and Seán O'Mahony, the anti-treaty TD for Fermanagh-Tyrone. In the event, she was unable to be present.[9] On the first anniversary of Brugha's death, a Mass was offered in the Carmelite church on Whitefriar Street in Dublin after which a procession marched to his grave in Glasnevin. Prayers were recited on O'Connell Street when the procession passed the spot where Brugha fell fatally wounded.[10] This was repeated in July 1924 when it was more extensively attended. On O'Connell Street, Seán T. O'Kelly gave an address from a platform erected opposite the ruins of the Hammam Hotel and Caitlín and her children were warmly welcomed by the crowd.[11]

In the August 1923 general election, Caitlín stood for the republican side in the revised four-seat Waterford constituency. Addressing an election meeting in Waterford on 9 August, de Valera pronounced Cathal Brugha 'the very soul of Ireland's resistance to England since 1916' and called on voters to select his widow as his successor. He described her as 'the faithful companion and confidante of Cathal in his work, the partner in his sacrifice, [who] can be no less true than he was'.[12] At a meeting in Dungarvan, Caitlín revealed it was with 'mixed feelings' that she had agreed to contest the election but 'her greatest feeling was one of pride that she had been chosen to follow in Cathal's footsteps'.[13] On the eve of the election there was little doubt, according to the *Waterford News*, that 'Mrs Brugha will be triumphant'.[14] And so it proved as she topped the poll. Caitlín was elected on the first count with 8,263 first preference votes (25.38 per cent), ahead of Captain William Redmond, who ran as an independent, in second place, John Butler for Labour in third, and Nicholas Wall for the Farmers' Party taking the final seat.[15] She was one of five women elected to the fourth Dáil. Four republicans were returned – Caitlín, Constance Markievicz, Mary MacSwiney and Kathleen Lynn – and Margaret Collins-O'Driscoll was elected for the pro-treaty Cumann na nGaedheal. In accordance with Sinn Féin's abstentionist policy, republican TDs refused to take their seats in protest at the oath of allegiance.[16] Female republican TDs faced particular hostility and derision. For instance, W.T. Cosgrave, president of the executive council, suggested that they would be better off saying the rosary or staying 'at home with knitting needles'.[17]

From 1922 Caitlín was particularly active in calling for the release of republican prisoners and drawing public attention to the privations suffered by their families.[18] She was a strong supporter of the Irish Prisoners' Dependents Fund and in March 1928 Cathal Brugha's bicycle was offered as the prize in a draw to raise money for the fund.[19] Caitlín acted as honorary secretary of the Sinn Féin re-organizing committee ahead of its ard fheis in October 1923 and subsequently served on the party's executive as honorary treasurer.[20] She refused to forsake Sinn Féin when de Valera established the Fianna Fáil party in 1926. Much like her husband, she held steadfast to her republican principles for the rest of her life. Sinn Féin went into sharp decline thereafter and only 200 delegates attended the October 1926 ard fheis. A reluctant Caitlín was prevailed on to serve as secretary on the party executive.[21] She was re-elected as a Sinn Féin TD to the short-lived fifth Dáil between June and August 1927, taking the fourth and last seat in the Waterford constituency. She was one of just five Sinn Féin TDs elected. Due to a lack of funds the party did not contest the September 1927 general election; this marked the end of Caitlín's political career. Unlike Oscar Traynor, for example, she did not belatedly join Fianna Fáil. In 1934 she resigned from Sinn Féin in protest at what she considered an unfair attack at the ard fheis on Mary MacSwiney, who had resigned the previous year. Caitlín opposed the continuation of Michael O'Flanagan (excluded from ecclesiastical office since the mid-1920s) as president of Sinn Féin because he had accepted a commission from the Fianna Fáil government to write Irish-language county histories for use in schools.[22] She welcomed his expulsion from Sinn Féin in January 1936 for participating in a re-enactment of the opening of the first Dáil on state-run radio: 'He is finished with Sinn Féin and it is none too soon'.[23] Both Caitlín and MacSwiney shared concerns about the drift of republicanism towards the left and the emergence of pro-communist voices.[24] Caitlín hoped that Sinn Féin would, in time, return to 'its former proud position' and retained an active interest in politics throughout her life.[25]

Although determined to protect her husband's legacy, a greater priority for Caitlín was safeguarding her family. According to one of her daughters, she considered emigrating to the United States to provide better opportunities for her children and to remove them from the bitterly divided political environment in Ireland and constant reminders of their personal tragedy. That Cathal Brugha would have wanted his children to grow up in Ireland ultimately convinced her to remain.[26] The family's financial position which had been comfortable was now uncertain. Brugha died intestate and left a total estate valued at £252, which included shares in Lalor Ltd and an insurance policy for £100.[27] Brugha never accepted payment for the services he rendered during the course of the first and second Dáil. As a matter of principle, Caitlín refused financial support from the Irish Free State government. Lalor's paid her a weekly allowance. Displaying independence, determination and business acumen, she established her own company with the financial assistance of her brother, Charles P. Kingston, a former secretary of Offaly County Council. As discussed in chapter 1, Caitlín grew up in a family business in Birr and assisted her mother to manage it following her father's death in 1904. Initially, Caitlín

23 Kingston's men's outfitters, O'Connell Street, c.1960s.

opened a shop on Nassau Street selling Irish leather goods along with other items. In 1924 this business was superseded by the establishment of Kingston's Ltd, a drapery business located in the Hammam Buildings, Upper O'Connell Street, on the site formerly occupied by the Hammam Hotel (see plate 23).

Charles was a director and Caitlín's partner in the company.[28] It soon developed a reputation as one of the leading menswear shops in Dublin. Its sales slogan, 'A Kingston shirt makes all the difference', became well known, not only in Dublin, but nationwide, while another advertising catchphrase emphasized that 'Kingston quality is the last word'.[29]

Fianna Fáil brought its own stringent narrative of the revolution when it came to power in 1932. During the reconstruction of Upper O'Connell Street following the civil war, a new street was created between O'Connell Street and Gloucester Street. Popularly, it became known as Cathal Brugha Street in the 1920s and this was given legal effect in August 1932.[30] In the same year, Gloucester Street was renamed Seán MacDermott Street. The shared geography of Cathal Brugha and Seán MacDermott Streets was a fitting tribute to their shared republicanism. Just as Cumann na nGaedheal commissioned busts of its political and revolutionary heroes, such as Collins and Griffith, during the 1920s, de Valera speedily followed suit by appropriating Brugha and Austin Stack to emphasize the republican credentials of the new government. Caitlín was outraged at the way her husband's memory was being applied and refused to loan his death mask for the making of a bust, just as she had refused pro-treatyites permission to attend her husband's funeral in 1922.[31] Undeterred, de Valera renamed the headquarters of the National Health Insurance at 9–10 Upper O'Connell Street after Brugha. A plaque containing an image of Brugha was to be erected on the building and unveiled by de Valera. The plaster cast of the plaque was stolen from a Dublin foundry before it was cast in bronze. It was widely believed at the time that Seán Russell, then IRA quartermaster-general and a friend of Caitlín, had stolen the plaque. In 1950 it was discovered hidden in the home of Úna Stack, widow of Austin Stack, following her death.[32] The National Health Insurance headquarters was duly renamed 'Áras Brugha', despite objections from Caitlín. When she wrote to the organizing committee to protest against the use of Cathal Brugha's name for political purposes, she was told 'it was impossible for them to retrace their steps'.[33] The commission for the bust of Brugha was later accepted by Oliver Sheppard, the renowned Tyrone-born sculptor, who agreed to base his model on photographic sources.[34] When it was announced in January 1939 that the bust would be displayed in Leinster House, Caitlín emphatically rejected what she considered an 'insult' to her husband's memory. In a letter to the press, she considered it

> a piece of gross impertinence … for men who have abandoned the ideals for which Cathal Brugha died to attempt to shelter themselves in the reflected glory of one who died for the Republic. I write this

letter in the hope that a sense of decency, if any such remains in these men, will prevent them from inflicting this gratuitous pain on the children and widow of Cathal Brugha.[35]

Sheppard's clay model was completed in May 1939 but due to the outbreak of the Second World War could not be sent to Brussels for casting in bronze. It was eventually cast in 1948 and five years later was put on display in the National Gallery of Ireland, a less contentious venue.[36] Caitlín privately commissioned the sculptor Albert Power to execute a bust of her late husband and allowed his death mask to be used. Unsurprisingly, it was regarded as a more life-like representation of Brugha.[37] In May 1952 the Fianna Fáil government renamed Portobello Barracks in Rathmines in memory of Cathal Brugha.[38]

Caitlín's role as a mother, public representative and businesswoman was supported by the assistance of her sister Máire, who had lived in the Brugha household since 1912 and worked on a part-time basis in the Kingston outfitter's business. Fidelma Brugha described her aunt as 'adorable' and an extraordinary help to her mother. The Brugha children were raised in an Irish-speaking environment. Máire Kingston was also a member of the Gaelic League and was well known to many leading members of the Irish independence movement. She died in December 1939.[39] During Caitlín's final days before her own death on 1 December 1959 she told her son Ruairí of the challenges she faced in trying to run a business and raise six children without the support of a husband.[40] She was buried alongside Cathal in Glasnevin cemetery.[41]

Turning now briefly to the Brugha children, it was hardly surprising that their father's legacy influenced some of their endeavours. Of the six, only Ruairí and Nóinín became politically active. For most of his working life Ruairí was managing director of Kingston's. He joined the IRA in 1933 and was involved in republican activities.[42] In the early hours of 31 March 1935, he was one of 'five suspicious looking men ... on bicycles without lights' who were observed at Bushy Park Road, Terenure. They were intercepted by a Garda patrol car and Ruairí, then aged seventeen, and another were taken into custody; the others escaped. He possessed application forms for IRA membership and posters in connection with the sale of Easter lilies, the emblem of modern active republicanism and a method of raising funds for republican causes.[43] His mother insisted that 'the son of Cathal Brugha, was merely posting up bills about the unveiling of a memorial to Liam Lynch and advertising the distribution of Easter lilies'. In a letter to the *Irish Press*, she complained: 'So it is a crime to honour one of the greatest soldiers of the

Republic, a crime to commemorate as in other years the glorious sacrifice of Easter Week'.[44] On the outbreak of the Second World War, Ruairí, along with many known republicans, was listed for detention in the Curragh internment camp and went on the run. Following a year in hiding, he was arrested and interned in 1940. Given his lineage, he was regarded by his fellow internees in the Curragh as a man 'of some standing'.[45] However, due to ill health, he was released on parole to the Mater Hospital on 27 November 1941 and his sentence was later remitted.[46]

Around this time, Nóinín – the second eldest child of Cathal and Caitlín – had also come to the attention of the police, who suggested that she was 'of considerable assistance and importance to the IRA and that such activities … should be terminated by her internment'.[47] A recommendation to that effect was issued to a Garda assistant commissioner on 11 July 1941. That no action was taken suggests that the police and political authorities may have been mindful of the sensitivities of interning the daughter of Cathal Brugha. The application for Nóinín's internment was reactivated by the detective branch in Dublin Castle on 23 April 1942. Superintendent S. Gantly stated that Nóinín worked in Kingston's drapery shop and 'used her position there to receive and issue IRA dispatches'. Concerned about the apparent reluctance of those in higher authority to act on his previous recommendation, Gantly was adamant that no 'distinction should be made between Miss Brugha and other women who have been interned in consequence of their activities with the IRA'.[48] As minister for justice from 1939 to 1948, Gerald Boland, older brother of Harry Boland, implemented a hard-line security policy against the IRA. About twenty republican women were interned in Mountjoy following the outbreak of the Second World War.[49] On 30 April 1942 Boland ordered Nóinín's internment. On the same day gardaí conducted simultaneous raids on the Brugha home in Rathmines and Kingston's drapery shop on O'Connell Street.[50] Nóinín was detained at Kingston's and taken to Mountjoy. Nóinín's internment aroused some disquiet. William L. Kelleher, an architect and civil engineer in Cork who described himself as a friend of Cathal Brugha, appealed to Minister Boland: 'for the honour of her father, and your brother, Harry, … LET THE GIRL GO HOME'.[51] Nóinín was granted parole on 30 July and, following the extension of her parole period on a number of occasions, Boland ordered her release from custody on 27 November 1943.[52]

During the search of the Brugha home on the day of Nóinín's arrest, the police unexpectedly found and detained Günther Schutz, a German agent who used the alias Hans Marschner.[53] He was one of a number of German agents who had arrived secretly in Ireland between August 1939 and December 1943. His mission included relaying daily weather reports, observing British convoy movements, making the IRA more interested in British activities in Northern Ireland, especially in the Belfast shipyards, and engagement in economic sabotage. Schutz parachuted into County Wexford in March 1941 and was arrested within a day. However, in February 1942 he escaped from Mountjoy with the assistance of the IRA. At the time of his re-arrest in April, the police believed that he had spent two weeks in the Brugha home.[54] Caitlín was not interrogated by the police, but Boland discussed whether proceedings should be taken against her with Taoiseach Éamon de Valera on 8 May. It was decided that 'no action should be taken against Mrs Brugha'.[55] In her memoir, Máire MacSwiney Brugha suggested that her mother-in-law 'harboured' Schutz because no one else would take him in and added: 'I think, as usual, the Republican movement was using Mrs Brugha'.[56]

Following his release from detention and having grown disillusioned with the IRA, Ruairí became active in Clann na Poblachta, a new political party led by Seán MacBride. He unsuccessfully contested the Waterford constituency for the party in the 1948 general election. In 1962 he joined Fianna Fáil and was active in promoting North-South relations through business, cultural and political circles. In 1969 Ruairí was elected to the Seanad and in the 1973 general election he was elected Fianna Fáil TD for the Dublin South constituency. He served as front bench spokesman for posts and telegraphs and later for Northern Ireland. Ruairí lost his Dáil seat in 1977 but later that year was nominated to serve as a member of the European Parliament. He failed to retain that seat in the first direct European parliamentary elections in 1979. An unsuccessful attempt to win a seat in the Dublin South constituency in the November 1982 general election brought his political career to an end. Ruairí Brugha carved out his own political course but always remained true to his family's republican values. In 1945 he married Máire MacSwiney, the only child of Terence and Muriel MacSwiney. He died in 2006.[57]

As this study has shown, the governing thesis of Brugha's life was the pursuit of an Irish republic, a constant that was placed above family bonds and his deep-seated commitment to the Irish language. Like many of his generation, Brugha embraced the projection of a distinctive cultural identity and took inspiration from Thomas Davis's fundamental linkage of language and nationality. He remained president of the Keating branch of the Gaelic League until his death. Dedication to the Irish language was a facet of Brugha's embrace of advanced republicanism. The pivotal moment in that journey occurred in 1908 when he was sworn into the IRB, which was committed to achieving an independent republic by force of arms. Through it, he became immersed in the Irish Volunteers during the political convulsions occasioned by the third home rule crisis and the outbreak of the First World War. Although not a member of the IRB military council, which plotted a pre-emptive insurrection, Brugha was trusted by it and was close to some of its members, most notably Éamonn Ceannt, his commanding officer in the 4th Battalion, Dublin Brigade. For Brugha, belief in an Irish republic had to be translated into action. His valiant single-handed defence of his position in the South Dublin Union, despite being severely wounded, became one of the most celebrated acts of bravery and defiance of the 1916 Rising. Were it not for the proximity of the union's hospital facilities, Brugha's race would have been run in 1916 rather than in 1922 when he consciously followed Ceannt's earlier example of dying for Ireland.

There has been a tendency to reduce Brugha's contribution to the Irish Revolution to a three-act melodrama of soldierly acts of heroic defiance in 1916 and 1922, and furious *ad hominem* attacks on Collins and Griffith for betraying the republic by signing the Anglo-Irish treaty and accepting dominion status. Likewise, the memorialization of Brugha – the naming of the street where he was mortally wounded, the renaming of a military barracks in Rathmines, and even a 24p commemorative stamp featuring Brugha in his Irish Volunteer uniform issued in 1987 – has narrowed the portrayal of Brugha to that of the soldier alone. This was cultivated by Caitlín in the context of the Irish civil war. Writing to her shortly after Brugha's death, Joe McGarrity wrote: 'May Cathal's unbending spirit inspire his comrades and the youth of Ireland to carry on and finish the work he died to accomplish. His death will be avenged and his principles vindicated.'[58] The invocation of Brugha's unyielding commitment to the republic, his courage and ultimate sacrifice were readily exploited by republican propagandists during and after the civil war. His was a new name to beatify, to add to the list of venerated Fenian dead, to be used endlessly as political shrapnel to fire at the Irish government and the public in defence of the sacred cause of the republic and the actions of a minority. For example, one contemporaneous handbill stated: 'Brugha and Boland gave their lives for the old cause which will never die: they were in a minority: so also were Tone, Emmet and Pearse.'[59] It is doubtful that Brugha would have concurred with McGarrity or crude handbills. He was anguished by the prospect of civil war and despondent when it became a reality. Between January and June 1922, he had tried unsuccessfully and at times inconsistently to prevent the division over the treaty culminating in fratricidal strife. There is no reason to doubt the reliability of Linda Kearns who recalled that Brugha hoped that his death would be worthwhile if it put a stop to the civil war.

Viewing Brugha solely through the prism of his martial exploits presents two difficulties. First, it obscures the significance of his overall contribution to the Irish Revolution. Second, it sustains a stereotype of a dour, sour, uncompromising, antagonistic, ruthless zealot such as that portrayed in Neil Jordan's 1996 film, *Michael Collins*. Based on a wide trawl of the surviving archival evidence, this study offers a more rounded perspective of an individual whose contribution to the Irish Revolution was greater than is typically realized. Brugha was certainly a zealot and his pursuit of an Irish republic was uncompromising. With the prestige of being a 1916 veteran and in the absence of jailed or interned colleagues, he embraced both the military and political wings of separatism after the Rising. Brugha played a galvanizing role in reviving and consolidating the Irish Volunteers in 1917 and 1918. He was also centrally involved in the reinvention of Sinn Féin from being a marginal political party to the dominant force it became by 1918. He helped to weld disparate nationalist elements together under the Sinn Féin banner with its demands for an Irish republic and international recognition at the Versailles peace conference in 1919. He served on Sinn Féin's national executive until poor health forced him to resign. Through all of this, Brugha stoically defied the effects of his injuries and the constant pain that he endured. This contributed to his dour and irritable demeanour and masked an innate kindness and generosity that were noted by several contemporaries.

By his own admission, Brugha was a reluctant politician. Elected TD for Waterford in December 1918, the honours of acting as speaker at the opening of the first Dáil on 21 January 1919 and fulfilling the role of temporary president until April 1919 were bestowed on him. During the War of Independence Brugha was both a constitutionalist and a militant. The authority and legitimacy of the Dáil were of paramount importance to him. As minister for defence in the underground Dáil, he was initially cautious about endorsing the guerrilla campaign pursued by the IRA, over which GHQ had but a tenuous control, and he urged restraint. For Brugha, political violence had to be justified and there were several examples where he criticized or prevented the killing of alleged spies because evidence of their supposed guilt was insufficient. At times, his role as a scrupulous minister gave way to more extreme stances such as his proposed plot to assassinate the British cabinet during the conscription crisis in 1918. But as we have argued, this was not a solo run by Brugha, who believed, mistakenly or not, that the gravity of the conscription crisis merited drastic action. This episode also revealed Brugha's tendency to lack judgement about the timing and consequences of particular actions. Understandably, his rivalry with Collins has attracted considerable comment, little of it favourable to Brugha as minister for defence. As discussed in this study, his wariness of Collins was often well-founded.

Their relationship was not always strained and they worked closely before 1920. After the Rising, Brugha became a vehement critic of the IRB and its secretive influence. This opposition became progressively more entrenched during the War of Independence and lay at the heart of Brugha's increasingly fractious relationship with Collins. Fundamentally, Brugha viewed the IRB, the source of Collins's remarkable influence, as undermining his role as minister for defence and the authority of the Dáil itself. In the context of the War of Independence, this stance was more high-minded and politically naïve than reflective of a personal jealousy as is often suggested. There were similar festering tensions between Brugha and Mulcahy that deepened during the truce period because Brugha attempted to reassert his authority as minister and that of the Dáil over the IRA. This partially explains his insistence on financial accountability, even in the murky world of IRA arms smuggling. Brugha's insistence on financial rectitude was an indelible legacy of his father's financial ruin.

Brugha's monolithic commitment to a republic blinded him to the magnitude of the Irish achievement in negotiating terms of settlement with the British government. Indeed, the agreement of a truce in July 1921 and the opening of negotiations all but guaranteed that compromise of some kind was inevitable and suggests an element of self-deception on Brugha's part. The Dáil's approval of the treaty was the supreme crisis of his career because it effectively disestablished his cherished republic and his life's work. His ferocious contribution to the treaty debates, fuelled by concerns that the IRB was used to sway the Dáil, irreparably damaged his reputation. Brugha's subsequent regret and earnest appeals for unity went largely unnoticed. Siding with de Valera in opposing the treaty, Brugha was won over to the concept of external association as a means of reconciling the demands of British imperialism and Irish nationalism. It demonstrated some flexibility of political thought. Brugha tried unsuccessfully to win public opinion over to the anti-treaty side but there was little sense of what future policy lay beyond that limited objective. When the result of the 1922 general election decisively rejected the anti-treaty position, Brugha's pessimism that conflict over the settlement could not be avoided given the stance of the IRA proved correct. He tried to restrain more bellicose republicans but was given no hearing at the IRA convention in March 1922. Brugha was a reluctant participant in the civil war, 'who consciously offered his own life as a final sacrifice to safeguard his trust' as de Valera expressed in a note of sympathy to Caitlín Brugha.[60] One of the most revealing contemporaneous assessments of Brugha was offered by Eoin MacNeill:

Cathal Brugha, in all that I ever knew of him, was an honest, honourable, brave and unselfish man. I have no doubt at all that he was a man who acknowledged the law in his conscience to be supreme in everything, and who with that in mind gave his wholehearted allegiance to Ireland, setting his duty to Ireland above life and all the claims and ties and affections that he found in life. What more can be said for any of us?[61]

Despite the failure of the republican ideal, it was a fitting tribute to Brugha's indomitable spirit.

Notes

Prologue

1   The number of biographies of Collins is extensive. For an overview see Anne Dolan & William Murphy, *Michael Collins: the man and the revolution* (Cork, 2018), pp 1–17.

2   On Boland, see David Fitzpatrick, *Harry Boland's Irish revolution* (Cork, 2003) and Jim Maher, *Harry Boland: a biography* (revised ed. Cork, 2020 [1998]). On Griffith, see Richard P. Davis, *Arthur Griffith* (Dundalk, 1976), Calton Younger, *Arthur Griffith* (Dublin, 1981), Brian Maye, *Arthur Griffith* (Dublin, 1997), Owen McGee, *Arthur Griffith* (Sallins, 2015), Colum Kenny, *The enigma of Arthur Griffith: 'father of us all'* (Newbridge, 2020).

3   *Wolfe Tone Weekly*, 2 July 1938.

4   An exception is Brian P. Murphy, *Patrick Pearse and the lost republican ideal* (Dublin, 1991).

5   J.J. O'Kelly (Bureau of Military History (hereafter BMH) Witness Statement (hereafter WS) 384, p. 20).

6   Liam Kavanagh to Ruairí Brugha, 21 May 1965 (in possession of Cathal MacSwiney Brugha).

7   Robert Barton to Ruairí Brugha, 6 May 1965, ibid.

8   James Quinn, 'Brugha, Cathal', *Dictionary of Irish biography* (hereafter *DIB*).

9   *Waterford News*, 14 July 1919.

10   *Irish Times*, 8 July 1922.

11   Brian P. Murphy, 'O'Kelly, John Joseph ('Sceilg'; Ua Ceallaigh, Seán)', *DIB*.

12   Seán Ua Ceallaigh [J.J. O'Kelly], *Cathal Brugha* (Dublin, 1942).

13   J.J. O'Kelly, *A trinity of martyrs. Terence MacSwiney, Cathal Brugha, Austin Stack. Anniversary lectures delivered by Sceilg at Sinn Féin headquarters* (Dublin, n.d. [1947]).

14   Murphy, 'O'Kelly, John Joseph ('Sceilg'; Ua Ceallaigh, Seán)', *DIB*.

15   Tomás Ó Dochartaigh, *Cathal Brugha: a shaol is a thréithe* (Dublin, 1969).

16   Ruairí Brugha to Florence O'Donoghue, 21 May 1966 (National Library of Ireland (hereafter NLI), Florence O'Donoghue papers, MS 31,319/2/14).

17   'The story of Cathal Brugha' featured in the *Wolfe Tone Annual 1962*.

18   *Wolfe Tone Weekly*, 13 Mar., 16 Apr., 2 July 1938.

19   Tom Barry, *Guerrilla days in Ireland* (Dublin, 1962 [1949]), p. 188.

20   Marie Coleman, 'O'Donoghue, Florence ('Florrie')', *DIB*. On the Bureau of Military History, see Diarmaid Ferriter, *A nation and not a rabble: the Irish Revolution, 1913–23* (London, 2015), pp 17–23.

21   *Irish Times* (hereafter *IT*) and *Irish Press* (hereafter *IP*), 26 Apr. 1966.

22   Brugha to O'Donoghue, 21 May 1966 (NLI, O'Donoghue papers, MS 31,319/2/140).

23   On this see Eve Morrison, 'Tea, sandbags, and Cathal Brugha: Kathy Barry's Civil War' in Oona Frawley (ed.), *Women and the decade of commemoration* (Indiana, 2021), p. 197.

24   Desmond Rushe review in *Irish Independent* (hereafter *II*), 10 July 1972.

25   *Evening Herald*, 10 July 1972; Anne Dolan, 'Clarke, Joseph Christopher', *DIB*.

26   Micheál Ó Cillín, 'Cathal Brugha 1874–1922', *Dublin Historical Record*, 38 (1984–5), 141–9; Máire MacSwiney Brugha, *History's daughter: a memoir from the only child of Terence MacSwiney* (Dublin, 2006), pp 262–73.

27 Fergus O'Farrell, *Cathal Brugha* (Dublin, 2018).

28 Peter Hart, 'The social structure of the IRA, 1916–23', *Historical Journal*, 42:1 (1999), 208.

CHAPTER 1 *Beginnings: early life, career and the Gaelic League*

1   Cathal Brugha, 'Connradh na Gaedhilge', *Leabhar na hÉireann/The Irish yearbook* (Dublin, 1909), 460–9.

2   Michael Hickey, *The Irish language movement, its genesis, growth and progress*, Gaelic League pamphlet no. 29 (Dublin, 1902).

3   Ó Dochartaigh, *Cathal Brugha*, p. 14.

4   Joe Mathew's genealogical research on the Burgess family has corrected a widely published inaccuracy that Brugha's grandfather was Richard Burgess rather than William (d. 18 Sept. 1883) (in possession of Cathal MacSwiney Brugha); *Slater's National Commercial Directory of Ireland 1846*, 201.

5   Examples include Terence de Vere White, *Kevin O'Higgins* (London, 1948), p. 52; Max Caufield, *Easter Rebellion* (Dublin, 1995 [1963]), p. 51; Andrew Boyle, *The riddle of Erskine Childers* (London, 1977), p. 257; Thomas Jones, *Whitehall diary, vol. III: Ireland 1918–1925*, ed. Keith Middlemas (London, 1971), p. 249.

6   Given as 'Maryanne' in several accounts but spelled 'Marianne' on the 1901 census and in her husband's probate listing.

7   St Michan's parish, Dublin city; Archdiocese of Dublin. Marriages (NLI, Microfilm 08833/03).

8   Birth certificate information could not be established in all cases. They were in order of birth: Elizabeth (1860), Edward (1862), Thomas (1863), Lucy Agnes (1865), Mary (1866), Frances (1868), Madeline (1869), Caroline, Pauline, Charles (1874), Adelaide (Ada), Eveleen, Alfred (1878) and Angela (1882).

9   Ó Dochartaigh, *Cathal Brugha*, p. 16.

10 *Thom's Directory 1860, 1864*; *Dublin Evening News*, 22 Aug. 1861.

11 *Dublin Weekly Nation*, 13 Sept. 1862.

12 *Tuam Herald*, 24 Jan. 1863.

13 *Dublin Daily Express*, 13 Oct. 1864.

14 Classified advertisements by Thomas Burgess in *IT*, 11 May 1863 and 15 July 1864.

15 *Freeman's Journal* (hereafter *FJ*), 28 Nov. 1867.

16 Mark Westgarth, 'A biographical dictionary of nineteenth century antique and curiosity dealers', *Regional Furniture*, 23 (2009), 76.

17 *London Evening Standard*, 10 Sept. 1870.

18 Census of England, Wales & Scotland, 1871; *Irishman*, 20 Dec. 1873.

19 *Thom's Directory 1874, 1877*.

20 *IT*, 21 Apr. 1881; *Thom's Directory 1881, 1899*.

21 Census of England, Wales & Scotland, 1881.

22 Ó Dochartaigh suggests that Burgess sought to establish a business in Melbourne, but this is not borne out by the bankruptcy proceedings in Sydney.

23 *Evening News*, 22 Feb. 1889. This was a Sydney newspaper.

24 *Advocate*, 23 Feb. 1889.

25 *IT*, 23 Apr. 1888; *London Evening Standard*, 7 July 1888.

26 *Evening News*, 22 Feb. 1889.

27 *Cork Constitution*, 11 Sept. 1889.

28 Ó Dochartaigh, *Cathal Brugha*, p. 16.

29 Joan Lawrence, *A pictorial history: Lavender Bay to the spit* (Alexandria, NSW, 1999), p. 106.

30 Ó Dochartaigh, *Cathal Brugha*, p. 17.

31 Austin Ó Briain to *IT*, 7 Aug. 2020.

32 *Saturday Herald*, 17 Apr. 1897; Frank Bouchier-Hayes, 'An Irishman's Diary', *IT*, 18 Aug. 2008.

33 *IP*, 26 May 1939.

34 *FJ*, 18 Apr. 1897.

35 *Evening Herald*, 2 Jan. 1899.

36 *Belfast Newsletter*, 4 Apr. 1899; *Evening Herald*, 3 and 4 Apr. 1899.

37 *Belfast Newsletter*, 11 Mar. 1901.

38 *Waterford News and Star*, 24 Aug. 1923.

39 Account by John McCann in *IP*, 21 Jan. 1952; Fidelma Brugha to Professor Éamon de Valera, 9 May 1971 (University College Dublin Archives (hereafter UCDA), Éamon de Valera papers, P150/3618) (Professor de Valera was Éamon de Valera's third child. He became professor of obstetrics and gynaecology at UCD in 1960); R.F. Foster, *Vivid faces: the revolutionary generation in Ireland 1890–1923* (London, 2014), pp 67–8.

40 Thomas Burgess death certificate, 11 Apr. 1899; *FJ*, 8 Apr. 1899.

41 Alfred Burgess (BMH WS 1,634, p. 1); Will of Thomas Burgess 1899, Ireland Calendar of Wills and Administrations, 1858–1920 (www.FamilySearch.org).

42 *IP*, 21 Jan. 1952.

43 Ó Dochartaigh, *Cathal Brugha*, p. 18; Ó Cillín, 'Cathal Brugha', 141.

44 Census of Ireland 1901: http://www.census.nationalarchives.ie/pages/1901/Dublin/ Rotunda/ Ardilaun_Terrace/1330115/.

45 *Irish Independent* (hereafter *II*), 9 Mar. 1907.

46 Dublin City Public Libraries and Archive, Electoral Rolls, 1908–1915.

47 Ó Dochartaigh, *Cathal Brugha*, p. 19.

48 *Waterford News and Star*, 24 Aug. 1923.

49 *United Irishman*, 17 Sept. 1932; Quinn, 'Brugha, Cathal', *DIB*; Brian Dillon Branch Sinn Féin, *Cathal Brugha*, (Cork, 1955), p. 4.

50 Robert Barton to Ruairí Brugha, 6 May 1965 (in possession of Cathal MacSwiney Brugha).

51 Ibid.

52 Alfred Burgess (BMH WS 1,634, p. 2).

53 Timothy G. McMahon, *Grand opportunity: the Gaelic revival and Irish society, 1893–1910* (New York, 2008), p. 88.

54 J.E. Dunleavy & G.W. Dunleavy, *Douglas Hyde: a maker of modern Ireland* (Berkeley, 1991), p. 202.

55 *FJ*, 10 June 1902, 20 Sept. 1902; *An Claidheamh Soluis*, 20 Sept. 1902, 4 Oct. 1902; *Kerry Sentinel*, 28 Oct. 1903.

56 Brian P. Murphy, *The Catholic Bulletin and republican Ireland with special reference to J.J. O'Kelly (Sceilg)* (Belfast, 2005), p. 47; https://comeheretome.com/2015/03/26/an-stad-north-frederick-street/.

57 Joseph Doolan, 'Cathal Brugha', lecture given in O'Donovan Rossa hall, Rathmines, 24 Feb. 1953.

58 Peadar Ó hAnnracháin, *Fé bhrat an Chonnartha* (Dublin, 1944), pp 99–100.

59 *Waterford News and Star*, 8 Jan. 1943.

60 Ibid., 1 Feb. 1924.

61 Foster, *Vivid faces*, p. 51.

62 Alfred Burgess (BMH WS 1,634, p. 1).

63 Ó Cillín, 'Cathal Brugha', 141.

64 *Irishman*, 20 Dec. 1873.

65 Census of Ireland, 1911.

66 Quinn, 'Brugha, Cathal', *DIB*; Senia Pašeta, *Before the revolution* (Cork, 1999), p. 44.

67 Piaras Béaslaí, 'Giants of the Gaelic revival movement – a veteran remembers', *II*, 17 May 1957. On this see Regina Uí Chollatáin, 'Ó Chéitinn go Conradh: the revivalists and the 1916 Rising', *Studies in Arts and Humanities*, 2:1 (2016), 52–66.

68 *II*, 7 July 1924.

69 Foster, *Vivid faces*, pp 67–8.

70 Brian P. Murphy's entry on Brugha in the *Oxford dictionary of national biography* states that he joined in 1906 but several other sources, including reports in *An Claidheamh Soluis*, suggest an earlier admission to the Keating branch.

71 Brian P. Murphy, 'O'Kelly, John Joseph ('Sceilg'; Ua Ceallaigh, Seán)', *DIB*; Patrick, Maume, *The long gestation: Irish nationalist life, 1891–1918* (Dublin, 1999), p. 27.

72 Murphy, 'O'Kelly, John Joseph ('Sceilg'; Ua Ceallaigh, Seán)', *DIB*; Brian P. Murphy, *Patrick Pearse and the lost republican ideal* (Dublin, 1991), p. 34.

73 On this controversy see Joost Augusteijn, *Patrick Pearse: the making of a revolutionary* (Basingstoke, 2010), p. 127.

74 Eoin Mac Cárthaigh, 'Dinneen, Patrick Stephen', *DIB*.

75 J.J. O'Kelly (BMH, WS 384, p. 16).

76 Ua Ceallaigh, *Cathal Brugha*, p. 11.

77 On this see Alvin Jackson, *Home rule: an Irish history* (London, 2003), pp 101–2.

78 'The IRB: some recollections and comments by Diarmuid Lynch', p. 5 (NLI, Diarmuid Lynch papers, MS 11,128).

79 Timothy G. McMahon, 'Douglas Hyde and the politics of the Gaelic League in 1914', *Éire-Ireland*, 53:1 & 2 (2018), 29–47.

80 *II*, 9 Nov. 1914.

81 Ua Ceallaigh, *Cathal Brugha*, pp 41–2; P.J. Mathews, *Revival: the Abbey Theatre, Sinn Féin, the Gaelic League and the Co-operative movement* (Cork, 2003), p. 25.

82 Patrick Maume, 'Hyde, Douglas (de hÍde, Dubhghlas)', *DIB*.

83 Dunleavy & Dunleavy, *Douglas Hyde*, p. 331.

84 *IT*, 2 July 1910; 'Obituary – Mr. V.J. Lalor', *IP*, 27 Sept. 1955; Ó Cillín, 'Cathal Brugha', 142.

85 Oliver Murphy, *The cruel clouds of war: a book of the sixty-eight former pupils and teachers of Belvedere College S.J. who lost their lives in the military conflicts of the 20th century* (Dublin, 2003), p. 89.

86 Joseph O'Doherty (Irish Military Archives (hereafter IMA), Military Service Pensions Collection (hereafter MSPC), MSP34REF16536); *IP*, 29 June 1967; Marie Coleman, 'O'Doherty, Joseph', *DIB*.

87 Robert Barton to Ruairí Brugha, 6 May 1965 (in possession of Cathal MacSwiney Brugha).

88 *FJ*, 28 Sept. 1911.

89 Ibid.

90 James Quinn, 'Ceannt, Éamonn', *DIB*.

91 Census of Ireland 1901; Senia Pašeta, 'Brugha, Caitlin [née Catherine Mary Kingston]', *Oxford dictionary of national biography* [https://doi-org.dcu.idm.oclc.org/10.1093/ref:odnb/92989].

92 *Leinster Leader*, 21 May 1904.

93 Ibid., 6 Aug. 1904.

94 Fidelma Brugha to Professor Éamon de Valera, 9 May 1971 (UCDA, de Valera papers, P150/3619); Mary McAuliffe, 'Remembering Caitlín Brugha, TD for Waterford, 1923–27', paper to 'Remembering Cathal Brugha Conference', Dungarvan, 4 Dec. 2018 [https://marymcauliffe.blog/2018/12/04/remembering-caitlin-brugha-td-for-waterford–1923–1927/].

95 *II*, 30 Dec. 1939.
96 *FJ*, 17 June 1912.
97 Ibid.
98 Ó Cillín, 'Cathal Brugha, 142; O'Kelly, *A trinity of martyrs*, p. 39.
99 *FJ*, 15 Jan. 1914; *Thom's Directory 1912, 1913, 1914*; Fidelma Brugha to Professor Éamon de Valera, 9 May 1971 (UCDA, de Valera papers, P150/3618).
100 Information from Cathal MacSwiney Brugha.
101 Ó Dochartaigh, *Cathal Brugha*, p. 20.
102 Piaras Béaslaí, 'Giants of the Gaelic revival movement – a veteran remembers', *II* 17 May 1957.
103 Ua Ceallaigh, *Cathal Brugha*, p. 116.

CHAPTER 2 *Republican: stalwart of the Irish Republican Brotherhood and Irish Volunteers*

1 Micheál Ó Siochrú, 'O'Neill, Owen Roe (Ó Néill, Eoghan Rua)', *DIB*.
2 M.J. Kelly, *The Fenian ideal and Irish nationalism, 1882–1916* (Woodbridge, 2006), p. 238.
3 Matthew Kelly, 'Radical nationalism, 1882–1916' in Thomas Bartlett (ed.), *The Cambridge history of Ireland, vol. IV: 1880 to the present* (Cambridge, 2018), p. 35.
4 Proinsias Mac Aonghusa, *Ar son na Gaeilge: Conradh na Gaeilge, 1893–1993* (Dublin, 1993), p. 132; Brian Feeney, *16 lives: Seán Mac Diarmada* (Dublin, 2015), p. 110.
5 Notes on the Inauguration of the Irish Volunteers at the Rink Meeting on 25th November 1913 (UCDA, Mulcahy papers, P7b/197).
6 Brian P. Murphy, 'O'Kelly, John Joseph ('Sceilg'; Ua Ceallaigh, Seán)', *DIB*.
7 J.J. O'Kelly (BMH WS 384, p. 13).
8 Florence O'Donoghue, 'Cathal Brugha' lecture, Apr. 1966 (NLI, O'Donoghue papers, MS 31,319/2/10); *Nationalist and Leinster Times*, 19 Aug. 1922.
9 Michael Laffan, *The resurrection of Ireland: the Sinn Féin party, 1916–1923* (Cambridge, 1999), p. 31.
10 P.S. O'Hegarty, 'Recollections of the IRB', p. 5, 7–11 Nov. 1917 (NLI, Roger Casement papers, MS 36,210). On O'Hegarty, see Kieron Curtis, *P.S. O'Hegarty (1879–1955): Sinn Féin Fenian* (London, 2010).
11 Kelly, *Fenian ideal*, p. 188.
12 Ibid.
13 O'Hegarty, 'Recollections of the IRB', p. 14.
14 Kelly, 'Radical nationalism', p. 53; Foster, *Vivid faces*, p. 170.
15 Diarmuid Lynch (BMH WS 4, pp 1–2).
16 John McKenna (BMH WS 1025, p. 1).
17 Jeremiah O'Connell (BMH WS 998, p. 1).
18 W.J. Dilworth (Office of National Education) to Fr P. Conor Browne (PP Caherciveen), 19 Oct. 1915 (UCDA, Eoin MacNeill papers, LA1/H/9).
19 Art O'Donnell (BMH WS 1,322, p. 3); Pádraig Ó Ruairc, *Blood on the Banner: the republican struggle in Clare* (Cork, 2009), p. 27.
20 Charles Townshend, *Easter 1916: the Irish rebellion* (London, 2005), p. 40.
21 Augusteijn, *Patrick Pearse*, pp 193–8.
22 For a comprehensive biography of Béaslaí, see Pádraig Ó Siadhail, *An Béaslaíoch: beatha agus saothar Phiarais Béaslaí* (Dublin, 2007).
23 Piaras Béaslaí, *Michael Collins and the making of a new Ireland*, i (2 vols, Dublin, 1926), pp 51–2.
24 Ibid. p. 52.
25 Murphy, *Lost republican ideal*, p. 39.

26 Précis of reports regarding secret societies, June 1911 (The National Archives (hereafter TNA), CO 904/13); Burgess, Charles (Brugha, Cathal), Easter Rising Records (TNA, WO 35/206/22); *FJ*, 23 June 1911.

27 *FJ*, 23 June 1911; Kelly, *Fenian ideal*, p. 59.

28 Ibid.; Précis of reports regarding secret societies, June 1911 (TNA, CO 904/13); Lindie Naughton, *Markievicz: a most outrageous rebel* (Newbridge, 2016), p. 92.

29 *Cork Examiner*, 23 June 1911.

30 James Quinn, 'Clarke, Thomas James ('Tom')', *DIB*.

31 Murphy, *Lost republican ideal*, p. 38.

32 Thomas Bartlett, 'Tone, Theobald Wolfe', *DIB*.

33 Marnie Hay, *Bulmer Hobson and the nationalist movement in twentieth-century Ireland* (Manchester, 2009), p. 103.

34 Richard Mulcahy, 'Notes on Cathal Brugha', 1 Feb. 1966 (UCDA, Mulcahy papers, P7/D/86).

35 Richard Mulcahy, 'Cathal Brugha', 28 Apr. 1967 (UCDA, Mulcahy papers, P7/D/86).

36 Gerard MacAtasney, *Seán Mac Diarmada: the mind of the revolution* (Manorhamilton, 2004), p. 62.

37 Mulcahy, 'Notes on Cathal Brugha', 1 Feb. 1966; 'Cathal Brugha', 28 Apr. 1967 (UCDA, Mulcahy papers, P7/D/86); O'Donoghue, 'Cathal Brugha' lecture, Apr. 1966 (NLI, O'Donoghue papers, MS 31,319/2/10).

38 O'Hegarty, 'Recollections of the IRB', p. 15.

39 Bulmer Hobson, 'The origin of Óglaigh na hÉireann', *An tÓglach*, 4:1 (Mar. 1931), 4; George Irvine (BMH WS 265, pp 1–2).

40 O'Rahilly to Ceannt, 10 Nov. 1913 (NLI, Éamonn Ceannt papers, MS 13,069/42).

41 Original draft of objects of the Irish Volunteers made by O'Rahilly, 11 Nov. 1913 (NLI, Documents relating to The O'Rahilly, MS 13,019).

42 Constitution of the Irish Republican Brotherhood [1873–1916] (NLI, Bulmer Hobson papers, MS 13,163).

43 MacNeill to Casement, 25 Nov. 1913 (NLI, Casement papers, MS 36,203/2); *FJ*, 26 Nov. 1913.

44 Bulmer Hobson, *A short history of the Irish Volunteers* (Dublin, 1918), pp 30–1.

45 *FJ*, 26 Nov. 1913.

46 Seán Mac Diarmada to Joseph McGarrity, 12 Dec. 1913 (NLI, Joseph McGarrity papers, MS 17,618); Hobson, 'The origin of Óglaigh na hÉireann', 6.

47 Kelly, *Fenian ideal*, p. 207.

48 MacNeill to Casement, 25 Nov. 1913 (NLI, Casement papers, MS 36,203/2).

49 'The IRB: some recollections and comments by Diarmuid Lynch' (NLI, Diarmuid Lynch papers, MS 11,128).

50 MacNeill to Casement, 27 Nov. 1913 (NLI, Casement papers, MS 36,203/2); Hobson (BMH WS 51, p. 7).

51 Memorandum for cabinet, 2 Apr. 1914 (TNA, CAB 37/119/51).

52 Diary entry by Ceannt for 25 Nov. 1913 (NLI, Ceannt papers, MS 21,810).

53 James Kenny (BMH WS 174, p. 1).

54 National Archives of Ireland (hereafter NAI), Census of Ireland 1911.

55 Minute book pertaining to Larkfield [1914] (NLI, George Walsh papers, P4955).

56 Séamus Murphy (BMH WS 1,756, p. 2); Henry S. Murray (BMH WS 300, p. 3).

57 James Rogers to Maurice Moore, 3 Oct. 1914 (NLI, Maurice Moore papers, MS 10,548/6).

58 Charles Townshend, *Political violence in Ireland: government and resistance since 1848* (Oxford, 1983), p. 266.

59 Receipt from Judge & Son to honorary secretaries Irish Volunteers, 9 Mar. 1914 (NLI, Ceannt papers, MS 13,069/40).

60 Hobson, *A short history*, p. 65.

61 Timothy Bowman, 'Irish paramilitarism and gun cultures, 1910–1921' in Karen Jones, Giacomo Macola, David Welch (eds), *A cultural history of firearms in the age of empire* (Farnham, Surrey, 2013), p. 279.

62 Redmond to Asquith, 2 Mar. 1914 (Bodleian Library, Asquith papers, MS Asquith 39 ff 134–41).

63 RIC Inspector-General's monthly report for Mar. 1914 (TNA, CO 904/92).

64 'Irish Volunteers: Table showing total number of branches and total number of members as set forth in weekly reports' (NLI, Joseph Brennan papers, MS 26,176).

65 *FJ*, 10 June 1914.

66 Seán Fitzgibbon (BMH WS 130, pp 7–8).

67 Piaras Béaslaí, 'Nation in revolt – 4', *II*, 8 Jan. 1953.

68 'Statement given to Joseph McGarrity, at his request, by Bulmer Hobson', 1934 (NLI, Hobson papers, MS 13,171).

69 Ibid.

70 Hobson, 'The origin of Óglaigh na hÉireann', 7; Hobson (BMH WS 31, p. 7).

71 Hobson (BMH WS 53, p. 6); Dorothy Macardle, *The Irish Republic* (Dublin, 1951), p. 113.

72 Darrell Figgis, *Recollections of the Irish war* (London, 1927), p. 45.

73 MacAtasney, *Seán Mac Diarmada*, p. 72.

74 James Kenny (BMH WS 174, p. 2).

75 *II*, 28, 29 July 1914; *FJ*, 28, 29 July 1914; *Report of the Royal Commission into the circumstances connected with the landing of arms at Howth on July 26th 1914* (Cd. 7631), p. 6; Robert Woollcombe, *All the blue bonnets: the history of The King's Own Scottish Borderers* (London, 1980), p. 99.

76 Matthew Nathan to secretary Treasury, 23 Oct. 1914, enclosing a police report on persons killed and injured (TNA, T1/11945). Those killed were James Brennan, Mary Duffy, Patrick Quinn and Sylvester Pidgeon.

77 Seán Fitzgibbon (BMH WS 130, p. 11).

78 Seán T. Ó Ceallaigh, *Seán T.* (Dublin, 1963), p. 136.

79 Seán Fitzgibbon (BMH WS 130, pp 12–13); Seán O'Byrne (BMH WS 986, pp 3–4).

80 *Report of the Royal Commission into the circumstances connected with the landing of arms at Howth on July 26th 1914* (Cd. 7631), pp 14–15.

81 Pearse to McGarrity, 28 July 1914 (NLI, McGarrity papers, MS 17,477/5).

82 'Return setting forth the strength of the Volunteers in September 1914, before the division into two bodies subsequently known as the National Volunteers and the Irish Volunteers', *Intelligence notes 1914*, p. 51 (TNA, CO 903/18).

83 Hobson, 'The origin of Óglaigh na hÉireann', 11.

84 David Fitzpatrick, 'The logic of collective sacrifice: Ireland and the British army, 1914–1918', *Historical Journal* 38:4 (1995), 1028.

85 *II*, 7 Sept. 1914; CI Dublin, Sept. 1914 (TNA, CO 904/94).

86 MacNeill to Redmond, 9 Aug. 1914 (NLI, MacNeill papers, MS 10,883); Pearse to McGarrity, 12 Aug. 1914 (NLI, McGarrity papers, MS 17,477/7); *Irish Volunteer*, 29 Aug. 1914.

87 Minutes of meeting of provisional committee, 10 Sept. 1914 (NLI, Hobson papers, MS 13,174/1).

88 BMH statement of Séamus Ó Conchubhair (Séamus O'Connor), p. 22 (UCDA, MacNeill papers, LA1/G/117); Béaslaí, 'Nation in revolt – 6', *II*, 12 Jan. 1953.

89 *FJ*, 21 Sept. 1914.

90 Statement by provisional committee on split with Redmond, 24 Sept. 1914 (NLI, Hobson papers, MS 13,174/10).

91 James Kenny (BMH WS 174, p. 4).

92 'Table showing the original strength of the Irish National Volunteers and indicating approximately how the various battalions divided as result of meetings held from 24 September, date of secession, up to and including 31 Oct. 1914' (NLI, John Redmond papers, MS 15,258).

93 Pearse to McGarrity, 26 Sept. 1914 (NLI, McGarrity papers, MS 17,477/8).

94 'The Present Crisis' manifesto issued by the executive committee of the Irish Volunteers, 15 July 1915 (NLI, Hobson papers, MS 13,174/2).

95 Return setting forth the strength of the Irish Volunteers, Dec. 1914, *Intelligence notes*, p. 54 (TNA, CO 903/18).

96 Pearse to McGarrity, 19 Oct. 1914 (NLI, McGarrity papers, MS 17,477/9).

97 Account of the first Irish Volunteer convention, Oct. 1914 (NLI, Hobson papers, MS 13,174/11).

98 *Irish Volunteer*, 10 Nov. 1915.

99 Ibid., 9 Jan. 1915.

100 James A. Gubbins (BMH WS 765, p. 11).

101 Dan Breen, *My fight for Irish freedom* (Dublin, 1989), p. 14.

102 John O'Callaghan, *Limerick: the Irish Revolution, 1912–23* (Dublin, 2018), p. 30.

103 Report of honorary secretary Irish Volunteers, 31 Oct. 1915 (UCDA, MacNeill papers, LA1/H/4).

104 Second Irish Volunteer Convention Agenda and motions, 31 Oct. 1915 (NLI, Hobson papers, MS 13,174/11).

105 Report on recruiting by General Purposes Committee, n.d. [Dec. 1915] (NLI, MacDonagh papers, MS 20,643/2).

106 Circular from Thomas Slater (hon. sec. pro tem. Dublin City and County Board) enclosing programme of lectures to end March 1915 (NLI, Hobson papers, MS 13,174/11).

107 Notes from lecture on street fighting, 3 May 1915 (NLI, Ceannt papers, MS 13,069/38).

108 Henry S. Murray (BMH WS 300, pp 10–11); Pearse to Ceannt, n.d. [1915] (NLI, Ceannt papers, MS 13,069/42).

109 Séamus Murphy (BMH WS 1,756, p. 7).

110 Charles J. O'Grady (BMH WS 282, p. 3).

111 *Irish Volunteer*, 20 Mar. 1915.

112 Henry S. Murray (BMH WS 300, p. 12).

113 Ó Dochartaigh, *Cathal Brugha*, pp 41, 43.

114 'J.J. O'Connell's memoir of the Irish Volunteers, 1914–16, 1917', ed. Daithí Ó Corráin, *Analecta Hibernica*, 47 (2016), 59–61.

115 'Cathal Brugha – Some reminiscences and reflections', *Waterford News and Star*, 1 Feb. 1924.

116 *Irish Volunteer*, 7 Feb. 1914.

CHAPTER 3 *Rebel: the 1916 Rising*

1 Memorandum of interview with the prime minister, 22 Feb. 1916 (Bodleian Library, Matthew Nathan papers, MS Nathan 469 ff 269–71).

2 See Townshend, *Easter 1916*; Michael Foy & Brian Barton, *The Easter Rising* (Stroud, 2004); Fearghal McGarry, *The Rising: Easter 1916* (Oxford, 2010).

3 O'Donoghue, 'Cathal Brugha' lecture, Apr. 1966; Ó Cillín, 'Cathal Brugha', 144; Ó Dochartaigh, *Cathal Brugha*, p. 47.

4   Caitlín Brugha to Robert Dudley Edwards, 10 Mar. 1935 (NLI, O'Donoghue papers, MS 31,299/1/1).

5   Thomas Treacy (BMH WS 590, pp 7–8); Eoin Swithin Walsh, *Kilkenny in times of revolution, 1900–1923* (Newbridge, 2018), pp 26–7.

6   Thomas Treacy (BMH WS 590, pp 8–10); Declan Dunne, *Peter's key: Peter Deloughry and the fight for Irish independence* (Cork, 2012), p. 66; Townshend, *Easter 1916*, p. 239.

7   Circular from Eoin MacNeill, 19 Apr. 1916 (UCDA, Terence MacSwiney papers, P48b/364).

8   Bulmer Hobson's account of Easter Week 1916, n.d. (NLI, McGarrity papers, MS 17,613).

9   Volunteer orders, 21 Apr. 1916 (NLI, Hobson papers, MS 13,174/16).

10 Séamus O'Kelly (BMH WS 471, pp 5–7).

11 Mary Gallagher, *16 lives: Éamonn Ceannt* (Dublin, 2014), p. 226.

12 Mary Josephine Mulcahy (BMH WS 399, pp 9–10).

13 Marcus Bourke, *The O'Rahilly* (Tralee, 1967), p. 118.

14 Note from MacNeill, Easter Sunday [23 Apr. 1916] (UCDA, de Valera papers, P150/462).

15 Áine Ceannt (BMH WS 264, pp 22–4).

16 Ibid., p. 24.

17 Seán T. O'Kelly (BMH WS 1,765, part 2, p. 239).

18 Notebook with entry dated 7 Jan. 1916 (NLI, Ceannt papers, MS 13,069/39).

19 'Notes as basis of account of my connection with Volunteers' n.d. [*c*.1949] (UCDA, de Valera papers, P150/447).

20 Áine Ceannt (BMH WS 264, p. 29); pension application of Áine Ceannt (IMA, MSPC, MSP34REF63426).

21 Áine Ceannt (BMH WS 264, p. 30).

22 Liam O'Flaherty (BMH WS 248, p. 2).

23 J.V. Joyce, 'Easter Week, 1916: the defence of the South Dublin Union', *An tÓglách*, 12 June 1926; James Kenny (BMH WS 174, p. 5).

24 Brugha to Ceannt, 24 Apr. 1916 (IMA, Áine Ceannt Collection, BMH CD/94/4/2).

25 Joyce, 'Easter Week, 1916'.

26 Ibid.; James Kenny (BMH WS 174, p. 5).

27 Townshend, *Easter 1916*, pp 172–3.

28 *Catholic Bulletin* 8:3 (Mar. 1918), 153–6; William Henry, *Supreme sacrifice: the story of Éamonn Ceannt 1881–1916* (Cork, 2005), pp 66–9; Gallagher, *Éamonn Ceannt*, p. 241.

29 William T. Cosgrave (BMH WS 268, p. 6b); Henry, *Supreme sacrifice*, p. 70.

30 Gallagher, *Éamonn Ceannt*, p. 243; Brian Barton, *From behind a closed door: secret court martial records of the 1916 Easter Rising* (Belfast, 2002), p. 184.

31 G.A. Hayes-McCoy, 'A military history of the 1916 Rising' in Kevin B. Nowlan (ed.), *The making of 1916: studies in the history of the Rising* (Dublin, 1969), pp 269–70.

32 George Irvine (BMH WS 265, p. 5).

33 James Coughlan (BMH WS 304, pp 8–11).

34 Annie Mannion (BMH WS 295, p. 3).

35 NAI, 30060/340, South Dublin Union Minute Books, 1916–17, Master's Report, p. 553.

36 Stannus Geoghegan, *Campaigns and history of the Royal Irish Regiment Vol. II* (London, 1927), pp 102–3.

37 James Coughlan (BMH WS 304, p. 12).

38 McGarry, *The Rising*, p. 191.

39 Joseph Doolan, 'Cathal Brugha: incident of Easter Week', n.d. [*c*.1934] (NLI, Personal narratives of the Rising of 1916 collection, MS 10,915/8).

40 James Coughlan (BMH WS 304, p. 15).

41 Joseph Doolan (BMH WS 199, p. 5).
42 Doolan, 'Cathal Brugha: incident of Easter Week'.
43 O'Donoghue, 'Cathal Brugha' lecture, Apr. 1966; Townshend, *Easter 1916*, pp 202–3; Gallagher, *Éamonn Ceannt*, pp 261–8.
44 Annie Mannion (BMH WS 295, p. 4).
45 Caulfield, *Easter Rebellion*, p. 226.
46 Townshend, *Easter 1916*, pp 202–3.
47 *Catholic Bulletin* 8:6 (1918), 310.
48 James Coughlan (BMH WS 304, p. 15); Joyce, 'Easter Week, 1916'; Ó Dochartaigh, *Cathal Brugha*, p. 52.
49 Caulfield, *Easter Rebellion*, p. 227.
50 Joyce, 'Easter Week, 1916'.
51 Ibid.; O'Donoghue, 'Cathal Brugha' lecture, Apr. 1966.
52 Joyce, 'Easter Week, 1916'; Pádraigín Clancy & Clare Eager (eds), *Ireland first: comóradh ár sinsir, 1916–2016: relatives remember: 4th Battalion Dublin Brigade 1916, South Dublin Union – Marrowbone Lane garrisons* (Dublin, 2016), p. 18.
53 Doolan, 'Cathal Brugha: incident of Easter Week'.
54 O'Donoghue, 'Cathal Brugha' lecture, Apr. 1966; Joyce, 'Easter Week, 1916'.
55 Caulfield, *Easter Rebellion*, p. 228.
56 Joyce, 'Easter Week, 1916'.
57 *Cathal Brugha* (Cork, 1955), p. 7 [pamphlet by Brian Dillon Branch, Sinn Féin].
58 James Coughlan (BMH WS 304, pp 21–2); William T. Cosgrave (BMH WS 268, p. 9); Doolan, 'Cathal Brugha: incident of Easter Week'.
59 Ó Dochartaigh, *Cathal Brugha*, p. 53. Eveleen was Ó Dochartaigh's mother.
60 Joyce, 'Easter Week, 1916'.
61 Ibid.
62 Ibid.; Caulfield, *Easter Rebellion*, p. 229.
63 Doolan (BMH WS 199, appendix p. 4); William T. Cosgrave (BMH WS 268, p. 9).
64 Joyce, 'Easter Week, 1916'.
65 Caulfield, *Easter Rebellion*, p. 229.
66 Townshend, *Easter 1916*, pp 243–5.
67 James Kenny (BMH WS 174, p. 6); James Coughlan (BMH WS 304, p. 24).
68 Townshend, *Easter 1916*, p. 250.
69 Piaras F. Mac Lochlainn (ed.), *Last words: letters and statements of the leaders executed after the Rising at Easter 1916* (Dublin, 1971), p. 131.
70 Copy Maxwell to Lord French, 29 Apr. 1916 (UCDA, de Valera papers, P150/512).
71 Barton, *From behind a closed door*, p. 186.
72 Áine Ceannt (BMH WS 264, p. 31); Henry, *Supreme sacrifice*, p. 95.
73 Áine Ceannt (BMH WS 264, p. 32).
74 Ibid.
75 Joseph Doolan (BMH WS 199, appendix p. 4); Quinn, 'Brugha, Cathal', *DIB*.
76 Áine Ceannt (BMH WS 264, p. 32).
77 Caitlín Brugha to Robert Dudley Edwards, 10 Mar. 1934 (NLI, O'Donoghue papers, MS 31,299/1/1).
78 Information from Cathal MacSwiney Brugha.
79 Copy Maxwell to Kitchener, 2 May 1916 (UCDA, de Valera papers, P150/512).
80 Copy Dillon to Maxwell, 8 May 1916, ibid.
81 Mac Lochlainn, *Last words*, p. 136.
82 Áine Ceannt (BMH WS 264, p. 35).

83 Brugha [signed C. Burgess] to Fr Albert, 14 June 1916 (Capuchin Archives, CA/IR/1/1/
2/1/2).
84 Brian A. Cusack (BMH WS 736, p. 6).
85 Pension application of William F. Staines (IMA, MSPC, DP5788).
86 *IP*, 6 Apr. 1934.
87 *Waterford News and Star*, 24 Aug. 1923; O'Higgins, 'The story of Cathal Brugha', p. 12;
Quinn, 'Brugha, Cathal', *DIB*.
88 Ó Dochartaigh, *Cathal Brugha*, p. 54.
89 Ibid.
90 *Waterford News and Star*, 24 Aug. 1923; Joseph Doolan (BMH WS 199, appendix, p. 5);
Sceilg's 'reminiscences of Brugha' as published in *Waterford News and Star*, 24 Aug. 1923.
91 Statement of activities of Mary Ellen Vaughan, Main Street, Milltown Malbay, n.d.
(courtesy of Mary Crawford).
92 Frank McGrath (BMH WS 1,557, p. 4).
93 Jeremiah O'Connell (BMH WS 998, pp 1–5).
94 Inspector general's confidential monthly report for June 1916 (TNA, CO 904/100).
95 On this see Daithí Ó Corráin, '"They blew up the best portion of our city and ... it is their
duty to replace it": compensation and reconstruction in the aftermath of the 1916 Rising',
Irish Historical Studies, 39:154 (2014), 272–95.
96 Claim by Lalor Ltd, 14 Ormond Quay Lower (NAI, Property Losses Ireland Committee,
PLIC/1/0905).
97 Murphy, 'O'Kelly, John Joseph ('Sceilg'; Ua Ceallaigh, Seán)', *DIB*.
98 Townshend, *Easter 1916*, p. 355.

CHAPTER 4 *Facilitator: Brugha and the reorganization of separatism, 1917–18*

1 Frank Henderson (BMH WS 821, p. 1).
2 William Murphy, *Political imprisonment and the Irish, 1912–1921* (Oxford, 2014), pp 54–5.
3 RIC inspector general monthly report for June 1916 (TNA, CO 904/100).
4 Frances Clarke, 'Clarke, Kathleen', *DIB*; Sinéad McCoole, *Easter widows* (Dublin, 2014), pp
263–4.
5 RIC inspector general monthly report for Aug. 1916 (TNA, CO 904/100). On the fund, see
Caoimhe Nic Dháibhéid, 'The Irish National Aid Association and the radicalisation of
public opinion in Ireland, 1916–1918', *Historical Journal*, 55:3 (2012), 705–29.
6 Laffan, *Resurrection*, p. 68; William Murphy, 'Imprisonment, 1915–18' in Crowley et al., *Atlas
of the Irish Revolution*, p. 321; Margaret Ward, *Unmanageable revolutionaries: women and Irish
nationalism* (London, 1995), pp 88–9; Liz Gillis, *Women of the Irish Revolution* (Cork, 2016),
p. 59; Ann Matthews, *Renegades: Irish republican women, 1900–1922* (Cork, 2010), p. 160.
7 Jason Knirck, *Women of the Dáil: gender, republicanism and the Anglo-Irish treaty* (Dublin,
2006), p. 116; Cal McCarthy, *Cumann na mBan and the Irish Revolution* (Cork, 2007), p. 73.
8 RIC inspector general monthly report for July 1916 (TNA, CO 904/100).
9 'J.J. O'Connell's memoir of the Irish Volunteers, 1914–16, 1917', 102.
10 Pension application of Liam Clarke (IMA, MSPC, MSP34REF8875); pension application
of Luke Kennedy (IMA, MSPC, MSP34REF21389); pension application of Gregory
Murphy (IMA, MSPC, MSP34REF10228).
11 Gerald Byrne (BMH WS 668, p. 2).
12 Pension application of Piaras Béaslaí (IMA, MSPC, 24SP295); pension application of
Thomas C. Hunter (IMA, MSPC, DP4587).
13 Nicholas Laffan (BMH WS 703, pp 1–2).

14 Henry S. Murray (BMH WS 601, p. 2).

15 Thomas J. Meldon (BMH WS 734, p. 32).

16 Michael Lynch (BMH WS 511, p. 29).

17 Richard Walsh (BMH WS 400, p. 21); Murphy, *Lost republican ideal*, p. 70.

18 Pension application of Liam Clarke (IMA, MSPC, MSP34REF8875); Gregory Murphy (BMH WS 150, p. 8); Richard Walsh (BMH WS 400, p. 22).

19 Various notes on Irish Volunteers after 1916 (UCDA, Mulcahy papers, P7b/200).

20 Thomas J. Meldon (BMH WS 734, p. 32).

21 Jeffrey Leddin, *The 'Labour Hercules': the Irish Citizen Army and Irish republicanism, 1913–23* (Newbridge, 2019), pp 190–1.

22 Foy & Barton, *Easter Rising*, p. 257.

23 Charles J. O'Grady (BMH WS 282, p. 7).

24 Henry S. Murray (BMH WS 601, p. 3).

25 Florence O'Donoghue, *Tomás MacCurtain* (Tralee, 1958), pp 116–17; Patrick Maume, 'MacCurtain, Tomás', *DIB*; Francis J. Costello, *Enduring the most: the life and death of Terence MacSwiney* (Dingle, 1995), pp 63–7.

26 MacSwiney to Brugha, 30 Sept. 1920 (UCDA, MacSwiney papers, P48b/416).

27 Diarmuid Lynch, *The IRB and the 1916 insurrection* (Cork, 1957), p. 32.

28 Ó Dochartaigh, *Cathal Brugha*, p. 59.

29 Pension application of Diarmuid O'Hegarty (IMA, MSPC, 24SP6568); William Murphy & Marie Coleman, 'O'Hegarty (Ó hÉigeartuigh), Diarmuid', *DIB*.

30 Patrick Long, 'Ó Murthuile, Seán', *DIB*.

31 Murphy, *Lost republican ideal*, pp 70–1.

32 Kathleen Clarke, *Revolutionary woman, Kathleen Clarke, 1878–1972: an autobiography*, ed. Helen Litton (Dublin, 1991), p. 141.

33 Ibid., p. 142.

34 Seán Matthews (BMH WS 1,022, pp 6–7).

35 Éamon T. Dore (BMH WS 392, p. 8).

36 Richard Walsh (BMH WS 400, p. 162).

37 Macardle, *Irish Republic*, p. 231.

38 James McGuill (BMH WS 353, p. 109).

39 Ibid., p. 113.

40 Pension application of Liam Clarke (IMA, MSPC, MSP34REF8875); Gregory Murphy (BMH WS 150, p. 8).

41 Richard Walsh (BMH WS 400, p. 29); Order by Irish Volunteers Executive, 22 May 1917 (NLI, Hobson papers, MS 13,174/5).

42 Order by Irish Volunteers Executive, 22 May 1917 (NLI, Hobson papers, MS 13,174/5).

43 Ibid.

44 Geraldine Plunkett Dillon, *All in the blood: a memoir of the Plunkett family, the 1916 Rising and the War of Independence*, ed. Honor Ó Brolcháin (Dublin, 2006), pp 253, 255; Murphy, *Lost republican ideal*, p. 80.

45 Linde Lunney & Enda Leaney, 'Dillon, Thomas Patrick', *DIB*.

46 Thomas Craven (IMA, MSPC, MSP34REF2994).

47 Óglaigh na hÉireann Training Order no. 1, 25 Aug. 1917 (NLI, Hobson papers, MS 13,174/5).

48 See John Burke, *Roscommon: the Irish Revolution, 1912–23* (Dublin, 2021), pp 43–50.

49 Archbishop Walsh to *Evening Herald*, 8 May 1917.

50 Handbill for Longford by-election [1917] (UCDA, de Valera papers, P150/541).

51 *II*, 22 May 1917; *FJ*, 22 May 1917; *IT*, 26 May 1917.

52 Maher, *Harry Boland*, pp 61–2; Peter Hart, *Mick: the real Michael Collins* (London, 2005), p. 106; Joseph O'Connor (BMH WS 487, p. 3).

53 Assistant under-secretary to chief secretary, 8 June 1917 (NAI, CSORP/1917/2221).

54 DMP chief commissioner to assistant under-secretary, 11 June 1917, ibid.

55 Ibid.; *FJ*, 11 June 1917.

56 DMP chief commissioner to assistant under-secretary, 11 June 1917 (NAI, CSORP/1917/2221); Eunan O'Halpin & Daithí Ó Corráin, *The dead of the Irish Revolution* (New Haven, 2020), p. 102

57 DMP chief commissioner to assistant under-secretary, 11 June 1917 (NAI, CSORP/1917/2221).

58 Assistant under-secretary to chief secretary, 12 June 1917, ibid.; *FJ*, 19 June 1917; *Nationalist*, 20 June 1917.

59 *Evening Herald*, 4 Jan. 1919.

60 Minute of a meeting of the war cabinet, 14 June 1917 (Bodleian Library, Henry Duke papers, Dep c. 715 f. 12); *II*, 16 June 1917.

61 James O'Connor to chief secretary, 4 Dec. 1917 (Bodleian Library, Duke papers, Dep c. 715 ff 216–17).

62 Michael Laffan, 'A political revolution' in Crowley et al., *Atlas of the Irish Revolution*, p. 306.

63 Laffan, *Resurrection*, p. 92.

64 Brian Farrell, *The founding of Dáil Éireann: parliament and nation building* (Dublin, 1971), p. 17; Laffan, 'The unification of Sinn Féin', 367–8; Denis Carroll, *They have fooled you again: Michael O'Flanagan (1876–1942): priest, republican, social critic* (Dublin, 1993), p. 67.

65 William O'Brien (BMH WS 1,766, p. 135).

66 Younger, *Arthur Griffith*, p. 66; Maye, *Arthur Griffith*, p. 127; Kenny, *Arthur Griffith*, p. 190.

67 Robert Brennan (BMH WS 779, p. 408).

68 Laffan, *Resurrection*, p. 118; Macardle, *Irish Republic*, pp 231–2.

69 'Elections at Ard Fheis, 1917' (UCDA, de Valera papers, P150/575).

70 Thomas Morrissey, *Laurence O'Neill (1864–1943), lord mayor of Dublin (1917–1924): patriot and man of peace* (Dublin, 2014), p. 91.

71 Austin Stack to de Valera, 29 Oct. 1917 (UCDA, de Valera papers, P150/562).

72 Laffan, *Resurrection*, p. 173; O'Farrell, *Cathal Brugha*, pp 32–3.

73 *FJ*, 26 Oct. 1917; *Evening Herald*, 26 Oct. 1917; Kevin O'Shiel (BMH WS 1,770, p. 691).

74 J.J. O'Kelly (BMH WS 427, p. 3); Laffan, *Resurrection*, p. 119.

75 *IT*, 26 Oct. 1917; *CE*, 26 Oct. 1917; *FJ*, 26 Oct. 1917.

76 *IT*, 26 Oct. 1917.

77 Townshend, *Easter Rising*, p. 333.

78 Ibid.

79 'Notes on Volunteer Convention 1917', 23 Aug. 1963 (UCDA, Mulcahy papers, P7b/198).

80 Ibid.

81 Copy MacNeill to de Valera, 22 Oct. 1917 (NLI, Hobson papers, MS 13,161/3). This is not mentioned in MacNeill's *Memoir of a revolutionary scholar*, ed. Brian Hughes (Dublin, 2016).

82 Bulmer Hobson (BMH WS 81, p. 17).

83 Frank Henderson (BMH WS 821, p. 16).

84 'Notes on Volunteer Convention 1917', 23 Aug. 1963 (UCDA, Mulcahy papers, P7b/198).

85 See, for example, Béaslaí, *Michael Collins*, vol. I, p. 114 and 'A nation in revolt – 23', *II*, 4 Feb. 1953; Macardle, *Irish Republic*, p. 235; Dr Risteárd Mulcahy to Béaslaí, 9 Jan. 1962 (NLI, Béaslaí papers, MS 33,930/18).

86 Laffan, *Resurrection*, pp 175–6.

87 Meeting of the Sinn Féin standing committee, 6 Feb. 1918; 10 Apr. 1918 (NLI, Sinn Fein Minute Book of Standing Committee, Jan. 1918–May 1919, P3269).

88 Various notes on the Irish Volunteers after 1916 (UCDA, Mulcahy papers, P7b/200).
89 Alan J. Ward, 'Lloyd George and the 1918 Irish conscription crisis', *Historical Journal* 25:1 (1974), 108.
90 Minutes of war cabinet, 25 Mar. 1918 (Bodleian Library, Duke papers, Dep c. 716 f. 127).
91 Cabinet conclusions, 27 Mar. 1918 (TNA, CAB 23/5, WC 374).
92 Minutes of war cabinet, 27 Mar. 1918 (Bodleian Library, Duke papers, Dep c. 716 ff 128–30).
93 RIC inspector general confidential report for the month of May 1918 (TNA, CO 904/105).
94 De Valera to O'Neill, 13 Apr. 1918 (NLI, Laurence O'Neill papers, MS 35,294/2).
95 Laffan, *Resurrection*, p. 138.
96 General Byrne to under-secretary, 20 Apr. 1918 (Bodleian Library, Duke papers, Dep c 716 f. 226).
97 Townshend, *Easter 1916*, pp 338–9.
98 Charles Townshend, *The republic: the fight for Irish independence* (London, 2013), p. 15.
99 Pension application of Richard Walsh (IMA, MSPC, MSP34REF18536).
100 Richard Walsh (BMH WS 400, pp 43–4).
101 Recommendation under regulation 14B of the Defence of the Realm Regulations, 17 May 1918 (TNA, CO 904/186/2).
102 David McCullagh, *De Valera, volume 1: rise 1882–1932* (Dublin, 2017), pp 147–8.
103 Macardle, *Irish Republic*, p. 269.
104 J.J. O'Kelly (BMH WS 384, pp 39–42).
105 O'Farrell, *Cathal Brugha*, p. 40; Seán Healy (BMH WS 1,479, p. 52).
106 Peter Hart, 'On the necessity of violence in the Irish Revolution' in Danine Farquarson & Seán Farrell (eds), *Shadows of the gunman: violence and culture in modern Ireland* (Cork, 2008), p. 23.
107 'Notes on Cathal Brugha', 1 Feb. 1966 (UCDA, Mulcahy papers, P7/D/86).
108 Richard Walsh (BMH WS 400, p. 40); Note dictated by de Valera on Volunteer executive, 13 Mar. 1964 (UCDA, de Valera papers, P150/609).
109 Hart, *Mick*, p. 292; Ernest Blythe (BMH WS 939, p. 127).
110 See pension application of Thomas Craven (IMA, MSPC, MSP34REF2994); pension application of James McNamara (IMA, MSPC, MSP34REF17660); Joseph Good (BMH WS 388); William Whelan (BMH WS 369); John Gaynor (BMH WS 1,447); Michael Rock (BMH WS 1,398).
111 Joseph Good (BMH WS 388, p.1); Joe Good, *Enchanted by dreams: the journal of a revolutionary* (Dingle, 1996), pp x–xi.
112 Pension application of Thomas Craven (IMA, MSPC, MSP34REF2994); Good, *Enchanted by dreams*, p. xi.
113 Bill Whelan (BMH WS 369, pp 5–6).
114 John Gaynor (BMH WS 1,447, p. 5); Bill Whelan (BMH WS 369, pp 7–8).
115 Statement of Thomas Barry regarding the activities of the Cork Brigade in London 1918, [1933] (NLI, O'Donoghue papers, MS 31,322/2); Barry's obituary, *Cork Examiner*, 30 May 1969; John Borgonovo, *The dynamics of war and revolution: Cork city, 1916–1918* (Cork, 2013), p. 197.
116 Pension application of Neil Kerr (IMA, MSPC, 24SP1206); Béaslaí, 'Michael Collins', *Cork Examiner*, 7 Aug. 1926.
117 Risteárd Mulcahy, *My father, the general: Richard Mulcahy and the military history of the revolution* (Dublin, 2009), p. 130.
118 Pádraig Ó Caoimh, *Richard Mulcahy: from the politics of war to the politics of peace, 1913–1924* (Newbridge, 2019), p. 47; 'Notes on Cathal Brugha', 1 Feb. 1966 (UCDA, Mulcahy papers, P7/D/86).

119 Mary MacDiarmada, *Art O'Brien and Irish nationalism in London, 1900–25* (Dublin, 2020), p. 60.

120 Pension application of John Joseph McGrath (IMA, MSPC, MSP34REF31710); Joseph Good (BMH WS 388, p. 41).

121 Statement of Thomas Barry [1933] (NLI, O'Donoghue papers, MS 31,322/2).

122 Joseph Good (BMH WS 388, p. 41); Bill Whelan (BMH WS 369, p. 6); 'Note on Cathal Brugha', 25 Apr. 1967 (UCDA, Mulcahy papers, P7/D/86).

123 Joseph Good (BMH WS 388, p. 42); Bill Whelan (BMH WS 369, p. 7); John Gaynor (BMH WS 1,447, p. 5).

124 John Gaynor (BMH WS 1,447, p. 7).

125 Ibid.

126 Joseph Good (BMH WS 388, p. 44); Bill Whelan (BMH WS 369, p. 7).

127 Bill Whelan (BMH WS 369, p. 7).

128 John Gaynor (BMH WS 1,447, p. 7).

129 Michael Lynch (BMH WS 511, p. 107).

130 J.J. O'Kelly (BMH WS 384, p. 41).

131 Pension application of John Joseph McGrath (IMA, MSPC, MSP34REF31710); Ernie O'Malley, *On another man's wound* (Revised ed. Dublin, 2002), p. 102.

132 O'Malley, *On another man's wound*, pp 102–3.

133 John Gaynor (BMH WS 1,447, pp 6–9).

134 Michael Lynch (BMH WS 511, p. 106).

135 Bill Whelan (BMH WS 369, p. 7).

136 O'Malley, *On another man's wound*, p. 113.

137 Joseph Good (BMH WS 388, p. 45); John Gaynor (BMH WS 1,447, p. 9); 'Note on Cathal Brugha', 25 Apr. 1967 (UCDA, Mulcahy papers, P7/D/86).

138 Mrs Batt O'Connor (BMH WS 330, p. 5); Richard Mulcahy, 'Conscription and the general headquarters staff', *Capuchin Annual*, 35 (1968), 388.

139 Mrs Batt O'Connor (BMH WS 330, pp 5–6); information from Cathal MacSwiney Brugha.

140 Meeting of standing committee, 26 Sept. 1918 (NLI, Sinn Fein Minute Book of Standing Committee, Jan. 1918–May 1919, P3269).

141 Farrell, *Founding of Dáil Éireann*, p. 26.

142 *IT*, 8 July 1922; *Waterford News and Star*, 1 Feb. 1924; O'Kelly, *Trinity of martyrs*, pp 38–9.

143 Pat McCarthy, *Waterford: the Irish Revolution, 1912–23* (Dublin, 2015), p. 55; Patrick Maume, 'O'Shee, James John', *DIB*.

144 'Notes on Cathal Brugha', 1 Feb. 1966 (UCDA, Mulcahy papers, P7/D/86); Long, 'Ó Murthuile, Seán', *DIB*.

145 Kathleen Lynn (BMH WS 357, p. 11); O'Kelly, 'Cathal Brugha – as I knew him', *Waterford News and Star*, 25 Aug. 1922; Ida Milne, *Stacking the coffins: influenza, war and revolution in Ireland, 1918–19* (Manchester, 2018), pp 118, 127.

146 Caitriona Foley, *The last Irish plague: the great flu epidemic in Ireland, 1918–19* (Dublin, 2011), p. 34.

147 RIC inspector general's monthly report for Nov. 1918 (TNA, CO 904/107).

148 *Dungarvan Observer*, 4 Dec. 1918, cited in McCarthy, *Waterford*, p. 56.

149 Pax Ó Faoláin interview in Uinseann Mac Eoin, *Survivors: the story of Ireland's struggle as told through some of her outstanding living people recalling events from the days of Davitt, through James Connolly, Brugha, Collins, Liam Mellows, and Rory O'Connor, to the present time* (Dublin 1980), p. 138.

150 Seditious literature reports, July–Dec. 1918 (TNA, CO 904/167).

151 *Cork Examiner*, 19 Dec. 1918; Waterford county inspector report for Dec. 1918 (TNA, CO 904/107).

152 Ibid.

153 Townshend, *Republic*, pp 58–60.

154 McCarthy, *Waterford*, pp 56–7.

155 See Brian Walker (ed.), *Parliamentary election results in Ireland, 1918–92* (Dublin, 1992), pp 4–9.

156 *Munster Express*, 4 Jan. 1919; *Waterford News and Star*, 15 July 1922.

157 Michael V. O'Donoghue (BMH WS 1,741, p. 43).

CHAPTER 5 *Minister: from the first Dáil to the Anglo-Irish truce, 1919–21*

1 *FJ*, 30 Dec. 1918.

2 Circular by Harry Boland and Tom Kelly, 2 Jan. 1919 (NLI, Piaras Béaslaí papers, MS 33,912/14).

3 Arthur Mitchell, *Revolutionary government in Ireland: Dáil Éireann, 1919–22* (Dublin, 1995), p. 9.

4 Dáil Éireann preliminary meeting, 7 Jan. 1919 (NLI, Béaslaí papers, MS 33,912/14).

5 Constitution of Dáil Éireann, 1 Apr. 1919 (NAI, DÉ 4/1/5) in *Documents on Irish foreign policy*, vol. I, document no. 6.

6 Townshend, *Republic*, pp 64–5.

7 Provisional constitution of Dáil drafted by select committee A, n.d. [Jan. 1919] (NLI, Béaslaí papers, MS 33,912/14).

8 Declaration of independence, 21 Jan. 1919, *Documents on Irish foreign policy*, vol. I, document no. 1.

9 Message to the free nations of the world, 21 Jan. 1919, ibid., document no. 2.

10 Emmet O'Connor, 'Neither democratic nor a programme: the Democratic Programme of 1919', *Irish Historical Studies* 40:157 (2016), 92–109.

11 Ibid., 102.

12 RIC inspector general monthly report for Jan. 1919 (TNA, CO 904/108).

13 *Cork Examiner*, 22 Jan. 1919.

14 Ua Ceallaigh, *Cathal Brugha*, p. 63.

15 Mary Daly, 'The first Dáil' in Crowley et al., *Atlas of the Irish Revolution*, p. 334.

16 Townshend, *Republic*, p. 66.

17 Mitchell, *Revolutionary government*, p. 14.

18 Townshend, *Republic*, pp 66–7.

19 Report of press censor for Jan. 1919 (TNA, CO 904/167).

20 Invitation to reception and dinner menu, Jan. 1919 (NLI, Béaslaí papers, MS 33,912/14).

21 *Cork Examiner*, 22 Jan. 1919; Notes by O'Brien on Cathal Brugha [n.d.] (NLI, William O'Brien papers, MS 15,704/7/4); Townshend, *Republic*, p. 53; Thomas J. Morrissey, *William O'Brien, 1881–1968: socialist, republican, Dáil deputy, editor and trade union leader* (Dublin, 2007), p. 165.

22 Notes by O'Brien on Cathal Brugha (NLI, O'Brien papers, MS 15,704/7/4).

23 Brian Farrell, 'The parliamentary road to independence' in Brian Farrell (ed.), *The creation of the Dáil: a volume of essays from the Thomas Davis lectures* (Dublin, 1994), pp 1–3.

24 *Waterford News and Star*, 25 Apr. 1919.

25 Report of press censor for Jan. 1919 (TNA, CO 904/167).

26 *FJ*, 1 Feb. 1919.

27 Report of press censor for Jan. 1919 (TNA, CO 904/167).

28 Seán T. Ó Ceallaigh [O'Kelly] (Paris) to Brugha, 7 Mar. 1919 (NAI, DFA ES Paris 1919) in *Documents on Irish foreign policy*, vol. I, document no. 5.

29 Gerard Keown, *First of small nations: the beginnings of Irish foreign policy in the interwar years, 1919–1932* (Oxford, 2016), pp 38–42; Laffan, *Resurrection*, p. 251.

30 Laffan, *Resurrection*, p. 251; Townshend, *Republic*, p. 68.

31 Gavan Duffy (Paris) to Brugha, 20 Apr. 1919 (NAI, DFA ES Paris 1919) in *Documents on Irish foreign policy*, vol. I, document no. 7.

32 Kenny, *Arthur Griffith*, p. 147.

33 Laffan, *Resurrection*, p. 221.

34 Quinn, 'Brugha, Cathal', *DIB*.

35 Quoted in Maryann Gialanella Valiulis, *Portrait of a revolutionary: General Richard Mulcahy and the founding of the Irish Free State* (Dublin, 1992), p. 40.

36 *Waterford News and Star*, 25 Apr. 1919.

37 Ronan Fanning, 'De Valera, Éamon', *DIB*.

38 J.J. O'Kelly (BMH WS 384, p. 45); O'Donoghue, 'Cathal Brugha' lecture, Apr. 1966 (NLI, O'Donoghue papers, MS 31,319/2/10); Ó Dochartaigh, *Cathal Brugha*, p. 95.

39 Townshend, *Republic*, pp 82–3.

40 'De Valera's recollections following his escape from Lincoln jail in 1919', 15 Nov. 1960 (UCDA, de Valera papers, P150/629); McCullagh, *Rise*, p. 154.

41 Ó Caoimh, *Richard Mulcahy*, p. 55; Michael Hopkinson, *The Irish War of Independence* (Dublin, 2002), pp 39–40.

42 *FJ*, 10 Mar. 1919; Ua Ceallaigh, *Cathal Brugha*, pp 71–3.

43 *Dungarvan Observer and Munster Industrial Advocate*, 15 Mar. 1919.

44 Ua Ceallaigh, *Cathal Brugha*, p. 76.

45 John M. Regan, *The Irish counter-revolution, 1921–1936: treatyite politics and settlement in independent Ireland* (Dublin, 1999), p. 9.

46 *Dáil debates*, 2 Apr. 1919, vol. F, no. 4; J.J. O'Kelly (BMH WS 384, pp 47–9); Ó Caoimh, *Richard Mulcahy*, p. 56.

47 Mitchell, *Revolutionary government*, p. 55.

48 Máire Comerford interview in Mac Eoin, *Survivors*, p. 42.

49 *Waterford News and Star*, 25 Apr. 1919.

50 Arthur Mitchell, 'Making the case for Irish independence' in Crowley et al., *Atlas of the Irish Revolution*, p. 474.

51 McCullagh, *Rise*, p. 159.

52 Ibid., p. 171; O'Donoghue, 'Cathal Brugha' lecture, Apr. 1966.

53 Ua Ceallaigh, *Cathal Brugha*, p. 83; Colmán Ó Huallacháin, Rónán Ó Huallacháin & Patrick Conlon, *The Irish and the Irish – a sociolinguistic analysis of the relationship between a people and their language* (Dublin, 1994), pp 79–80.

54 Murphy, 'O'Kelly, John Joseph', *DIB*; Mitchell, *Revolutionary government*, p. 94.

55 Brian P. Murphy, *The Catholic Bulletin and Republican Ireland with special reference to J.J. O'Kelly (Sceilg)* (Belfast, 2005), p. 27.

56 *Irish without a teacher* compiled by Lil Ní Aodha & Breandán Ó hAodha (Dublin, 1920); Ó Dochartaigh, *Cathal Brugha*, pp 166–7.

57 David Fitzpatrick, *The two Irelands, 1912–1939* (Oxford, 1998), p. 83.

58 Kevin O'Shiel (BMH WS 1,770, p. 905).

59 Ibid., p. 963.

60 Ibid., p. 962; Mary Kotsonouris, *The Dáil courts, 1920–24* (Dublin, 1994), p. 26.

61 Fergus Campbell (ed.), 'The last land war? Kevin O'Shiel's memoir of the Irish Revolution (1916–21)', *Archivium Hibernicum*, 57 (2003), 168, 189.

62 Charles Townshend, *The British campaign in Ireland, 1919–1921: the development of political and military policies* (London, 1975).

63 Townshend, *Republic*, p. 105.

64 Ibid., p. 152.

65 Laffan, *Resurrection*, pp 277–84; Townshend, *Republic*, pp 86–9.

66 Laffan, *Resurrection*, p. 282.

67 Mulcahy, *My father*, p. 39; Ó Caoimh, *Richard Mulcahy*, p. 62.

68 Mitchell, *Revolutionary government*, p. 68.

69 Ó Caoimh, *Richard Mulcahy*, p. 57.

70 *Dáil debates*, 20 Aug. 1919, vol. F, no. 13.

71 Richard Walsh (BMH WS 400, p. 55); Memorandum by Richard Mulcahy on 'the oath and the IRB and the Dáil', 14 Jan. 1965 (UCDA, Mulcahy papers, P7/D/17).

72 Ó Caoimh, *Richard Mulcahy*, p. 62.

73 Ibid., p. 57.

74 *Dáil debates*, 20 Aug. 1919, vol. F, no. 13.

75 Townshend, *Republic*, p. 87.

76 Memorandum by Richard Mulcahy on 'the oath and the IRB and the Dáil', 14 Jan. 1965 (UCDA, Mulcahy papers, P7/D/17).

77 *Dáil debates*, 20 Aug. 1919, vol. F, no. 13; Laffan, *Resurrection*, p. 282; Townshend, *Republic*, p. 87.

78 Evidence of Michael Staines in the pension application of Joseph O'Doherty (IMA, MSPC, MSP34REF16536).

79 Lynch (BMH WS 511, p. 78).

80 Ibid.

81 Michael McDonnell (BMH WS 225, p. 4); Ernest Blythe (BMH WS 939, p. 110); T. Ryle Dwyer, *The Squad and the intelligence operations of Michael Collins* (Cork, 2005), pp 46–52.

82 Fitzpatrick, *Two Irelands*, p. 124.

83 C.S. Andrews, *Dublin made me* (Dublin, 1979), p. 201.

84 Good, *Enchanted by dreams*, p. 111; Robert Barton (BMH, WS 979, p. 25).

85 Barton (BMH WS 979, p. 25).

86 Hart, *Mick*, p. 261.

87 Regan, *Irish counter-revolution* p. 8.

88 Ernest Blythe (BMH WS 939, pp 126–7).

89 Frank Henderson (BMH WS 821, pp 102–3).

90 Hart, *Mick*, pp 35, 71.

91 Mulcahy's reflections on 'The question of the chief of staff position' (UCDA, Mulcahy papers, P7/D/96).

92 Mulcahy, 'Notes on Cathal Brugha', 1 Feb. 1966, ibid.

93 Mulcahy, *My father*, p. 132.

94 Dolan & Murphy, *Michael Collins*, p. 122.

95 Seumas Robinson (BMH WS 1,721, p. 37); O'Malley, *On another man's wound*, p. 327.

96 O'Malley, *On another man's wound*, p. 327.

97 Laurence Nugent (BMH WS 907, p. 223); León Ó Broin, *Revolutionary underground: the story of the Irish republican brotherhood, 1858–1923* (Dublin, 1975), p. 200.

98 Dan McCarthy (BMH WS 722, p. 24).

99 Francis Pakenham & Thomas P. O'Neill, *Éamon de Valera* (London, 1970), p. 118.

100 Mitchell, *Revolutionary government*, p. 78.

101 Ó Broin, *Revolutionary underground*, p. 202.

102 Ibid., p. 231.

103 Pension application of Michael Lynch (IMA, MSPC, MSP34REF9462); Lynch (BMH WS 511, pp 30–2).

104 Dolan & Murphy, *Michael Collins*, p. 150.

105 Andy Bielenberg, 'Female fatalities in County Cork during the Irish War of Independence and the case of Mrs Lindsay' in Linda Connolly (ed.), *Women and the Irish Revolution* (Newbridge, 2020), pp 154–8; Townshend, *Republic*, p. 300; O'Halpin & Ó Corráin, *Dead of the Irish Revolution*, pp 332–4.

106 Minister for defence to Ethel Benson, 29 July 1921 (NLI, Seán O'Mahony papers, MS 44,045).

107 Bielenberg, 'The case of Mrs Lindsay', p. 161.

108 Ó Caoimh, *Richard Mulcahy*, pp 60–1.

109 Mulcahy, 'Cathal Brugha', 28 Apr. 1967 (UCDA, Mulcahy papers, P7/D/86).

110 Mulcahy, *My father*, p. 134.

111 Seán Saunders (BMH WS 817, p. 4); Liam Kavanagh to Ruairí Brugha, 21 May 1965 (in possession of Cathal MacSwiney Brugha).

112 Mitchell, *Revolutionary government*, p. 79; Kavanagh to Ruairí Brugha, 21 May 1965; information from Andrea O'Reilly.

113 J.J. O'Kelly (BMH, WS 384, pp 57–9); Béaslaí, *Michael Collins*, i, p. 19.

114 Mitchell, *Revolutionary government*, p. 79.

115 Máire Comerford interview in Mac Eoin, *Survivors*, p. 42.

116 Barton to Ruairí Brugha, 6 May 1965.

117 Pension application of Joseph O'Doherty (IMA, MSPC, MSPC34REF16536).

118 O'Kelly (BMH WS 384, p. 57); Townshend, *Republic*, p. 87.

119 Robert Brennan (BMH WS 779, p. 22); Brennan, 'Fearless Cathal', *IP*, 20 June 1957. Brennan claims that the source of this information was the notorious Dublin Castle intelligence officer, Captain Jocelyn Hardy.

120 Robert Nugent (BMH WS 907, p. 223).

121 Ibid.; O'Farrell, *Cathal Brugha*, p. 56.

122 Kavanagh to Brugha, 21 May 1965.

123 Tomás Ó Dochartaigh, 'Cathal Brugha', *IP*, 29 June 1967.

124 *Voice of Labour*, 17 May 1919; *Watchword of Labour*, 4 Oct., 18 Oct., 25 Oct. 1919; Fitzpatrick, *Politics and Irish life*, p. 217.

125 Mrs Batt O'Connor (BMH, WS 330, pp 4–7).

126 *IP*, 9 July 1932 and 4 Apr. 1933; Brennan, 'Fearless Cathal', *IP*, 20 June 1957; Frank Gallagher, *The four glorious years* (Dublin, 1953), pp 152–3.

127 Bridie O'Reilly (BMH WS 454, p. 5).

128 *II*, 25 Oct. 1920; *Evening Echo*, 25 Oct. 1920; Ó Dochartaigh, *Cathal Brugha*, pp 134–5.

129 Gallagher, *Four glorious years*, p. 152.

130 Margaret Ward, *Hannah Sheehy Skeffington, feminism and the Irish Revolution* (Dublin, 2019), p. 183.

131 Obituary for Mrs Ellen Humphreys, *IP*, 9 June 1939; Áine O'Rahilly (BMH WS 333, p. 10); Ó Dochartaigh, *Cathal Brugha*, p. 133.

132 J.J. O'Kelly (BMH WS 384, p. 57).

133 Dublin Castle file no. 180, Burgess, Charles (Brugha, Cathal) (TNA, WO 35/206/22).

134 Dolan & Murphy, *Michael Collins*, p. 117.

135 Ernie O'Malley, 'Bloody Sunday' in *Dublin's fighting story 1916–1921: told by the men who made it* (Tralee, 1949), p. 131; Ó Caoimh, *Richard Mulcahy*, p. 61; Townshend, *Republic*, p. 203; Dwyer, *The squad*, p. 192; Ferriter, *A nation and not a rabble*, p. 203.

136 Note on Cathal Brugha, 25 Apr. 1967 (UCDA, Mulcahy papers, P7/D/86).

137 On those killed see O'Halpin & Ó Corráin, *Dead of the Irish Revolution*, pp 222–33; Anne Dolan, 'Killing and Bloody Sunday, November 1920', *Historical Journal*, 49:3 (2006), 789–810.

138 'Talk given by Mulcahy to the Association Old Dublin Brigade', 31 Jan. 1964 (UCDA, Mulcahy papers, P7/D/6); 'Notes on Cathal Brugha', 1 Feb. 1966 (UCDA, Mulcahy papers, P7/D/86); Mulcahy, *My father*, pp 133–4.

139 Alfred Burgess (BMH WS 1,634, pp 6–7).

140 J.J. O'Kelly (BMH WS 384, p. 13).

141 Macready to John Anderson, 11 Jan. 1921 (TNA, John Anderson papers, CO 904/188).

142 Townshend, *Republic*, p. 223; Hopkinson, *Irish War of Independence*, pp 183–5.

143 O'Donoghue, 'Cathal Brugha' lecture, Apr. 1966; Hart, *Mick*, pp 271–2.

144 Recollections by de Valera of his arrival home from America in Dec. 1920, Feb. 1962 (UCDA, de Valera papers, P150/1414).

145 Ibid.

146 *Dáil debates*, 11 Mar. 1921, vol. F, no. 20; Fitzpatrick, *Politics and Irish life*, p. 166.

147 Ó Caoimh, *Richard Mulcahy*, p. 67; Mulcahy, *My father*, p. 69.

148 Patrick G. Daly (BMH WS 814, p. 20).

149 Frank Owen, *Tempestuous journey: Lloyd George, his life and times* (London, 1954), p. 569; Tim Pat Coogan, *Michael Collins: a biography* (London, 1990), p. 179.

150 Review of *Tempestuous journey* by Samiel J. Hurwitz, *Political Science Quarterly*, 70:4 (Dec. 1955), 616.

151 Seán McLoughlin (BMH WS 290, pp 46–7); Charlie McGuire, 'McLoughlin, Seán', *DIB*.

152 McLoughlin (BMH WS 290, p. 47; Emmet O'Connor, *Reds and the green: Ireland, Russia and the internationals, 1919–43* (Dublin, 2004), p. 38.

153 Brugha to de Valera, 16 May 1921 (UCDA, de Valera papers, P150/1387); Gerard Noonan, *The IRA in Britain, 1919–1923: 'in the heart of enemy lines'* (Liverpool, 2014), p. 195; see also W.H. Kautt, *Arming the Irish Revolution: gunrunning and arms smuggling, 1911–1922* (Kansas, 2021), pp 161–3.

154 Hart, *Mick*, p. 263.

155 McCullagh, *Rise*, p. 199.

156 Hart, *Mick*, p. 263; Mulcahy, *My father*, p. 85.

157 Robert Briscoe interview with Ernie O'Malley, 1948–54 (UCDA, O'Malley notebooks, P17b/97).

158 Béaslaí, *Michael Collins*, ii, p. 106.

159 Mitchell, *Revolutionary government*, pp 230–1; Hart, *Mick*, pp 262–3.

160 Mulcahy's notes on Brugha, Stack and other members of GHQ staff and cabinet (UCDA, Mulcahy papers, P7/D/96); McCullagh, *Rise*, p. 190.

161 See Hart, *Mick*, p. 263.

162 Brugha to Boland, 2 Mar. 1921 (UCDA, de Valera papers, P150/1128).

163 Boland to Brugha, 14 Apr. 1921; Brugha to Boland, 22 Apr. 1921; Boland to Brugha, 15 July 1921 (UCDA, de Valera papers, P150/1128); Fitzpatrick, *Boland*, p. 216.

164 Boland to Brugha, 19 July 1921 (UCDA, de Valera papers, P150/1128).

165 Brugha to Boland, 9 Aug. 1921, ibid.

166 Seán Nunan (BMH WS 1,744, pp 15–16); Fitzpatrick, *Boland*, pp 181–2.

167 Nunan (BMH WS 1,744, p. 16); Mitchell, *Revolutionary government*, p. 231; O'Farrell, *Cathal Brugha*, p. 69.

168 Hart, *Mick*, p. 261.

169 See, for example, Béaslaí, *Michael Collins*, i, p. 212; Peter Hart, 'Michael Collins and the assassination of Sir Henry Wilson', *Irish Historical Studies*, 28:110 (Nov. 1992), 150–70.

170 Joost Augusteijn, *From public defiance to guerrilla warfare: the experience of ordinary volunteers in the Irish War of Independence, 1916–1921* (Dublin, 1996), pp 327–8.

171 Michael McDonnell (BMH WS 225, pp 2–3).

172 Patrick A. Murray (BMH WS 1,584, pp 17–20); Murray to Florrie O'Donoghue, 14 Jan. 1959 (NLI, O'Donoghue papers, MS 31,296/1/13); Patrick Maume, 'MacSwiney, Terence James', *DIB*. Francis Costello suggests that the mission was to rescue MacSwiney from prison, see Costello, *Enduring the most*, p. 160.

173 Murray (BMH WS 1,584, p. 20).

174 MacSwiney to Brugha, 30 Sept. 1920 (UCDA, MacSwiney papers, P48b/416).

175 Brugha to Muriel MacSwiney, 3 Nov. 1920 (NLI, Art O'Brien papers, MS 8,447/9).

176 Ibid.

177 Seán Healy (BMH WS 1,479, pp 46–53); Stephen Foley (BMH WS 1,669, pp 8–9); Maye, *Griffith*, p. 146.

178 Seán MacKeon [Mac Eoin] (BMH WS 1,716, pp 161–4).

179 Dolan & Murphy, *Michael Collins*, p. 117.

180 MacKeon (BMH WS 1,716, p. 164); Pádraic O'Farrell, *The blacksmith of Ballinalee: Seán Mac Eoin* (Mullingar, 1993), p. 48.

181 Matt Feehan (editor *Sunday Press*) to Florence O'Donoghue, 17 Dec. 1958 (NLI, O'Donoghue papers, MS 31,296/1/2).

182 O'Donoghue, 'Alleged plan to assassinate British cabinet?', 25 Jan. 1959 (NLI, O'Donoghue papers, MS 31,296/2/5).

183 McCullagh, *Rise*, p. 201.

184 *IT*, 29 Apr. 1921.

185 Michael Hopkinson (ed.), *The last days of Dublin Castle: the Mark Sturgis diaries* (Dublin, 1999), p. 166.

186 McCullagh, *Rise*, p.206; Mitchell, *Revolutionary government*, p. 298.

187 Ernest Blythe (BMH WS 939, pp 129–30); Townshend, *Republic*, p. 308.

CHAPTER 6 *Custodian: truce, treaty and split*

1 Maher, *Harry Boland*, p. 195.

2 Diarmaid Ferriter, *Between two hells: the Irish civil war* (London, 2021), p. 4.

3 Morrissey, *William O'Brien*, p. 199.

4 *II*, 11 July 1921.

5 Terms of the truce, 12 July 1921 (NAI, DÉ/2/304/14/1).

6 Ibid.

7 Ó Dochartaigh, *Cathal Brugha*, p. 135.

8 Ibid., p. 161.

9 Máire Comerford, *On dangerous ground: a memoir of the Irish Revolution*, ed. Hilary Dully (Dublin, 2021), p. 211.

10 J.J. O'Kelly, 'Cathal Brugha – as I knew him', *Waterford News and Star*, 25 Aug. 1922; Ó Dochartaigh, *Cathal Brugha*, p. 161.

11 Mícheál Ó Fathartaigh & Liam Weeks, *Birth of a state: the Anglo-Irish treaty* (Newbridge, 2021), p. 56.

12 Austin Stack's account in Úna C. Stack (BMH WS 418, p. 37); Ó Dochartaigh, *Cathal Brugha*, pp 168–9; McCullagh, *Rise*, pp 212–14.

13 De Valera to William O'Brien as cited in McCullagh, *Rise*, p. 214.

14 McCullagh, *Rise*, pp 215–16.

15 Farrell, *Founding of Dáil Éireann*, pp 63, 70–3.

16 Laffan, *Resurrection*, p. 348.

17 *Dáil debates*, 14 Sept. 1921, vol. S, no. 10; Townshend, *Republic*, p. 332.

18 Michael Laffan, *Judging W.T. Cosgrave* (Dublin, 2014), p. 76.

19 Instructions to plenipotentiaries from Dáil cabinet, 7 Oct. 1921 (NAI, DÉ/4/5/1).

20 De Valera to McGarrity, 21 Dec. 1921 (NLI, McGarrity papers, MS 17,440).

21 Townshend, *Republic*, p. 332.

22 Caitlín Brugha to editor, *IP*, 30 Mar. 1937. The offending review was published in the *Irish Press* on 23 Mar. 1937.

23 *Weekly IT*, 18 Feb. 1922.

24 Townshend, *Republic*, p. 326.

25 Mulcahy as quoted in Valiulis, *Richard Mulcahy*, p. 44.

26 Colonel J. Brind, 'The military situation in Ireland at the end of Sept. 1921' (NAI, DÉ/2/304/14/1).

27 Minister for defence to officers in the [Irish] Republican Army, 25 Oct. 1921 (NLI, Moore papers, MS 10,544/1/39); Brian Hughes, *Defying the IRA?: intimidation, coercion, and communities during the Irish Revolution* (Liverpool, 2016), p. 176.

28 Minister for defence to Mrs O'Dempsey, 25 Oct. 1921 (NAI, DÉ/2/463). On the killing, see O'Halpin & Ó Corráin, *Dead of the Irish Revolution*, pp 341–3.

29 Valiulis, *Richard Mulcahy*, p. 101.

30 Brugha to Gearóid O'Sullivan (adjutant-general), 30 July 1921 (UCDA, Mulcahy papers, P7a/1); McCullagh, *Rise*, p. 226; Ó Caoimh, *Richard Mulcahy*, p. 72.

31 Brugha to O'Sullivan, 30 July 1921 (UCDA, Mulcahy papers, P7a/1).

32 Mulcahy to Brugha, 2 Sept. 1921, ibid.

33 Brugha to Mulcahy, 6 Sept. 1921, ibid.

34 Ibid., 12–13 Sept. 1921, ibid.

35 Mulcahy to de Valera, n.d. [Sept. 1921], ibid.

36 McCullagh, *Rise*, p. 227.

37 Mulcahy as cited in McCullagh, *Rise*, p. 228; Ó Caoimh, *Richard Mulcahy*, p. 73.

38 McCullagh, *Rise*, p. 228.

39 J. Anthony Gaughan, *Austin Stack: portrait of a separatist* (Dublin, 1977), p. 141.

40 Fearghal McGarry, *Eoin O'Duffy: a self-made hero* (Oxford, 2005), p. 83.

41 Ó Caoimh, *Richard Mulcahy*, p. 74; Hart, *Mick*, pp 289–90.

42 Minister for defence to Charlie Daly, 17 Nov. 1921, reproduced in Síobhra Aiken, Fearghal Mac Bhloscaidh, Liam Ó Duibhir & Diarmuid Ó Tuama (eds), *The men will talk to me: Ernie O'Malley's interviews with the Northern Divisions* (Newbridge, 2018), p. 55.

43 O'Duffy to minister for defence, 24 Nov. 1921 (NLI, Eoin O'Duffy papers, MS 48,281/2/1).

44 Brugha to O'Duffy, 25 Nov. 1921 (NLI, O'Duffy papers, MS 48,281/2/2).

45 Ibid.

46 O'Duffy to minister for defence, n.d. [Nov. 1921] (NLI, O'Duffy papers, MS 48,281/2/3).

47 Mulcahy's notes on Brugha, Stack and other members of GHQ staff and cabinet (UCDA, Mulcahy papers, P7/D/96); McGarry, *Eoin O'Duffy*, p. 86.

48 McCullagh, *Rise*, p. 228; Townshend, *Republic*, pp 328–9; Hart, *Mick*, p. 289.

49 McGarry, *Eoin O'Duffy*, pp 86–7.

50 Tom Garvin, *1922: the birth of Irish democracy* (Dublin, 1996), p. 59.

51 McCullagh, *Rise*, p. 228; Townshend, *Republic*, pp 328–9; Hart, *Mick*, p. 289.

52 O'Duffy (deputy chief of staff) to all divisional commandants, 30 Nov. 1921, reproduced in Aiken et al. (eds), *The men will talk to me*, pp 55–6.

53 Mulcahy's notes on Brugha, Stack and other members of GHQ staff and cabinet (UCDA, Mulcahy papers, P7/D/96); Townshend, *Republic*, p. 330.

54 McCullagh, *Rise*, p. 229.

55 Mulcahy's notes on Brugha, Stack and other members of GHQ staff and cabinet (UCDA, Mulcahy papers, P7/D/96).

56 Townshend, *Republic*, p. 330.

57 Robert C. Barton (BMH WS 979, pp 32–3).
58 Report from quartermaster-general to minister for defence, 19 Dec. 1921 (UCDA, de Valera papers, P150/1335).
59 Ibid.
60 Pension application by Gilbert Barrington (IMA, MSPC, MSP34REF58934); Pension application of Richard Purcell (IMA, MSPC, 24SP13486); Gilbert Barrington (BMH WS 773, p. 13).
61 Notes by O'Brien on Cathal Brugha, n.d. (NLI, O'Brien papers, MS 15,704/7/4).
62 Ibid.; J. Anthony Gaughan, *Thomas Johnson 1872–1963: first leader of the Labour Party in Dáil Éireann* (Dublin, 1980), p. 191.
63 Notes by O'Brien on Cathal Brugha, n.d. (NLI, O'Brien papers, MS 15,704/7/4); O'Connor, *Reds and the green*, p. 56.
64 Nicholas Mansergh, *The unresolved question: the Anglo-Irish settlement and its undoing, 1912–72* (New Haven, 1972), p. 178.
65 Memorandum on defence by Erskine Childers, 7 Nov. 1921 (NAI, DÉ/2/304/14/1).
66 Austin Stack in Úna Stack (BMH WS 418, p. 48).
67 Michael Brennan (BMH WS 1,068, pp 116–18); Edward Lynch (BMH WS 1,333, pp 14–15); Kautt, *Arming the Irish Revolution*, p. 117.
68 Lynch (BMH WS 1,333, pp 15–23); *Cork Examiner*, 19 Jan. 1922; Meda Ryan, *Michael Collins and the women who spied for Ireland* (Cork, 1996), p. 119; Peter Hart, '"Operations abroad": the IRA in Britain, 1919–23', *English Historical Review*, 115:460 (2000), 87.
69 Brennan (BMH WS 1,068, p. 120).
70 Stack in Úna Stack (BMH WS 418, p. 54).
71 Mitchell, *Revolutionary government*, p. 323.
72 Maye, *Arthur Griffith*, p. 226.
73 Stack in Úna Stack (BMH WS 418, pp 52–3); Michael Hopkinson, *Green against green: the Irish civil war* (Dublin, 1988), p. 30; Townshend, *Republic*, pp 347–8.
74 *II*, 7 Dec. 1921.
75 Patrick Maume, 'O'Doherty, Thomas', *DIB*.
76 Recollections of de Valera of a visit to Bishop O'Doherty of Clonfert in Dec. 1921, 19 Jan. 1963 (UCDA, de Valera papers, P150/1537); McCullagh, *Rise*, p. 240.
77 McCullagh, *Rise*, p. 242.
78 Gaughan, *Thomas Johnson*, p. 192; O'Connor, *Reds and the green*, p. 56.
79 Dáil cabinet minutes, 8 Dec. 1921 (NAI, DÉ/1/3).
80 Laurence O'Neill as quoted in Morrissey, *Laurence O'Neill*, p. 205.
81 Macardle, *Irish Republic*, p. 634.
82 Ibid., pp 634–8.
83 Alfred Burgess (BMH WS 1,634, p. 2).
84 Ibid., p. 3.
85 *Cork Examiner*, 16 Dec. 1921.
86 *FJ*, 16 Dec. 1921.
87 Ó Fathartaigh & Weeks, *Birth of a state*, p. 97.
88 *FJ*, 9 Dec. 1921.
89 *IT*, 9 Dec. 1921.
90 *Dáil debates*, 21 Dec. 1921, vol. T, no. 8.
91 Townshend, *Republic*, p. 360.
92 *Dáil debates*, 7 Jan. 1922, vol. T, no. 15.
93 Ibid.
94 Ibid.

95   Ibid.
96   Ibid.
97   Máire Comerford interview in Mac Eoin, *Survivors*, p. 45.
98   *FJ*, 9 Jan. 1922.
99   Andrews, *Dublin made me*, p. 207.
100 Jennie Wyse Power to Nancy Wyse Power, 7 Jan. 1922, cited in Matthews, *Renegades*, p. 306.
101 *Dáil debates*, 7 Jan. 1922, vol. T, no. 15.
102 RTÉ, *Treaty live*, broadcast on 7 Jan. 2022.
103 *Dáil debates*, 9 Jan. 1922, vol. T, no. 16.
104 Ibid.
105 Ibid.
106 Frank Pakenham, *Peace by ordeal: the negotiation of the Anglo-Irish treaty* (London, 1935), p. 96.
107 Béaslaí, *Michael Collins*, ii, p. 224.
108 Murphy, *Lost republican ideal*, p. 136.
109 Brugha to O'Duffy, 12 Jan. 1922 (NLI, O'Duffy papers, MS 48,281/2/3).
110 J.J. O'Kelly, 'Cathal Brugha – as I knew him', *Waterford News and Star*, 24 Aug. 1923.

CHAPTER 7 *Martyr: civil war, death and funeral*

1   Béaslaí, *Michael Collins*, ii, p. 266.
2   Laffan, *Resurrection*, p. 361.
3   *Dáil debates*, 9 Jan. 1922, vol. T, no. 16.
4   *II*, 10 Apr. 1922.
5   Notes by Brugha on the treaty, n.d. [1922] (in possession of Cathal MacSwiney Brugha).
6   *Tipperary Star*, 11 Mar. 1922.
7   Laffan, *Resurrection*, pp 366–7.
8   *Weekly IT*, 18 Feb. 1922.
9   McCullagh, *Rise*, pp 264, 268–70.
10   *Weekly IT*, 18 Feb. 1922; Ua Ceallaigh, *Cathal Brugha*, pp 250–1.
11   Matthews, *Renegades*, p. 309; Lawrence William White, 'MacDonagh, Joseph', *DIB*.
12   Cathal Brugha, 'Was it for this?', *Poblacht na hÉireann*, 21 Feb. 1922: Ua Ceallaigh, *Cathal Brugha*, pp 256–7.
13   *IT*, 20 Feb. 1922.
14   Ibid., 21 Feb. 1922.
15   *Cork Examiner*, 20 Feb. 1922.
16   Laffan, *Resurrection*, pp 372–3.
17   *Weekly IT*, 25 Feb. 1922.
18   Laffan, *Resurrection*, p. 374.
19   Margaret Ward, 'Women in the Irish Free State: gender and the legacy of revolution' in Crowley et al., *Atlas of the Irish Revolution*, p. 814.
20   *Dáil debates*, 2 Mar. 1922, vol. S2, no. 3.
21   *Weekly IT*, 11 Mar. 1922.
22   *II*, 17 Mar. 1922.
23   Transcript notes taken by Francis D. McManus of speech made by Austin Stack, delivered in Providence, US, 20 Mar. 1922, p. 8 (NLI, Austin Stack papers, MS 17,088/4).
24   *IT*, 18 Mar. 1922.
25   *II*, 11 Mar. 1922; *IT*, 18 Mar. 1922.
26   *II*, 18 Mar. 1922.

27 Hopkinson, *Green against green*, p. 40.

28 John Borgonovo, 'IRA conventions' in Crowley et al., *Atlas of the Irish Revolution*, p. 670.

29 Hopkinson, *Green against green*, p. 41.

30 Ibid., p. 58.

31 Ibid., p. 66; Ó Caoimh, *Richard Mulcahy*, p. 107.

32 Hopkinson, *Green against green*, p. 67; Lawrence William White, 'O'Connor, Rory', *DIB*.

33 Macardle, *Irish republic*, p. 693.

34 Brugha to editor *II*, 25 Mar. 1922.

35 Morrissey, *Laurence O'Neill*, p. 212.

36 *Irish Catholic Directory 1923*, 598–600.

37 Kostick, *Revolution in Ireland*, pp 173–4.

38 Maye, *Arthur Griffith*, p. 253.

39 Ibid., p. 254.

40 McCullagh, *Rise*, pp 276–7; Morrissey, *Laurence O'Neill*, p. 214.

41 *Dáil debates*, 17 May 1922, vol. S2, no. 11.

42 Ibid.

43 On this see Alan Parkinson, *Belfast's unholy war: the troubles of the 1920s* (Dublin, 2004); Brian Feeney, *Antrim: the Irish Revolution, 1912–23* (Dublin, 2021).

44 Ibid.

45 J.J. O'Kelly (BMH WS 384, pp 52–3).

46 *Dáil debates*, 17 May 1922, vol. S2, no. 11.

47 Michael Gallagher, 'The pact general election of 1922', *Irish Historical Studies*, 21:84 (1979), 404–21; Laffan, *Resurrection*, pp 387–8.

48 *FJ*, 24 May 1922.

49 Laffan, *Resurrection*, p. 392.

50 *Waterford News and Star*, 16 June 1922; *Nationalist and Munster Advertiser*, 14 June 1922; Maher, *Harry Boland*, pp 285–6.

51 Waterford-Tipperary East, general election, 16 June 1922, electionsireland.org.

52 J.J. O'Kelly, 'Cathal Brugha as I knew him', *Waterford News and Star*, 24 Aug. 1923.

53 Keith Jeffery, 'Wilson, Sir Henry Hughes', *DIB*.

54 Morrissey, *Laurence O'Neill*, p. 215.

55 Robert Brennan (BMH WS 779, p. 711).

56 McCullagh, *Rise*, pp 286–6.

57 O'Kelly, *A trinity of martyrs*, p. 87; Ó Dochartaigh, *Cathal Brugha*, p. 244.

58 Brendan Considine (IMA, MSPC, MSP34REF18235).

59 Hopkinson, *Green against green*, p.123; Townshend, *Republic*, p. 409.

60 Robert C. Barton (BMH WS 979, p. 46); Hopkinson, *Green against green*, p. 123.

61 Comerford, *On dangerous ground*, p. 271.

62 Ibid., pp 269–70.

63 For a detailed examination, see Michael Fewer, *The battle of the Four Courts: the first three days of the Irish civil war* (London, 2018), pp 224–34.

64 John F. Homan, 'Memorandum of ambulance work and efforts for peace', July 1922 (NAI, Department of An Taoiseach, S8138).

65 Linda McWhinney (BMH WS 404, p. 19). In 1929 Kearns married Wilson Charles MacWhinney; *Poblacht na hÉireann*, 7 July 1922; Townshend, *Republic*, p. 410; Ward, *Unmanageable revolutionaries*, p. 129.

66 Macardle, *Irish Republic*, p. 753.

67 Eve Morrison, 'One woman's war', *IT*, 22 May 2013, supplement, 'Stories of the Irish Revolution'.

68 Comerford, *On dangerous ground*, p. 272.

69 *Poblacht na hÉireann*, 7 July 1922.

70 John O'Sheehan to editor, *Sunday Independent*, 21 July 1957; pension application of John O'Sheehan (IMA, MSPC, MSP34REF60017).

71 Report from Captain Dalton, Amiens Street, 3 July 1922 (NLI, Ernie O'Malley papers, MS 10,973/11/15): Ua Ceallaigh, *Cathal Brugha*, p. 299.

72 *Ulster Herald*, 15 July 1922.

73 Calton Younger, *Ireland's civil war* (London, 1968), p. 332.

74 Statement of Seán M. Glynn regarding the fighting in Dublin, June–July 1922, n.d. (UCDA, de Valera papers, P150/3631); Townshend, *Republic*, p. 410.

75 Kathleen Barry-Moloney to editor, *IP*, 28 July 1932. In 1924 Kathleen Barry married Jim Moloney.

76 Homan, 'Memorandum of ambulance work and efforts for peace', July 1922.

77 Linda McWhinney (BMH WS 404, p. 20).

78 Ibid.

79 *Observer*, 9 July 1922.

80 Linda McWhinney (BMH WS 404, p. 19); *Poblacht na hÉireann*, 7 July 1922.

81 Gallagher, *Four glorious years*, p. 379.

82 Linda McWhinney (BMH WS 404, p. 19).

83 *II*, 7 July 1922.

84 See p. 65.

85 'The faith of Cathal Brugha', note found after his death in July 1922 (NLI, McGarrity papers, MS 17,654/6/14); *Dáil debates*, 7 Jan. 1922, vol. T, no. 15.

86 Seán Brady's recollections of Cathal Brugha, 7 Feb. 1966 (UCDA, de Valera papers, P150/1634).

87 Linda McWhinney (BMH WS 404, p. 20); O'Donoghue, 'Cathal Brugha' lecture, Apr. 1966 (NLI, O'Donoghue papers, MS 31,319/2/10); Seán Brady's recollections of Cathal Brugha, 7 Feb. 1966; Seán Kearns, 'MacWhinney, Linda Kearns', *DIB*.

88 Linda McWhinney (BMH WS 404, p. 20).

89 *Evening Herald*, 8 July 1922.

90 De Valera to Brugha, 6 July 1922 (copy in possession of Cathal MacSwiney Brugha). See also McCullagh, *Rise*, p. 289.

91 *FJ*, 8 July 1922.

92 *II*, 8 July 1922; Michael Davern (BMH WS 1,348, p. 62).

93 Dublin City Coroner's Register, 1916–27 (NAI, CC/2004/75).

94 *Poblacht na hÉireann*, 11 July 1922.

95 Downing to O'Kelly, 14 July 1922, cited in Ó Dochartaigh, *Cathal Brugha*, p. 259; Patrick Murray, *Oracles of God: the Roman Catholic Church and Irish politics, 1922–37* (Dublin, 2000), pp 168–9.

96 *Nationalist and Leinster Times*, 15 July 1922.

97 Ibid.; *FJ*, 8 July 1922; *II*, 11 July 1922.

98 Anne Clare, *Unlikely rebels: the Gifford girls and the fight for Irish freedom* (Cork, 2011), p. 230; McCarthy, *Cumann na mBan*, p. 201.

99 Mellows to Diarmuid O'Hegarty, 9 July 1922 (NLI, Erskine Childers papers, MS 48,060/2).

100 *Derry Journal*, 12 July 1922.

101 McCullagh, *Rise*, p. 289.

102 Ó Dochartaigh, *Cathal Brugha*, p. 256.

103 Boland to McGarrity, 13 July 1922 (NLI, McGarrity papers, MS 17,424/2/8); Fitzpatrick, *Boland*, p. 313.

104 O'Donoghue, 'Cathal Brugha', lecture, Apr. 1966 (NLI, O'Donoghue papers, MS 31,319/2/10).
105 Fitzpatrick, *Boland*, pp 3–4.
106 *IT*, 8 July 1922.
107 Caitlín Brugha to Edmund Downey, 8 Aug. 1922 (NLI, Edmund Downey papers, MS 49,552/1); John Rouse, 'Downey, Edmund', *DIB*.

CHAPTER 8 *After Cathal*

1 McAuliffe, 'Remembering Caitlín Brugha'.
2 *Poblacht na hÉireann* (Scottish edition), 30 Sept. 1922.
3 Ibid.
4 *Poblacht na hÉireann*, 6 July 1922.
5 *II*, 7 Dec. 1922.
6 Noonan, *IRA in Britain*, p. 254.
7 Caitlín Brugha to an unknown person, 15 Jan. 1923 (NLI, O'Brien papers, MS 8,433/5/3).
8 Laffan, *Resurrection*, p. 437.
9 *Manchester Evening News*, 18, 20 Jan. 1922; *Manchester Guardian*, 22 Jan. 1923.
10 *IT*, 9 July 1923.
11 *II*, 7 July 1924.
12 *Sinn Féin*, 11 Aug. 1923.
13 McAuliffe, 'Remembering Caitlín Brugha'.
14 *Waterford News*, 24 Aug. 1923.
15 Ibid., 7 Sept. 1923; electionsireland.org 4th Dáil.
16 Claire McGinn, 'Women's political representation in Dáil Éireann in revolutionary and post-revolutionary Ireland' in Linda Connolly (ed.), *Women and the Irish Revolution* (Newbridge, 2020), p. 97.
17 Ibid., p. 96; McAuliffe, 'Remembering Caitlín Brugha'.
18 *II*, 20 Nov. 1922; *IT*, 18 July, 18 Sept., 9 Oct., 6 Nov. 1923.
19 *The Nation*, 10 Mar. 1928.
20 *IT*, 7 Sept. 1923, 6 Nov. 1924.
21 Ward, *Unmanageable revolutionaries*, p. 203.
22 Caitlín Brugha to Joseph Fowler, 3 Jan. 1935 (NLI, Joseph H. Fowler papers, MS 27,097/12); Carroll, *They have fooled you again*, p. 203.
23 Brugha to Fowler, 25 Jan. 1936 (NLI, Fowler papers, MS 27,097/13); Patrick Maume, 'O'Flanagan, Michael', *DIB*.
24 Mary MacSwiney to Caitlín Brugha, 23 Jan. 1935 (UCDA, Caitlín Brugha papers, P15/8).
25 Ibid.
26 Fidelma Brugha to Professor Éamon de Valera, 9 May 1971 (UCDA, de Valera papers, P150/3618).
27 *Meath Chronicle*, 27 Jan. 1923.
28 *Midlands Counties Advertiser*, 14 Dec. 1939; MacSwiney Brugha, *History's daughter*, p. 189.
29 MacSwiney Brugha, *History's daughter*, p. 190; *II*, 30 Oct. 1942.
30 Séamus Conboy, 'Changing Dublin street names, 1880s to 1940s', *Dublin Historical Record*, 64:2 (2011), 217.
31 Sighle Bhreathnach-Lynch, *Expressions of nationhood in bronze and stone: Albert G. Power, RHA* (Newbridge, 2019), pp 201–2; Anne Dolan, *Commemorating the Irish civil war: history and memory, 1923–2000* (Cambridge, 2003), p. 71.
32 Brian Hanley, 'Russell, Seán', *DIB*; Bhreathnach-Lynch, *Expressions of nationhood*, p. 121.
33 *IP*, 5 July 1934; Dolan, *Commemorating the Irish civil war*, p. 71.

34 John Turpin, 'Portraits of Irish patriots by Oliver Sheppard, 1865–1941', *Éire-Ireland*, 30:4 (1996), 151–2.

35 *IT* and *II*, 26 Jan. 1939.

36 Turpin, 'Portraits', 152–3.

37 Bhreathnach-Lynch, *Expressions of nationhood*, p. 148.

38 *Cork Examiner*, 26 May 1952.

39 Fidelma Brugha to Professor Éamon de Valera, 9 May 1971 (UCDA, de Valera papers, P150/3618); *IP*, 11 Dec. 1939; *Midland Counties Advertiser*, 14 Dec. 1939.

40 MacSwiney Brugha, *History's daughter*, p. 273.

41 *Evening Herald*, 1 and 3 Dec. 1959.

42 MacSwiney, *History's daughter*, pp 188–9.

43 Garda Síochána report on the arrest of Ruairí Brugha, 31 Mar. 1935 (NAI, DJ, 2008/117/585); *IP*, 2 Apr. 1935.

44 *IP*, 1 Apr. 1935.

45 Report on 'Rory Brugha – Conviction by Special Criminal Court, 1941' (NAI, TAOIS/3/S12318).

46 Ibid.

47 Application for internment warrant for Miss Nóinín Brugha, 11 July 1941 (NAI, DJ, 2011/25/730). In some police documents Nóinín is incorrectly referred to as 'Nodlag'.

48 Superintendent S. Gantly to Garda assistant commissioner, 23 Apr. 1942 (NAI, DJ, 2011/25/730).

49 Ward, *Unmanageable revolutionaries*, p. 246.

50 Order of minister for justice, Gerald Boland, 30 Apr. 1942 and report by S. Gantly to Garda assistant commissioner, 2 May 1943, on detention of 'Noneen Brugha' (NAI, DJ, 2011/25/730).

51 William L. Kelleher to minister for justice, 22 June 1942, ibid.

52 Orders of minister for justice, 30 July 1942 and 27 Nov. 1943, ibid.

53 Report by Gantly to Garda assistant commissioner, 2 May 1943, ibid.

54 Ibid.; James Scannell, 'German espionage in South County Dublin', *Dublin Historical Record*, 55:1 (2002), 98–9; Eunan O'Halpin, *Defending Ireland: the Irish state and its enemies since 1922* (Oxford, 1999), pp 241–2; *II*, 1 May 1942.

55 Handwritten note by Gerald Boland, 8 May 1942 (NAI, DJ, 2011/25/730).

56 MacSwiney Brugha, *History's daughter*, p. 196.

57 Ibid., pp 188–226; Patrick Maume, 'Brugha, Ruairí', *DIB*.

58 McGarrity to Caitlín Brugha, n.d. [1922] (NLI, McGarrity papers, MS 17,525/35).

59 Sinn Féin handbill, n.d. [1922].

60 De Valera to Caitlín Brugha, n.d. (in possession of Cathal MacSwiney Brugha).

61 Eoin MacNeill, 'In memory of Cathal Brugha', *The Free State*, 13 July 1922.

Select bibliography

PRIMARY SOURCES

MANUSCRIPTS

Dublin
Dublin City Libraries & Archive
Electoral Rolls, 1908–1915

Irish Military Archives
Bureau of Military History
Civil War operations and intelligence reports collection
Military Service Pensions Collection

National Archives of Ireland
Chief Secretary's Office Registered Papers
Dáil Éireann Records (DÉ2, DÉ4)
Department of An Taoiseach
Department of Justice
Dublin City Coroner's Register, 1916–27
Property Losses (Ireland) Committee
South Dublin Union Minute Books

National Library of Ireland
Piaras Béaslaí papers
Joseph Brennan papers
Roger Casement papers
Éamonn Ceannt papers
Erskine Childers papers
Edmund Downey papers
Joseph H. Fowler papers
Bulmer Hobson papers
Diarmuid Lynch papers
Thomas MacDonagh papers
Eoin MacNeill papers
Joseph McGarrity papers
Maurice Moore papers
Art O'Brien papers
William O'Brien papers
Florence O'Donoghue papers
Eoin O'Duffy papers

Seán O'Mahony papers
Laurence O'Neill papers
Documents relating to The O'Rahilly
Personal narratives of the Rising of 1916 collection
John Redmond papers
Sinn Féin papers
Austin Stack papers
George Walsh papers

University College Dublin Archives
Caitlín Brugha papers
Éamon de Valera papers
Eoin MacNeill papers
Terence MacSwiney papers
Richard Mulcahy papers
Seán O'Mahony papers
Ernie O'Malley notebooks
Ernie O'Malley papers

London
The National Archives
Cabinet records
Colonial Office records
Home Office records
War Office records

Oxford
Bodleian Library
H.H. Asquith papers
Henry Duke papers
Matthew Nathan papers

OFFICAL RECORDS

Census of Ireland 1901, 1911
Census of England, Wales & Scotland 1871, 1881
Dáil Éireann parliamentary debates
Hansard 5 (Commons) parliamentary debates
Report of the Royal Commission into the circumstances connected with the landing of arms at Howth on July 26th 1914 (Cd. 7631)
Report of the Royal Commission on the rebellion in Ireland: minutes of evidence and appendix of documents, House of Commons, 1916 (Cd. 8311)
Report of the Royal Commission on the rebellion in Ireland. House of Commons, 1916 (Cd. 8279)

NEWSPAPERS AND PERIODICALS

Advocate (Australia)
An Claidheamh Soluis
An tÓglach
Belfast Newsletter
Capuchin Annual
Catholic Bulletin
Cork Examiner
Derry Journal
Dublin Daily Express
Dublin Evening News
Dublin Weekly Nation
Dungarvan Observer and Munster Industrial Advocate
Evening Herald
Evening News (Australia)
Freeman's Journal
Free State
Irish Catholic Directory
Irish Independent
Irish Press
Irish Times
Irish Volunteer
London Evening Standard

Manchester Evening News
Manchester Guardian
Meath Chronicle
Midlands Counties Advertiser
Munster Express
The Nation
Nationalist and Leinster Times
Nationalist and Munster Advertiser
Poblacht na hÉireann
Saturday Herald
Slater's National Commercial Directory of Ireland
Sunday Independent
Thom's Directory
Tipperary Star
Tuam Herald
Watchword of Labour
Waterford News and Star
Wolfe Tone Annual
Wolfe Tone Weekly
Ulster Herald
United Irishman
Voice of Labour

SELECT SECONDARY SOURCES

PUBLISHED WORKS

Dublin's fighting story 1916–1921: told by the men who made it (Tralee, 1949).

Aiken, Síobhra, Fearghal Mac Bhloscaidh, Liam Ó Duibhir & Diarmuid Ó Tuama (eds), *The men will talk to me: Ernie O'Malley's interviews with the Northern Divisions* (Newbridge, 2018).

Andrews, C.S., *Dublin made me* (Dublin, 1979).

Augusteijn, Joost, *From public defiance to guerilla warfare: the experience of ordinary Volunteers in the Irish War of Independence, 1916–1921* (Dublin, 1996).

——, *Patrick Pearse: the making of a revolutionary* (Basingstoke, 2010).

Barry, Tom, *Guerrilla days in Ireland* (Dublin, 1962 [1949]).

Barton, Brian, *From behind a closed door: secret court martial records of the 1916 Easter Rising* (Belfast, 2002).

Béaslaí, Piaras, *Michael Collins and the making of a new Ireland* (2 vols, Dublin, 1926).

Bhreathnach-Lynch, Sighle, *Expressions of nationhood in bronze and stone: Albert G. Power, RHA* (Newbridge, 2019).

Bielenberg, Andy, 'Female fatalities in County Cork during the Irish War of Independence and the case of Mrs Lindsay' in Linda Connolly (ed.), *Women and the Irish Revolution* (Newbridge, 2020), pp 148–63.

Borgonovo, John, *The dynamics of war and revolution: Cork city, 1916–1918* (Cork, 2013).

Bourke, Marcus, *The O'Rahilly* (Tralee, 1967).

Bowman, Timothy, 'Irish paramilitarism and gun cultures, 1910–1921' in Karen Jones, Giacomo Macola & David Welch (eds), *A cultural history of firearms in the age of empire* (Farnham, Surrey, 2013), pp 267–84.

Breen, Dan, *My fight for Irish freedom* (Dublin, 1989 [1924]).

Brugha, Máire MacSwiney, *History's daughter: a memoir from the only child of Terence MacSwiney* (Dublin, 2006).

Burke, John, *Roscommon: the Irish Revolution, 1912–23* (Dublin, 2021).

Campbell, Fergus (ed.), 'The last land war? Kevin O'Shiel's memoir of the Irish Revolution (1916–21)', *Archivium Hibernicum*, 57 (2003), 155–200.

Carroll, Denis, *They have fooled you again: Michael O'Flanagan (1876–1942), priest, republican, social critic* (2nd ed., Dublin, 2016 [1993]).

Caulfield, Max, *The Easter Rebellion* (Dublin, 1995 [1963]).

Clancy, Pádraigín & Clare Eager (eds), *Ireland first: comóradh ár sinsir, 1916–2016: relatives remember: 4th Battalion Dublin Brigade 1916, South Dublin Union – Marrowbone Lane garrisons* (Dublin, 2016).

Clare, Anne, *Unlikely rebels: the Gifford girls and the fight for Irish freedom* (Cork, 2011).

Clarke, Kathleen, *Revolutionary woman, Kathleen Clarke, 1878–1972: an autobiography*, ed. Helen Litton (Dublin, 1991).

Comerford, Máire, *On dangerous ground: a memoir of the Irish Revolution*, ed. Hilary Dully (Dublin, 2021).

Conboy, Séamus, 'Changing Dublin street names, 1880s to 1940s', *Dublin Historical Record*, 64:2 (2011), 205–55.

Coogan, Tim Pat, *Michael Collins: a biography* (London, 1990).

Costello, Francis, *Enduring the most: the life and death of Terence MacSwiney* (Dingle, 1995).

——, *The Irish Revolution and its aftermath, 1916–1923: years of revolt* (Dublin, 2003).

Crowley, John, Donal Ó Drisceoil & Mike Murphy (eds), *Atlas of the Irish Revolution* (Cork, 2017).

Curtis, Kieron, *P.S. O'Hegarty (1879–1955): Sinn Féin Fenian* (London, 2010).

Dolan, Anne, *Commemorating the Irish civil war: history and memory, 1923–2000* (Cambridge, 2003).

——, 'Killing and Bloody Sunday, November 1920', *Historical Journal*, 49:3 (2006), 789–810.

Dolan, Anne & William Murphy, *Michael Collins: the man and the revolution* (Cork, 2018).

Dunleavy, J.E. & G.W. Dunleavy, *Douglas Hyde: a maker of modern Ireland* (Berkeley, 1991).

Dunne, Declan, *Peter's key: Peter Deloughry and the fight for Irish independence* (Cork, 2012).

Dwyer, T. Ryle, *The Squad and the intelligence operations of Michael Collins* (Cork, 2005).

Fanning, Ronan, Michael Kennedy, Dermot Keogh & Eunan O'Halpin, *Documents on Irish foreign policy, vol. I, 1919–1922* (Dublin, 1998).

Farrell, Brian, *The founding of Dáil Éireann: parliament and nation building* (Dublin, 1971).

Farrell, Brian (ed.), *The creation of the Dáil: a volume of essays from the Thomas Davis lectures* (Dublin, 1994).

Feeney, Brian, *16 lives: Seán Mac Diarmada* (Dublin, 2015).

——, *Antrim: the Irish Revolution, 1912–23* (Dublin, 2021).

Ferriter, Diarmaid, *A nation and not a rabble: the Irish Revolution, 1913–23* (London, 2015).

——, *Between two hells: the Irish civil war* (London, 2021).

Fewer, Michael, *The battle of the Four Courts: the first three days of the Irish civil war* (London, 2018).

Figgis, Darrell, *Recollections of the Irish war* (London, 1927).

Fitzpatrick, David, *Politics and Irish life, 1913–21: provincial experiences of war and revolution* (2nd ed., Cork, 1998 [1977]).

——, 'The logic of collective sacrifice: Ireland and the British army, 1914–1918', *Historical Journal*, 38:4 (1995), 1017–30.

——, *The two Irelands, 1912–1939* (Oxford, 1998).

——, *Harry Boland's Irish Revolution* (Cork, 2003).

Foley, Caitriona, *The last Irish plague: the great flu epidemic in Ireland, 1918–19* (Dublin, 2011).

Foster, Gavin M., *The Irish civil war and society: politics, class, and conflict* (New York, 2015).

Foster, Roy, *Vivid faces: the revolutionary generation in Ireland, 1890–1923* (London, 2014).

Foy, Michael & Brian Barton, *The Easter Rising* (Stroud, 1999).

Gallagher, Frank, *The four glorious years* (Dublin, 1953).

Gallagher, Mary, *16 lives: Éamonn Ceannt* (Dublin, 2014).

Gallagher, Michael, 'The pact general election of 1922', *Irish Historical Studies*, 21:84 (1981), 404–21.

Garvin, Tom, *1922: the birth of Irish democracy* (Dublin, 1996).

Gaughan, J. Anthony, *Austin Stack: portrait of a separatist* (Dublin, 1977).

——, *Thomas Johnson, 1872–1963: first leader of the Labour Party in Dáil Éireann* (Dublin, 1980).

Geoghegan, Stannus, *Campaigns and history of the Royal Irish Regiment, vol. II* (London, 1927).

Gillis, Liz, *Women of the Irish Revolution* (Cork, 2016).

Good, Joe, *Enchanted by dreams: the journal of a revolutionary* (Dingle, 1996).

Greaves, C. Desmond, *The Irish Transport and General Workers' Union: the formative years, 1909–1923* (Dublin, 1982).

Hart, Peter, 'Michael Collins and the assassination of Sir Henry Wilson', *Irish Historical Studies*, 28:110 (1992), 150–70.

——, 'The social structure of the IRA, 1916–23', *Historical Journal*, 42:1 (1999), 207–31.

——, "Operations abroad": the IRA in Britain, 1919–23', *English Historical Review*, 115:460 (2000), 71–102.

——, *Mick: the real Michael Collins* (London, 2005).

——, 'On the necessity of violence in the Irish Revolution' in Danine Farquarson & Seán Farrell (eds), *Shadows of the gunman: violence and culture in modern Ireland* (Cork, 2008), pp 14–37.

Hay, Marnie, *Bulmer Hobson and the nationalist movement in twentieth-century Ireland* (Manchester, 2009).

Hayes-McCoy, G. A., 'A military history of the 1916 Rising' in Kevin B. Nowlan (ed.), *The making of 1916: studies in the history of the Rising* (Dublin, 1969), pp 255–338.

Henry, William, *Supreme sacrifice: the story of Éamonn Ceannt, 1881–1916* (Cork, 2005).

Hickey, Michael, *The Irish language movement, its genesis, growth and progress*, Gaelic League pamphlet no. 29 (Dublin, 1902).

Hobson, Bulmer, *A short history of the Irish Volunteers* (Dublin, 1918).

——, 'The origin of Óglaigh na hÉireann', *An tÓglach*, 4:1 (Mar. 1931).

Hopkinson, Michael, *Green against green: the Irish civil war* (Dublin, 1988).

——, *The Irish War of Independence* (Dublin, 2002).

Hopkinson, Michael (ed.), *The last days of Dublin Castle: the Mark Sturgis diaries* (Dublin, 1999).

Hughes, Brian, *Defying the IRA?: intimidation, coercion, and communities during the Irish Revolution* (Liverpool, 2016).

Jackson, Alvin, *Home rule: an Irish history, 1800–2000* (Oxford, 2003).

Kautt, W.H., *Arming the Irish Revolution: gunrunning and arms smuggling, 1911–1922* (Kansas, 2021).

Kelly, Matthew J., *The Fenian ideal and Irish nationalism, 1882–1916* (Woodbridge, 2006).

——, 'Radical nationalism, 1882–1916' in Thomas Bartlett (ed.), *The Cambridge history of Ireland, vol. IV: 1880 to the present* (Cambridge, 2018), pp 31–61.

Keown, Gerard, *First of small nations: the beginnings of Irish foreign policy in the interwar years, 1919–1932* (Oxford, 2016).

Kenny, Colum, *The enigma of Arthur Griffith: 'father of us all'* (Newbridge, 2020).

Kissane, Bill, *The politics of the Irish civil war* (Oxford, 2005).

Knirck, Jason, *Women of the Dáil: gender, republicanism and the Anglo-Irish treaty* (Dublin, 2006).

Kotsonouris, Mary, *The Dáil courts, 1920–24* (Dublin, 1994).

Kostick, Conor, *Revolution in Ireland: popular militancy, 1917–23* (London, 1996).

Laffan, Michael, 'The unification of Sinn Féin in 1917', *Irish Historical Studies*, 17:67 (1971), 353–79.

——, *The resurrection of Ireland: the Sinn Féin party, 1916–1923* (Cambridge, 1999).

——, *Judging W.T. Cosgrave* (Dublin, 2014).

Lawrence, Joan, *A pictorial history: Lavender Bay to the spit* (Alexandria, NSW, 1999).

Leddin, Jeffrey, *The 'Labour Hercules': the Irish Citizen Army and Irish republicanism, 1913–23* (Newbridge, 2019).

Lynch, Diarmuid, *The IRB and the 1916 insurrection* (Cork, 1957).

Mac Aonghusa, Proinsias, *Ar son na Gaeilge: Conradh na Gaeilge, 1893–1993* (Dublin, 1993).

MacAtasney, Gerard, *Seán Mac Diarmada: the mind of the revolution* (Manorhamilton, 2004).

MacDiarmada, Mary, *Art O'Brien and Irish nationalism in London, 1900–25* (Dublin, 2020).

Mac Eoin, Uinseann, *Survivors: the story of Ireland's struggle as told through some of her outstanding living people recalling events from the days of Davitt, through James Connolly, Brugha, Collins, Liam Mellows, and Rory O'Connor, to the present time* (Dublin 1980).

Mac Lochlainn, Piaras F. (ed.), *Last words: letters and statements of the leaders executed after the Rising at Easter 1916* (Dublin, 1971).

MacNeill, Eoin, *Memoir of a revolutionary scholar*, ed. Brian Hughes (Dublin, 2016).

McCarthy, Cal, *Cumann na mBan and the Irish Revolution* (Dublin, 2007).

McCarthy, Pat, *Waterford: the Irish Revolution, 1912–23* (Dublin, 2015).

McCoole, Sinéad, *Easter widows: seven Irish women who lived in the shadow of the 1916 Rising* (Dublin, 2014).

McCullagh, David, *De Valera, volume 1: rise, 1882–1932* (Dublin, 2017).

McGarry, Fearghal, *Eoin O'Duffy: a self-made hero* (Oxford, 2005).

——, *The Rising: Ireland 1916* (2nd ed., Oxford, 2016 [2010]).

McGee, Owen, *The IRB: the Irish Republican Brotherhood from the Land League to Sinn Féin* (Dublin, 2006).

McGinn, Claire, 'Women's political representation in Dáil Éireann in revolutionary and post-revolutionary Ireland' in Linda Connolly (ed.), *Women and the Irish Revolution* (Newbridge, 2020), pp 85–102.

McMahon, Timothy, *Grand opportunity: the Gaelic revival and Irish society, 1893–1910* (Syracuse, 2008).

——, 'Douglas Hyde and the politics of the Gaelic League in 1914', *Éire-Ireland*, 53:1 & 2 (2018), 29–47.

Macardle, Dorothy, *The Irish Republic* (4th ed., London, 1968 [1937]).

Maher, Jim, *Harry Boland: a biography* (revised ed., Cork, 2020).

Mansergh, Nicholas, *The unresolved question: the Anglo-Irish settlement and its undoing, 1912–72* (New Haven, 1972).

Matthews, Ann, *Renegades: Irish republican women, 1900–1922* (Cork, 2010).

Mathews, P.J., *Revival: the Abbey Theatre, Sinn Féin, the Gaelic League and the Co-operative movement* (Cork, 2003).

Maye, Brian, *Arthur Griffith* (Dublin, 1997).

Maume, Patrick, *The long gestation: Irish nationalist life, 1891–1918* (Dublin, 1999).

Milne, Ida, *Stacking the coffins: influenza, war and revolution in Ireland, 1918–19* (Manchester, 2018).

Mitchell, Arthur, *Revolutionary government in Ireland: Dáil Éireann, 1919–22* (Dublin, 1995).

——, 'Making the case for Irish independence' in Crowley et al., *Atlas of the Irish Revolution*, pp 471–8.

Morrissey, Thomas, *William O'Brien, 1881–1968: socialist, republican, Dáil deputy, editor and trade union leader* (Dublin, 2007).

——, *Laurence O'Neill (1864–1943), lord mayor of Dublin (1917–1924): patriot and man of peace* (Dublin, 2014).

Morrison, Eve, 'Tea, sandbags, and Cathal Brugha: Kathy Barry's civil war' in Oona Frawley (ed.), *Women and the decade of commemoration* (Indiana, 2021), pp 189–204.

Mulcahy, Risteárd, *My father, the general: Richard Mulcahy and the military history of the revolution* (Dublin, 2009).

Murphy, Brian P., *Patrick Pearse and the lost republican ideal* (Dublin, 1991).

——, *The Catholic Bulletin and republican Ireland with special reference to J.J. O'Kelly (Sceilg)* (Belfast, 2005).

Murphy, Oliver, *The cruel clouds of war: a book of the sixty-eight former pupils and teachers of Belvedere College S.J. who lost their lives in the military conflicts of the 20th century* (Dublin, 2003).

Murphy, William, *Political imprisonment and the Irish, 1912–1921* (Oxford, 2014).

——, 'Imprisonment, 1915–18' in Crowley et al., *Atlas of the Irish Revolution*, pp 319–22.

Murray, Patrick, *Oracles of God: the Roman Catholic Church and Irish politics, 1922–37* (Dublin, 2000).

Naughton, Lindie, *Markievicz: a most outrageous rebel* (Newbridge, 2016).

Ní Aodha, Lil & Breandán Ó hAodha (compiled by), *Irish without a teacher* (Dublin, 1920).

Nic Dháibhéid, Caoimhe, 'The Irish National Aid Association and the radicalisation of public opinion in Ireland, 1916–1918', *Historical Journal*, 55:3 (2012), 705–29.

Noonan, Gerard, *The IRA in Britain, 1919–1923: 'in the heart of enemy lines'* (Liverpool, 2014).

Ó Broin, León, *Revolutionary underground: the story of the Irish Republican Brotherhood, 1858–1923* (Dublin, 1975).

Ó Caoimh, Pádraig, *Richard Mulcahy: from the politics of war to the politics of peace, 1913-1924* (Newbridge, 2019).

Ó Ceallaigh, Seán T., *Seán T.* (Dublin, 1963).

Ó Cillín, Micheál, 'Cathal Brugha 1874–1922', *Dublin Historical Record*, 38 (1984–85), 141–9.

Ó Corráin, Daithí, 'J.J. O'Connell's memoir of the Irish Volunteers, 1914–16, 1917', *Analecta Hibernica*, 47 (2016), 1–102.

——, '"They blew up the best portion of our city and … it is their duty to replace it": compensation and reconstruction in the aftermath of the 1916 Rising', *Irish Historical Studies*, 39:154 (2014), 272–95.

Ó Dochartaigh, Tomás, *Cathal Brugha: a shaol is a thréithe* (Dublin, 1969).

Ó Fathartaigh, Mícheál & Liam Weeks, *Birth of a state: the Anglo-Irish treaty* (Newbridge, 2021).

Ó hAnnracháin, Peadar, *Fé bhrat an Chonnartha* (Dublin, 1944).

Ó Huallacháin, Colmán, Rónán Ó Huallacháin & Patrick Conlon, *The Irish and the Irish – a sociolinguistic analysis of the relationship between a people and their language* (Dublin, 1994).

Ó Ruairc, Pádraig, *Blood on the Banner: the republican struggle in Clare* (Cork, 2009).

Ó Siadhail, Pádraig, *An Béaslaíoch: beatha agus saothar Phiarais Béaslaí* (Dublin, 2007).

O'Callaghan, John, *Limerick: the Irish Revolution, 1912–23* (Dublin, 2018).

O'Connor, Emmet, *Reds and the green: Ireland, Russia and the internationals, 1919–43* (Dublin, 2004).

——, 'Neither democratic nor a programme: the Democratic Programme of 1919', *Irish Historical Studies*, 40:157 (2016), 92–109.

O'Donoghue, Florence, *Tomás MacCurtain* (Tralee, 1958).

O'Farrell, Fergus, *Cathal Brugha* (Dublin, 2018).

O'Farrell, Pádraic, *The blacksmith of Ballinalee: Seán Mac Eoin* (Mullingar, 1993).

O'Halpin, Eunan, *Defending Ireland: the Irish state and its enemies since 1922* (Oxford, 1999).

O'Halpin, Eunan & Daithí Ó Corráin, *The dead of the Irish Revolution* (New Haven, 2020).

O'Kelly, J.J., *A trinity of martyrs: Terence MacSwiney, Cathal Brugha, Austin Stack* (Dublin, 1947).

O'Malley, Ernie, *On another man's wound. A personal history of Ireland's War of Independence* (Dublin, 2002 [1936]).

Owen, Frank, *Tempestuous journey: Lloyd George his life and times* (London, 1954).

Pakenham, Frank, *Peace by ordeal: the negotiation of the Anglo-Irish treaty* (London, 1935).

Pakenham, Francis & Thomas Patrick O'Neill, *Éamon de Valera* (London, 1970).

Pašeta, Senia, *Before the revolution* (Cork, 1999).

——, *Irish nationalist women, 1900–1918* (Cambridge, 2013).

Plunkett Dillon, Geraldine, *All in the blood: a memoir of the Plunkett family, the 1916 Rising and the War of Independence*, ed. Honor Ó Brolcháin (Dublin, 2006).

Regan, John M., *The Irish counter-revolution, 1921–1936: treatyite politics and settlement in independent Ireland* (Dublin, 1999).

Ryan, Meda, *Michael Collins and the women who spied for Ireland* (Cork, 1996).

Scannell, James, 'German espionage in south County Dublin', *Dublin Historical Record*, 55:1 (2002), 88–101.

Swithin Walsh, Eoin, *Kilkenny in times of revolution, 1900–1923* (Newbridge, 2018).

Townshend, Charles, *The British campaign in Ireland, 1919–1921: the development of political and military policies* (London, 1975).

——, *Easter 1916: the Irish rebellion* (London, 2006).

——, *The Republic: the fight for Irish independence 1918–1923* (London, 2013).

Turpin, John, 'Portraits of Irish patriots by Oliver Sheppard, 1865–1941', *Éire-Ireland*, 30:4 (1996), 134–53.

Ua Ceallaigh, Seán, *Cathal Brugha* (Dublin, 1942).

Uí Chollatáin, Regina, 'Ó Chéitinn go Conradh: the revivalists and the 1916 Rising', *Studies in Arts and Humanities*, 2:1 (2016), 52–66.

Walker, Brian (ed.), *Parliamentary election results in Ireland, 1918–92* (Dublin, 1992).

Ward, Alan J., 'Lloyd George and the 1918 Irish conscription crisis', *Historical Journal*, 25:1 (1974), 107–29.

Ward, Margaret, *Unmanageable revolutionaries: women and Irish nationalism* (London, 1995).

——, 'Women in the Irish Free State: gender and the legacy of revolution' in Crowley et al., *Atlas of the Irish Revolution*, pp 814–17.

—— *Hannah Sheehy Skeffington, feminism and the Irish Revolution* (Dublin, 2019).

Westgarth, Mark, 'A biographical dictionary of nineteenth-century antique and curiosity dealers', *Regional Furniture*, 23 (2009), 1–207.

Younger, Calton, *Ireland's civil war* (London, 1968).

Valiulis, Maryann Gialanella, *Portrait of a revolutionary: General Richard Mulcahy and the founding of the Irish Free State* (Dublin, 1992).

INTERNET SOURCES

ElectionsIreland.org.

McAuliffe, Mary, 'Remembering Caitlín Brugha, TD for Waterford, 1923–1927', https://marymcauliffe.blog/2018/12/04/remembering-caitlin-brugha-td-for-waterford–1923–1927/.

McGuire, James & James Quinn (eds), *Dictionary of Irish biography* (Cambridge, 2009) http://dib.cambridge.org.

Oxford Dictionary of national biography.

Index